GHOST
LIGHT

GHOST LIGHT

A Rogue's Guide on
How to Break the Rules
& Follow Your Inner Knowing

ANDREA
ST. AMAND

ANDREA
ST. AMAND

CHARLESTON

Ghost Light

Copyright © 2025 by Andrea St. Amand

All rights reserved.

Edited by Meg Calvin | www.megcalvin.com
Line editing and book design by Jodi McPhee
Cover art by Emily Werner | www.instagram.com/mygreenthumbart/
Rabbit art by Cassidy Lee | www.instagram.com/canvas_by_cass/

ISBN (Paperback): 979-8-218-78889-6

Printed in the U.S.A.

To Fire Horse,
without whom, many of my
explorations and accomplishments
may have remained in the recesses
of my imagination,
festering and taunting me,
until the more persistent few
tiptoed their way
into a world less meaningful
and a life less bold.

READER BONUS

ARE YOU AN EMPATH TRYING TO SUCCEED IN A NON-EMPATH WORLD?

A Special Gift for Readers of Ghost Light

Dear Reader,

Thank you for picking up **Ghost Light!** Before you dive in, I want to offer you a nugget of knowledge that goes beyond the traditional "introvert vs. extrovert" conversation.

Here's what I've discovered: Instead of focusing on whether you're introverted or extroverted, determine, instead, whether you're empathic.

The word "empath" seems to be overused lately. **In fact, scientifically-based empathy only affects approximately 20% of the population!**

(**Pro Tip:** Empathy and sensitivity are NOT the same! These topics are covered in much more detail in the pages of this book.)

For now, consider:

Do you walk into meetings or public gatherings and instantly feel grumpy or irritated by what you can only describe as "too much noise"... even when everyone else seems to be thriving and calm?

Do you feel extroverted, but networking or social events can leave you drained, even when they go well?

Are you picky about the fabric that touches your skin?

If you answered yes to any of these questions, you're not "too sensitive." It might be that your brain functions in a way researchers call empathic.

THE PROBLEM

Most empaths try to succeed using strategies designed for people whose brains process and react to information completely differently. It's like running Mac software on a PC — it doesn't work, and you'll burn out trying.

THE SOLUTION

Knowledge is power. You might not identify as "sensitive" or "empathic," but your brain and body might be sending you red-alert signals to the contrary. Understanding whether your brain functions as empathic — and learning how you can leverage this phenomenon — can turn what might seem like a weakness into your individual superpower, in both your personal and professional life.

TAKE YOUR PERSONALIZED, 15-MINUTE VIDEO QUIZ HERE: www.andreasaintamand.com/free-resources

This knowledge changed my life, even though I was skeptical and reluctant to accept it.

Join me in this video, so you, too, can discover:

- ✳ Are you an empath?
- ✳ If so, what type of empath are you? Where do you fall on the scale? What does this mean for your personal and professional life?

Alternatively:

- ✳ Are you highly sensitive, but your brain does NOT react to the world empathically?
- ✳ How can you use this knowledge to live with less stress and more authenticity?

Remember, knowledge is power. There are no right or wrong answers here. The more you know about yourself, the more you can show up in the world as your fullest most-glorious self.

JOIN ME IN THE VIDEO QUIZ HERE:
www.andreasaintamand.com/free-resources

This isn't about spiritual awakening, though it could be — it's about strategic advantage.

Stop trying to succeed like everyone else. The most successful empaths, or sensitive people, aren't the ones who've "toughened up." They're the ones who've learned to work WITH their wiring, not against it.

Let's find out exactly if you're an empath, and if so, what kind.

I'll see you in the video!

Andrea St. Amand
Author, *Ghost Light*

Advance Praise For *Ghost Light*

Runner–Up Winner, William Faulkner–William Wisdom Creative Writing Competition, NonFiction, Selected by the Faulkner Society, New Orleans, Louisiana.

"A mesmerizing page-turner, even as the topics may tempt you out of your comfort zone. Andrea St. Amand approaches the supernatural with realism and humor, turning the extraordinary into digestible — albeit at times, bloody — bite-size morsels. Given Bram's interest in the occult, I think he would be pleased with his role in this book."

—**Dacre Stoker, International Bestselling Author, Great–Grandnephew of Bram Stoker, www.dacrestoker.com**

"Close as sharing a dream or a heartbeat, St. Amand spins tales both ordinary and fantastic, whispering her truths in a language that readers will understand like some long forgotten memory. Bittersweet and revelatory, she retraces an extraordinary life filled with the strange and the transcendent. But ultimately, the power in this work rises from the staggeringly vulnerable human experiences of an esoteric poet. A soulful act of shimmering courage."

—**Kimberly Brock, award-winning author of *The Fabled Earth*, www.kimberlybrockbooks.com**

"An unflinching revelation into the costs and unexpected gifts of a generational dynasty."

—**Rachel Strickland, Artist, Writer, and Founder of The Audacity Project, www.rachelstricklandcreative.com**

If you turn one more page, you acknowledge the following:

This book is based on my experiences, as I have interpreted them. My experiences are Horrid and Majestic.

Usually at once. You may cry or laugh in the wrong places.

This book ventures heart-felt-ly into themes, situations and references to depression, anxiety, suicide, emotional and sexual abuse, failure, death, loss, disruptive grief/complicated bereavement, PTSD —

— and learning and healing from it all.

I'm a hypersensitive outlier as far as humans go, ravenous to consume the world's stranger offerings. So I should also warn you that this book contains ghosts, vampires, warlocks, angels, devils, hoodoo, witchcraft, dead people, souls communicating from other dimensions, wonder, synchronicities, miracles, and many other ideas of the supernatural —

— with healthy doses of analysis and skepticism.

If you make it to the end, I hope you leave my world feeling not so alone with or outcast by your own Majestic and Horrid Experiences.

The most dangerous risk of reading this book is that you remember … magical living is as close as your fingertips, should you choose to reach out and touch it.

Proceed with caution or proceed unflinchingly.

I recommend both.

Uncle Charlie called it a curse.

Aunt Jill called it a hoax.

Bridging that divide is pretty much what this book is about.

PLAYBILL

WELCOME TO THE GREEN ROOM

ACT ONE

Fleshy Bones & Bloody Ghosts:
The Sordid & The Sublime

ONE

IN THE 1980s, a nicely dressed, older man approached Dad in front of the bank on Main Street. He seemed slightly nervous, checking over his shoulder as he stopped on the sidewalk. Dad, a criminal defense lawyer, grew curious as to what troubles might tumble out of the man's mouth.

"Jack," the man said to Dad, "I don't know what rumors you heard about your grandparents and Charlie or what you believe, but will you listen if I tell you a story?"

Not what Dad expected. But his grandparents and Uncle Charlie were fascinating, not to mention well-known in the 1910s and 20s. Dad leaned his good ear toward the man.

The man talked fast. "I know about all the seances and such they held at their house. I never went to those. Can't speak to them. But when I was eleven, I worked one summer helping out your grandmother's brother, your Uncle Charlie, in his fields. We were in the middle of nowhere, outside town. No radios, no sound coming from anywhere."

He took a breath as if he'd screwed up the entirety of his life's allotment of courage to say what needed to come next. "Suddenly, Charlie stood straight up. He was so pale that his face looked gray. He broke into an awful sweat. I thought he would pass out. Thought he was sick or something.

"He turned his face up to the sky, and I swear to you, music started pouring out of him. Out of his chest. Out of his body. *Music.* Loud, everywhere at once.

"It was the most powerful, glorious thing I ever heard. I can't describe it as anything but inhuman. It was the music of angels or the heavens." The man swallowed, squirming under the weight of this confession before he continued.

"Charlie had no control over himself, like he was in a trance. I don't know how long we stood glued to the ground, with Charlie held captive by some force, and me, unable to blink or breathe. I finally got the presence of mind to run. I was never so scared in all my life. I ran and ran, all the way home. Never went back. And never told anyone."

He stared at Dad, perhaps weighing the odds that Dad would cart him off to the looney bin. But Dad listened with rapt attention.

He continued. "No matter what you heard about Charlie and your grandmother, something there is real. I don't know what you believe, but, buddy, after hearing heaven's music pour out of a man's chest, I believed."

Dad thanked the man profusely. He didn't have time to ask further questions or even think of any. The man had already moved on.

It wasn't the first wild tale Dad heard from otherwise seemingly credible people about the elders in the family. His grandmother, Sabina, and her brother Charlie were mediums of some renown in the area. Uncle Charlie apparently had a spirit horn that he claimed would help him hear into other dimensions during the seances Grandma held in her front parlor.

By all accounts, when Uncle Charlie tuned-in to the Great Beyond, as they called it, he fell into a trance and lost control of his faculties. He channeled voices or the dreaded music erupted out of him. If luck were with him, it happened during a seance.

But in front of the wrong audience, he was left exhausted and embarrassed, convinced he was cursed. Even during the worst of times, though, a knowing lingered. *Something* miraculous had happened.

Charlie and his sister, Grandma Sabina, held seances in Grandma's front parlor in the small but booming coal king town of Fayetteville, West Virginia. Sabina married an idealistic writer who ran his own newspaper, J. Alfred Taylor. "Alf" would go on to become a United States Congressman and wildly popular politician amongst the working class in a state run by the rail and coal barons.

He harbored a zealously progressive philosophy on social issues during a time when people were murdered for fighting for women's voting rights and worker's rights. It is no small wonder that Alf was also interested in pushing the edges of consciousness, through hosting seances run by his wife and brother-in-law.

Dad liked hearing stories of his Grandma Sabina and Uncle Charlie. Perhaps because he'd witnessed numerous bizarre moments with Grandma in her house and with his own mother, the stories of strangers helped validate his.

Purportedly, even President Coolidge and his family held seances in the White House in the 1920s.

Dad never doubted the existence of the spirit world or the after-life. He just wasn't sure what to do with it. After college, he'd almost gone into seminary but my mother refused to become a preacher's wife. He chose law school instead.

I didn't learn *any* of this family lore about communicating with the Great Beyond on the regular until I hit my mid-thirties. If I'd been brought up with the Taylor legends, normalized as part of the ancestral tapestry, rather than them being tucked away in the attic as an odd but insignificant interest, it sure would have helped.

⸿

Instead, I suffered over three decades of perceiving reality in a way no one else did, desperately trying to act normal.

I had been through lots of therapy to get my emotional and mental state in order, I was a partner in a big law firm, and owned a gorgeous house with my husband in the historic district of Charleston, South Carolina, mere blocks off the harbor and with a rooftop view of the city.

I made it. Faked-it-til-I-made-it Normal.

Normal meant stable, successful, yet for me, miserable in a way I couldn't wrap my arms around. I worked on a great team with interesting cases and smart, caring colleagues. Without my job, we'd have to sell the house and move out of downtown.

And then what would I do? I had no idea what I wanted, and I couldn't see a way out.

Until one day, when I was thirty-five, the wheels came off the bus.

I was working late in the office, when I heard a large dog walking down the hall, paws hitting the carpet, the light jingle of a dog tag, and the leash toggling against the collar.

I jumped up to see who brought their dog in for company, and found no one in the hall. After a search, I discovered that only one other colleague remained in the office.

I poked my head in his door. "Hey! You got your dog in here?"

"Wha — ?" He looked confused.

"I heard a dog coming down the hall."

"No, no dog. I didn't hear anything."

The law firm was cloaked in security, with locked doors and key card entries. We were on the fifth floor. That late at night, the opening and closing of any door, elevator, or stairwell echoed through the office. I hadn't heard anyone leaving, and I realized I hadn't heard anyone coming either.

I knew I heard the dog.

"Time to go home?" he suggested.

Halfway home, I wondered if I had turned off the space heater under my desk. My mind spun into hysteria, as it did every single time I left work and my irrational obsession over the heater kicked in.

If I didn't turn it off, it would overheat and burn down the office, then the entire building, including the bank on the first floor, then spread to the hotel next door, and then the art museum down the street. Soon, the entire historic district would be in flames like the city hadn't seen since 1886, all because I was an airhead and left the dang heater running.

It was easier to go back to the office than argue with my compulsive thoughts, or worse, jolt awake in the middle of the night with my head on fire over the heater. After my audible hallucination with the dog, I was too embarrassed to call my colleague still at the office and ask him to check.

As always, the heater was off. The yellow sticky notes on my computer screen, my calendar, and my keyboard were all in place. *TURN OFF HEATER.*

I finally arrived home, frustrated with myself and with hearing a non-existent dog. I opened the pantry to start a late-evening dinner, when a huge, misshapen dark object hurtled off the top shelf and toward my head.

"Aaaaaa!" I ducked, expecting to find a bag of rice or potatoes had fallen off the shelf. Nothing. Nothing landed on me. Nothing lay on the floor.

What the hell?

The following morning, back at the office, otherwise absorbed in my computer screen, another dark object fell into my sight from my peripheral vision. I cried out and jerked away. If someone had asked, I would have sworn a piano fell through the ceiling.

I broke into a cold sweat.

Secretly, I feared that all the therapy in the world couldn't save me. I *knew* I wasn't crazy in any standard-issue loony toon way. I was well-equipped with an arsenal of mental and emotional health tools.

Maybe, though, some veil in my brain had finally thinned to the point where I couldn't discern the difference between what was "real" and what were mere shapes and sounds projecting out from my imagination. I feared the inexplicable crazy, the kind for which no treatment existed, was finally erupting once and for all.

If I continued to respond to sounds other people didn't hear, and bob and weave from sights other people didn't see, I wouldn't have to worry about my career options. The firm would have no choice but to fire me and report me to the lawyers' Bar Association.

Mom and Dad divorced when I was still a baby. Mom moved the dachshund and me three hours away from Dad, back home with her parents, Kitty and Ambrose.

Apparently, the first time I saw Papa Ambrose, who the family called Pops, I catapulted my nine-month-old self out of Mom's arms to get to him. A family friend captured the event on camera, which is a good thing, or no one would have believed it, given Pops' overly critical and less-than-affectionate nature.

From that point forward, Pops was my best friend. As a bonus, his sister lived just down the street.

Aunt Lily wore bright red lipstick and drank and smoked with reckless abandon. From my perspective, Lily was a non-stop hoot. Apparently, the dachshund thought so too, because the dog frequently left our house on her own short-legged accord, preferring to party with Lily for days on end rather than comply with our household's rules.

When it was time to get the dog back, Grandma Kitty and I wrapped ourselves in white sheets and tiptoed around Lily's backyard at dusk, hoping to catch Lily tipsy enough that she'd think she saw a ghost floating outside her window. Maybe Grandma thought she'd eventually scare Lily into sobriety.

On a morning just before my fourth birthday, the phone rang. If I spoke clearly, the adults allowed me to answer the telephone. I picked up the receiver in the finished basement where I played and delivered the "hello, you've reached" spiel.

An older woman on the other end sniffled, and her voice broke when she said, "Andrea, honey, go get your grandmother."

I pounded up the stairs on a mission, long pigtails bobbing, burst into the kitchen and announced, "Lily died."

Everyone scrambled. Grandma ran to the hall phone. Pops hurled himself out the door and down the street. Mom asked in that measured parental tone, "Who called?" She probably wondered what moron told a kid on the phone that someone died.

Turns out, Pops found Lily safe in her house, soaking in a bath of bubbles up to her chin, thin ankles crossed on the edge of the tub, wondering what the fuss was about.

We learned that Grandma Kitty's mother had passed away. I got a slight talking-to about relaying accurate information and not scaring everyone by jumping to conclusions. Then there was the question of why I thought someone died in the first place.

I felt relieved that my favorite aunt was still with us, but certain about my announcement.

Lily died around three o'clock that afternoon.

⁕

Once Lily crossed into the Great Beyond, the fact of an afterlife seemed just as solid to me as the proven effects of gravity. You roll off the bed, you fall to the floor. Slip off the monkey bars, hit the ground fast and hard. Lily simply moved from down the street over to the Beyond.

I could not, however, wrap my head around what the afterlife was like. Grandma Kitty's description of streets paved with gold sounded awfully monochromatic.

I didn't go to Sunday School every single week because Mom assured me that attendance was a choice. But what little I heard in Sunday School fell flat on the details of a Heavenly Promise.

Not to mention that apparently, one Sunday morning when the Grands were at church and we decidedly weren't, I woke up, walked downstairs and told Mom, "When I was up in Heaven, before I was born, we were all looking down, and God decided you needed me."

Mom found that interesting, but claimed to have no knowledge of the conversation.

I persisted. "Don't you remember? You were there."

"Andrea, if that's what you remember, then that's what happened. But sometimes, not everyone else in your dreams will remember things exactly as you do."

One thing I knew for certain from that before-I-was-born-memory-dream: the very air crackled with endless possibility. There was nothing so dull as streets merely paved with gold. In fact, the whole Kingdom of Glory business peddled to us down on Earth lacked enough imagination and flair to suit me — or Lily.

"What do we *do* in heaven?" I repeatedly asked Grandma Kitty as she patiently tucked me into bed each night.

"Anything you want. You can walk and play on the streets of gold and enjoy the music."

I already walked and played here on Earth. Shouldn't we be doing something different Over There? Like, flying through walls? Talking to trees?

Suspicious, I asked about the music.

"Oh!" Grandma Kitty lit up and clasped her hands to her chest. She loved music. "There's glorious singing from the angels, like the choir at church."

That did it. I'd heard my fair share of the church choir and their buttoned-up Protestant hymns. The idea of listening to that racket for all of eternity made me want to jump out the window. Gravity being a thing, however, I was desperately afraid I wouldn't survive the leap and would end up in Grandma's heaven. I managed to bring on my first existential crisis before age five.

Fortunately, I had a roommate in the form of a six-inch man-toy who lived in the closet until after dark. He was skinny, with wooden legs, and sported red and white vertically-striped pants. When I couldn't sleep, he'd show off how he could step through the window onto the outside sill, elongate his legs two stories to the ground, and roam the streets until morning.

I was stuck in a body that came with different rules. I peered out the window after him, envying his freedom. Something about his abilities, his very existence, made sense, when a lot of other things didn't.

Such as how Grandma and Dad treated each other. Pops could get on Grandma's last nerve, but Dad manufactured all new ways to send Grandma over the edge, at least according to how she spoke of him behind his back.

Dad played out of the same rule book, but more lightheartedly, laughing to me about Grandma's controlling ways and how she hen-pecked poor Pops. But Dad was always polite to her face.

Dad moved into an apartment around the corner and started a law practice in town. Every now and then, he'd pick me up for a sleepover. Not having a clue what to do with a four-year-old, he took me to the grocery store to buy all the junk food I wasn't allowed to eat at home. We'd stay up all hours of the night, playing records and going through coins he'd gathered from his global travels.

The following morning, I returned to Grandma and Pops, hair wrestled into lopsided pigtails, high on Froot Loops, drenched in Dad's clinging cigar smoke, and happy.

More often than not, though, Friday or Saturday evening had me waiting at the end of the driveway. No call from Dad, no pickup, just a no-show.

"Must be busy," Grandma said through pursed lips.

Mom had a strict rule that Dad couldn't put me in the car if he'd had even one drink. So he just disappeared. I didn't understand why Grandma couldn't walk me around the corner, bang on his door, and drop me off.

"Because he might be in there laid up drunk as a skunk," Grandma explained. "So it's better if you just stay home with me. You won't come home reeking like a smokestack."

I didn't like Grandma's tone when she talked about Dad.

While I was disappointed, I wasn't devastated. Pops did all the things with a kid a dad would do. Taught me to play badminton, ride a bike, plant a garden.

One Saturday morning, I got all dressed up, but instead of waiting on Dad, Grandma announced my cousin Shaun was coming to walk me to my first movie. Shaun was about 14, closer enough to my age to be way cooler than Dad or Pops. Aunt Lily had been Shaun's grandmother, and since she died, Grandma and Pops moved into that role for Shaun.

He took me to the cartoon, *The Rescuers*, and we chatted about the characters all the way home. I asked him about their lives and what they did when they weren't in a movie. All of Shaun's answers made sense.

I told him about my roommate, Man-Toy. Shaun was fascinated and asked where he lived.

"In the closet. Where Grandma stores her shoes."

"Ah. So he can slip through walls and dimensions through a portal."

"What?"

"It's a door. But you might not be able to see it."

Emboldened, I shared our conversation with Grandma one day as she rummaged through shoe boxes. "A man lives in there." I proudly let her know what she certainly was already aware of.

"There's no man in the closet." Her voice was kind and firm, likely meant to scare away baddies.

I was so stunned she didn't know about him, I couldn't even argue with her. I waited until she left and hunted for him, climbing under the winter coats, over shoe racks, all the way to the back wall. No little man. No secret door.

The next time I saw Man-Toy, I called Grandma into the room. "He's right there on the dresser," I whispered in the dark, worried he'd disappear if I spoke too loud.

"That's your mother's perfume bottle. I bought it for her birthday. It's just your imagination turning it into a little man."

I could clearly differentiate between the Emeraude bottle and my tiny friend. I *knew* what I was seeing. I *knew* he was there.

"But Shaun said Man-Toy can come and go through an invisible door."

"Don't you listen to everything Shaun says. He can't always be trusted." *That* idea was devastating. Shaun was my new favorite human. I stayed silent as Grandma hugged me goodnight. "I'm so glad I don't have to share you with your Dad tonight. Aren't you happy to be here in your own bed? Lay down and I'll rub your back."

A terrible notion sparked to life. Grandma could be right. What if there was no Man-Toy? Shaun hadn't seen him. He just believed me where Grandma didn't.

But, if I made up something in my mind, shouldn't it stay in my mind? How could my imagination conjure something into a three-dimensional little man six feet away from me? That prospect was disturbing.

⊙⚉⋘⊙⊙⚉⊙

That movie outing was the first and last time Shaun took me out as a child or babysat me. Shortly thereafter, he came to the back door, visibly upset, and asked Grandma and Pops to come outside. I stayed inside next to the open kitchen window so I could hear every word.

I heard Shaun confessing that he had done something stupid, something that might hit the papers, and he was there to apologize for any embarrassment caused to the family. Apparently, he broke into the public library with a few friends after hours and stole computers. The cops easily arrested them.

Pops said calmly, "You don't need to apologize to us. You need to apologize to the library and to yourself."

Grandma tsked, her voice louder and more shrill. "That's just about the dumbest thing I ever heard of. You didn't think you would get caught? You've embarrassed your mother! Those friends of yours don't sound like friends to me."

Pops spoke again. "I hope you'll see that was a poor decision. You always have choices in life, and this time, you made the wrong one. But next time, make a better one."

Shaun left, dejected, his shoulders drooping with shame. I felt terrible for him. Grandma turned on Pops. "I told you he's headed down the wrong path. But you can't blame him. His mother is heading down the same road as your sister. Drinking and smoking and spending money like water."

"He'll be just like your side of the family if he doesn't watch out," Pops retorted.

Shaun never fully got back into the good graces of Grandma and Pops, if he had them to begin with. Shaun was a science geek, fascinated by electronics and mechanics. He took radios and gadgets apart to see how they worked, then put them back together again. Even before the library debacle, Pops wouldn't let him touch any of the electronics gathering dust in our basement, not even an old radio that didn't work anymore. "He'll ruin it," Pops said.

Shortly after the library break-in, Shaun had an accident with his chemistry set. Shaun's mother called, flustered and in a tizzy, hoping to talk with my mom. My mom and Shaun's mom were cousins, and they were also close friends.

When she arrived, another hushed family powwow ensued outside on the patio. I could see through the window that Mom had pulled out her mental health nursing face as she listened to her cousin. Grandma and Pops left them out there and caught me eavesdropping at the kitchen window.

I expected her to pretend like all was okay, but Grandma hissed, "Ambrose, there was no 'accident.' Shaun tried to kill himself with that chemistry set."

Pops clicked his tongue. "We don't know that. Maybe he's just not careful. That's why I can't let him play with the radio downstairs."

There were undercurrents too subtle for me to comprehend. But their treatment of Shaun as a second-class citizen seeped into me, and I started to grow a protective boundary between us when he came by to visit. The same boundary of distrust formed between Man-Toy and me.

When I was six, Mom and I moved into our own apartment in the next town over. The man-toy stayed tucked in the closet at Grandma and Papa's house. To his credit, he came out faithfully every time we returned for overnight stays, yet by then, I had grown wary of him.

❦

During this time, I experienced horrific night terrors. In the middle of the night, the sound of timber crackling, then the smell of smoke awakened me. I'd open my eyes, see the wall next to my bed shimmering from heat, invisible flames threatening to collapse the structure, and I knew, without a doubt, I was dreaming.

Sometimes, I dared to place my hand on the wall, telling my slowly waking mind, "The wall is not hot. The house is not on fire. The wall is real. The smoke is not."

Other nights, the lumps in the comforter at the bottom of the bed were rats. I tucked my feet way into my body so they wouldn't bite me and simultaneously told myself there was no way my bed was teeming with rats. Every now and then, I screwed-up the courage to shove my feet back to the bottom of the bed, where I found only cool sheets.

None of my friends at slumber parties appeared to have night terrors, or shape-shifting, talking doll besties that were inarguably real. Something was different with the way I saw things.

⁕

I was eight or nine, settled in for the night, when I first heard my bedroom door creak open and the unmistakable sound of footsteps approaching on the carpet. I wasn't yet asleep and assumed it was Mom. I looked over the covers and saw no one. I yanked the blankets back over my face, suddenly scared. The footsteps continued toward me. They reached the end of the bed. *Someone* was in my room.

I don't remember if I heard her voice, in my head, announcing herself, caught a whiff of scented lipstick and cigarette smoke, or if I just knew. Lily. I kept my head buried under the covers, but I relaxed. The presence was too familiar to be frightening.

I told my mom about the door opening and the footsteps the following morning. Because the Grandma-meet-Man-Toy attempt bombed, I knew to leave out my conclusion that the visitor was Lily.

"You probably heard footsteps from the people upstairs," Mom suggested helpfully. "I'm certain no one was in your room."

No. Way. I knew the difference between hearing people walking around upstairs and footsteps on my own carpet. Plus, I felt the unmistakable presence of *someone else* with me, just like with the man-toy.

The footsteps, the scent, and the slight weight at the foot of the bed, as if someone perched there, indicated Lily's presence visiting, night after night. It felt like she checked in on me at the end of the day.

Instead of dreading the sound of feet padding across the carpet, I missed her when I fell asleep without hearing them.

⌖

This juxtaposition between what I experienced as "real" versus what I knew was the dream world intruding into my waking world may have been what propelled me into the library. I became a voracious reader of all things supernatural, tearing through every ghost book I could get my hands on, and reading books written for children above my age. From ghosts, I moved on to stories about witches, dream states, magical parallel dimensions, and astral travel, anything that wasn't mired in strict reality or stuffy religion.

I remember a book about a girl who communicated with her deceased grandmother, honed her telepathic skills, referred to as ESP in the 1980s, and at one point, this girl even spoke with her future self. I checked out and read that book so many times, the binding crumbled.

Other books crept into my awareness as well. Books that offered a more scientific explanation for why my perception of the world's reality seemed so different than everyone else's.

Mom was a psychiatric nurse. She had interesting books on the shelf, including Sylvia Plath's *The Bell Jar*.

Lo and behold! There were other people out there who heard voices and saw beings, experienced full-on sensory perceptions that were as real as anything else. In other words, the experiences took place *outside* their heads. Not relegated to the shameful space of "just your imagination." They were objective.

But the more I investigated these sorts of books, the more I understood that if an experience is objective, other people should witness it too.

If not …

TWO

❧

FORTUNATELY, THERE WAS a madhouse around the corner that offered the promise of asylum. In those years, this clever asylum existed in the form of a rickety but sizable wooden stage, glaring spotlights and a cavernous auditorium.

As soon as I stepped my six-year-old foot onto that stage during my first-grade dance recital, the madhouse whispered, *Welcome home.*

Mom was agile and loved to dance but worried she lacked co-ordination. She vowed that her daughter would feel comfortable moving in her body. She enrolled me in creative movement classes at my Montessori kindergarten where Mr. Rose visited once a week to teach us how to twinkle like a star and sprinkle like rain.

I loved those sessions so much that in first grade Saturdays meant proper tap and ballet classes at Beckley Dance Theater. Mr. Rose's baritone voice filled the studio, jovially admonishing us to "prance like cats, not tromp like elephants!"

By the end of the year, despite our first-grade class failing to master these critical life skills, Mr. Rose had the grace to put us on stage, in a real theater.

Five minutes before our turn to shine, all us little girls single-filed it against the wall in the backstage hallway. Everyone but me chattered away the moments. I looked up and down our line. Our first-grade costumes were so ugly I felt embarrassed. Families paid good money for those scratchy, sequined getups.

But one more show tune later, a nudge in the back through the stage door, past the wings and into the lights, I was a goner. From first-time user to mach 10 addicted. *Hey, if anyone wants to stick me in a hideous, bright orange tutu ever again and toss me in front of an audience, let's do it!*

If there had been an asylum attendant lurking in the wings offstage with a clipboard and a list of possible inmates, he would have placed a check next to my name.

With the notation: *Exhibits abnormally heightened response to the stimulus. Mania. May be prone to hysteria when endorphins and adrenaline run low. Long-term treatment likely.*

Not surprisingly, the following day, an adrenaline crash pounded down my door and delivered a horrible blow. I had to wait an *entire year* to get back onstage again. There were no other performing opportunities in our small town between that moment and the second-grade recital, one year away.

Irritable, crying, uncomfortable in my skin, I had no idea how I would survive.

Like I said, addicted.

My great-grandmother, Sabina, and her brother Charlie, the ones who held the seances and talked with spirits, had a younger sister, Grace. Aunt Grace had an irrepressible need to — guess what? Dance.

When Grace disappeared from Fayetteville in 1923, this spirit-communicating family faced, head on, the worst-case scenario. Grace must have hopped on the train to Cincinnati to become a "dancer."

In those days, entertainment venues glittered Cincinnati, primarily catering to burlesque appetites. Thankfully, Granddad Alf Taylor, the congressman, knew what to do. He and his buddies boarded the next train west, determined to coax Grace into returning home before she brought on permanent damage to everyone's reputation.

The Find Grace party started with where the men *knew* she would be: the most low-rent strip club in town — because who else would hire a runaway large on a dream but short on talent?

Grace wasn't there.

They hit one club after another, each venue a step up toward respectability, drinking and patronizing their way through a sleazy town they seemed to know an awful lot about.

The search and rescue crew finally decided to regroup over dinner, even considering the prospect of involving law enforcement. Because they'd earned it, they chose the most prestigious establishment in Cincinnati, with proper, late-night supper club entertainment.

Who had the prettiest legs kicking it up onstage? Aunt Grace.

Any woman in the family would have started the search there first. But the men either discounted Grace's drive and talent, or wanted an excuse to take the long road looking for her. After all they'd witnessed of Cincinnati's nightlife, they were so relieved that Grace worked as a real showgirl in a high-class establishment, they let her stay in Cincinnati.

On Grace's part, it's hard to say if she needed to dance, or if she needed to get out of a small town, and dancing was her golden ticket. Regardless, she earned her headdress as far as the patriarchs were concerned. They returned home Grace-less, but puffed out their chests with pride when telling the story.

Somehow, I managed to bide time each year between recitals, and starting in third grade, the Christmas ballet, *The Nutcracker*, blessedly broke up the year.

Dad married my fabulous stepmother, Drema, about this time. Dark, short hair, always coiffed and immaculately dressed, she cut a striking figure. She was the opposite of my little-make-up, com-fy-clothed, no-fuss-no-muss pretty Mom.

Drema worked her way up from a teenaged dishwasher in the kitchen of a nursing home to the regional president of several major national healthcare corporations, living and traveling all over the country. She embodied the sky's-the-limit, you-can-have-it-all-if-you-work-hard attitude.

Back then, she and Dad still lived close enough to attend every *Nutcracker* performance, which they did, even when they had to sit through two hours of older girls clunking around before the eight-year-olds tiptoed out at the end to parade for 60 seconds in angel costumes. Even under those circumstances, Dad and Drema dressed to the nines, better than your average Sunday church clothes, making me feel like the show was worth going all out for.

Drema always introduced me as "the daughter she never had but always wanted," and lavished me with cute skirts and jeans and jewelry.

Grandma Kitty observed with disapproval, "Honey, you shouldn't allow yourself to be bought like that."

To which Mom gently commented, "Drema is wonderful, and she's a positive addition to Jack's life. All a mother can ever ask for is for someone to be good to your child."

So color me baffled when the summer I was nine, Grandma called Dad a hero. "Put on your tennis shoes. I need to show you something." She took my hand and marched me uptown. I felt too old to be holding hands with an adult, but Grandma was more serious than normal and walked at a clip.

We reached Dad's office on Main Street and stopped across the street. Dad had the corner office, with windows on two sides. His desk was positioned by the windows.

"Are we going in?" I asked. Dad's secretary, Lisa, always welcomed me when I stopped by, whether Dad was in or not. Grandma, in spite of her mouthiness about her former son-in-law, never failed to point out his law office with pride every time we drove by.

"No, honey. No one's in there today. Do you see those holes in the window?"

I nodded.

"Those are bullet holes. A man went in there yesterday and shot up the place. But your dad's okay. You might hear about it on the news, and I thought you needed to see it and hear about it for yourself first."

"Was Dad there? Was Lisa there?"

"Yes. A woman came in, wanting a divorce from her husband. The husband went crazy. He turned the gun on your dad. So your dad pulled out his gun and shot him. Killed him."

My eyes widened. If Grandma hadn't been so matter-of-fact, my eyes probably would have popped out of my head.

I knew where Dad sat at his desk. I could see from the holes that it was a miracle those bullets didn't hit Dad on their way to the window.

Grandma continued, "That man was out of his mind. Your dad had no choice. He saved Lisa's life, and he saved his own life. But you might not hear from him for a while. He'll need some down time after this."

"Dad had a gun?" Dad was vocal about supporting the idea of the Second Amendment while hating guns.

"He bought it two days ago. Put it in his desk drawer. Good thing too."

Grandma tugged at my hand, pulling me toward our next errand. I had no idea how she knew what she knew, but that was that. End of discussion.

⁓⁓⁓⁓

My addiction to dancing soon bled out of the theater and into the studio. When I was in ballet class or rehearsal, every aspect of my humanity - mental, emotional, physical and imaginative - melded into one seamless, expansive expression.

I soon grasped that within the technique itself there exists the promise that a sequence can be perfected, such that a human will transcend mere steps and become, for a fleeting moment, the living embodiment of Something More. I became rabid in that pursuit.

Mr. Rose fueled the fire with stories of glamor, of how to walk into every room with the command of royalty, and of former students who became professional dancers in far away cities. During those hours, everything was possible.

I threw myself into as many classes as the Beckley Dance Theater school would allow me to take. Year after year, I pestered Mom to call Mr. Rose to see if there was any way to take more classes, and how much they would cost. Alas, until I grew older, the offerings were limited.

Something about this limitation didn't sit right. I believed in my bones that somewhere, out there in the world, existed a place where girls could dance every single day after school. Or skip the banality of school altogether and practice only what mattered, like perfecting dance techniques to a soaring score, or casting spells to make the walls shimmer and candles twirl.

⁘

Perhaps further propelling my need to escape into Something More was a group of bullies in the neighborhood.

Mom and I lived in a basement apartment at the furthest end of the street from school. The apartment's front door was down a sloping walkway, around the back of the house, and looked out into a large, beautiful yard that descended into forest and a creek.

Vivi was the only nice kid in the neighborhood. She was one year older than me and lived at the opposite end of the street, closer to school. Between us lay a gauntlet of cruelty.

Mornings were usually quiet as I walked up to Vivi's house, and from there, we trekked to school together every single weekday, rain, shine or sideways blowing snow. Maybe in the morning, the parents of the unholy terrors hadn't yet left for work, or they carted their hateful spawn to school by car.

But afternoons were sheer hell. While Vivi could have played with the neighborhood brats, she stayed by my side on the way home from school. However, by virtue of where she lived, she and I parted ways at the top of the street, and I was left to tiptoe down to my block alone.

If I could just get around the side of our house and into the back-yard without anyone noticing... If the babysitter would leave *General Hospital* for five minutes and come meet me on the sidewalk...

The sitter, Cruella, was a teenager in high school, so she held ulti-mate moral authority over everyone. She never smiled, and she could shoot a look so cold, flames straight from hell would freeze.

Most afternoons, she waited for me, glued to the TV set inside our apartment, while on my way home, my very existence insulted the trolls as I made my way through their gauntlet. "Get away from my house, Swamp Rat! Don't touch my sidewalk! Scurry back to where you belong."

"Throw the ball at her, run her off! Vermin!"

"We should get a BB gun and shoot you!"

"You're not one of us."

Kids have an uncanny instinct for sniffing out and ruthlessly shunning the oddball in the crowd.

But truer words were never spoken. Thank God.

I recalled seeing a fleeting conversation on Oprah, between Cruella's channel flipping, where a guest broke down sobbing over her childhood mistreatment. A grown adult crying on national television!

It seemed mortifying to let anyone know they got to you. So I adopted Cruella's haughty expression, never blinked, walked straight ahead and never crossed the street. I just quietly swore, *One day, they'll beg to be my friend. In the meanwhile, be invisible.*

I really just wanted to enjoy my walk home in peace. It seemed deeply wrong for those kids to put so much effort into robbing some-one of something so simple.

Cruella did come out to the front of the house every now and again, once I screwed-up the courage to ask her to walk me home. "Why are they yelling at you?"

"I don't know. I don't know why they don't leave me alone if they hate me so much."

"Well, you must have done something to make them do this to you." I should have known Cruella was worse than they were. Rumor had it that I wasn't the only younger child she tormented.

She shook her head in disgust. "No wonder you don't have friends. There's something not right about you. Why can't you just be normal?"

That year, I stopped going to the bathroom at school. Maybe it was to control the only thing I could, my bladder. I'd walk to the bathroom with the other girls in my class, none of whom lived on my street or were mean girls, but I couldn't bring myself to leave the group to go into the stall. Or maybe I love a challenge and wanted my after-school walk to be even more miserable by adding in the rush factor to get home.

Lo and behold, one day, Cruella wasn't at my house when I arrived. I didn't have a key. I waited and waited outside, hopping around on the patio and finally peed down my wooly tights and into the snow.

Just as I breathed in relief, Cruella zipped around the corner with three of her high school friends. She spotted a sizable yellow spot near where I stood in the snow, with steam rising.

"What did you do?" she demanded. "*Pee?*" She angrily stamped fresh snow over the yellow spot to cover it up.

Her friends looked on in horror. "Oh, *this* is who you babysit." They'd already heard about me. But I guess no one expected to find that I was still feral.

As if I couldn't hear, Cruella hissed, "Now you know what I was talking about." She shook her finger in my face and spat, "Do not tell your mother. She will be furious. I don't want to hear a word out of you for the rest of the day."

They then had no problem going inside my house, watching our TV, eating up all our food, and leaving a mess in the kitchen.

Mom was pretty upset with the sitter when she found out why my tights were in the sink. I don't know what words were had, whether Mom wanted to fire her and get someone else or what.

I know at some point, desperate to prove my worth to the kids on the street and to my sitter, who by all accounts was the coolest in the neighborhood, I told Mom she could keep working with us. But Mom made sure I had a key after that.

My afternoon mantra then became, *If I can just get to ballet…* Once in dance class, I felt human again, normal even. My limbs grew lighter, and instead of wishing I could disappear, Mr. Rose encouraged us to be seen and to feel good in our bodies. Maybe there was a value to my existence, after all, something I was beginning to doubt.

⚬᷎⸱⸱⸱⸱⸱⸱⸱⸱

A television show aired on Thursday nights that convinced me Something More was real, and the kids around me, Cruella included, were leftover Neanderthals pretending to be modern humans. They were not my future.

Fame. According to the television, there *was* a place where kids unabashedly pursued Something More. They might not have lived in a full-on magical reality, but the theater was the next best thing. These kids went to school to focus on performing. Every. Single. Day.

A few years later, *Double Trouble* started, another show about two young ballerinas in New York. New York City! It dawned on me that some people had the luck of being born in a different place in the world, and in those places, even within the tangible confines of life on Earth, Something More existed. The kids on TV were proof of that, and I grew thoroughly jealous of them.

Those kids lived life out loud, filled with dazzling, human-made beauty, attended schools where they engaged with exciting topics and conversations, and generally did awe-inspiring, stimulating stuff all the time. They even walked down the street to and from school unaccosted by their peers.

In other words, that cube in the living room showed me a world where opportunities abounded, and children flourished. There didn't seem to be a ceiling on the pursuit of brilliance or merely imagining it.

From where I sat, however, Mr. Rose and his technicolor world only seemed to exist in the studio. The magical reality I craved only existed in make-believe books. Outside the studio, the theater and my fantastical books, the world shrank to gray, unnaturally restrictive at best and downright harmful on a daily basis. Where I lived had to be the culprit.

My parents were educated, held good jobs, and Mom and I lived on a pretty street, in a breathtaking area of cliffs and gorges, creeks and forests that Pops took us exploring through every weekend.

But even Dad and Drema moved up and out to the state's capital, where Drema was offered a promotion and where Grandma said, "Maybe your Dad will now live up to his potential as a lawyer."

Grandma and Pops never hesitated to credit my dad as a *good* lawyer if anyone asked, but Grandma privately held onto the notion that he must be leaving opportunities on the table if he only worked on Main Street in a small, dying coal town.

Children don't grasp that one day they'll age into self-determination, so I spent many days and nights wondering why I had the bad luck to be born where Nothing Good was the only thing that ever happened, and Apathy was the only host of any gathering.

Maddeningly, everyone — including other children — seemed to have signed an unspoken social contract that Not Enough was acceptable, and human-created beauty was an ideal that didn't belong to us.

I am positive and grateful by nature, but these attitudes didn't resonate with me from the get-go. Grace's blood ran in my blood. While Mom and Pops and Grandma Kitty may not have understood my full-on embrace of a magical reality, Pops preached travel and education more fervently than the Bible. They even started a savings account in my name with the admonishment that I not spend the money on a car or material items but on seeing the world.

It is not surprising that from age ten onward, every cell in my body harbored one single-minded focus: Get Out.

The following year, when it came time to either try out for the cheerleading team and maybe, finally, be part of the in-crowd, I tossed my dance bag over my shoulder for the extra ballet classes I was finally old enough to take.

Even on Friday afternoons, when I was frequently the only kid who showed up for that additional pointe class to work on strength and technique. After I wore out my muscles and toes, I fell into my familiar favorite books about ghosts, telepathy, and girls who talked with their deceased ancestors.

Until one of the long-deceased ballerinas in a *DanceMagazine* photo leapt off the page and into my room.

⟡⟡⟡

Her black-and-white picture in that month's *DanceMagazine* revealed that she was a typical Balanchine ballerina, characterized by impossibly long, thin limbs, a short torso and a neck like a swan. Her dramatic, dark gaze bore into me as I sat on the floor of my bedroom flipping through the magazine.

She seemed to come to life. It was subtle, but sure enough, something *above* the page hovered over her image and shimmered.

I was home alone for the evening while Mom was in class for her Master's. Clearly, without enough human interaction for too many hours in a row, my imagination had run away with itself for its own cruel entertainment.

I closed the magazine, but unable to resist, quickly re-opened it.

The air hovering over the photograph appeared to move again, this time forming into a ball. Clear plasma, the size of a small tennis ball, with twinkling electric blue dots, appeared to gel between me and the photograph.

"Hello?" My voice sounded skeptical, and unnaturally loud in my room.

Thankfully, no one spoke back, even as I was certain I was not alone. The hair on the back of my neck stood on end.

Then the ball *moved.* In my head, I repeated, *Hello!* It seemed a lot less kooky to continue this conversation telepathically. It came closer, moved away, then danced up and down around me. I smiled and felt the energy ball smile back.

Oooh, boy, I thought, *a twinkling ball is "smiling"*?

I noted that I wasn't seeing any portion of a human or animal figure form, but I was sensing playfulness, and even something of an interaction. Then, unmistakably, I began to feel more than one presence around me. It seemed like my room was crowded with people — and suddenly noisy.

The longer I watched the energy ball, and truly made out a defined shape *outside my head*, in 3-D reality, the more I knew I wasn't making up the entire experience.

I wondered briefly if the plasma-like ghost ball really was the spirit of a true ballerina, gracing me with her presence, or if the photograph had triggered something in me that allowed me to discern and interact with shapes and forms I couldn't ordinarily see.

The latter made sense, as far as any of this was rational. In contrast, the notion that a real dancer from New York City Ballet would take time out of her afterlife to visit *me* in Beckley, West Virginia struck me as preposterously impossible.

Hours seemed to pass before Mom finally arrived home. By then, the fact that the energy ball remained tootling around my room — I could see it clear as day, and I could still sense a crowd of invisible people — freaked me the hell out.

Why couldn't I just be normal?! I couldn't hide my rattled state, and obviously, I needed an adult to help shoo everyone out of the house.

I urgently dragged Mom into my room and plunged into a blubbering confession of the evening's events, culminating with, "You can't see the ball? Twinkling blue dots?? *IT'S RIGHT THERE!*" I jabbed at mid-air, then shook the helpless magazine.

Mom adjusted her glasses and viewed the photograph intently, playing along like any psychiatric nurse worth her salt. "That dancer sure does have an intense look on her face. I can see how this is a disturbing picture." She closed the magazine.

The ball dissipated. Suddenly, there was no one in the room but Mom and me. The air stopped sizzling.

Mom straightened up. "I've left you alone too long with your supernatural books." She headed into the living room where my beloved friends were stacked next to a comfy reading chair.

"Nooooooo!" I cried.

"If these books about witches and flying ghosts are scaring you, I think we need a break from them." Mom piled the books by the door to return to the library.

I sobbed harder. The books were innocent. The stories inside their covers were make-believe. What I saw and felt in my room was *real*. Then again, perhaps I couldn't tell the difference.

"Pick one that we don't take back right away. But how about we also see if there are any new Nancy Drew mysteries."

Mom reminded me that, "You're lucky I allow you to choose your own books. Grandma wouldn't let me read anything interesting or popular, including after I went away to college! She even read all of my letters from friends before I got to read them."

I stared wide-eyed at Mom. Personal privacy reigned supreme in our household.

She warned, "But if you pick books that upset you, I'm going to have to start vetting what you read first, like Grandma did."

The books weren't the problem. The problem was me.

If I was going to be like one of the kids on *Fame* when I grew up — and it looked like that was my only way out — I had to avoid indulging whatever it was in my head that made me act like a lunatic.

If I was unacceptably off, like the kids up the street said, well then, I didn't need to voluntarily hand over additional evidence for their file. I needed to show up in the studio the following day as a normal person. No more supernatural stories. Ghosts were for babies and weirdos.

⁘

In the fall of sixth grade, my ballet friends and I squeezed into Mom's car, more girls than seatbelts, for a road trip to a scholarship audition to ballet summer schools. None of us would have attended a summer school for ballet if we weren't on scholarship. The travel, tuition and room and board would have been prohibitively expensive, on top of the already astronomical cost of pointe shoes.

Mr. Rose pounded into our heads that the entire adventure was for Fun Only. But just in case, we had to dance big and dance our way to the front.

He added, "Maybe if you dance well, Mr. Noble will remember you in future years." Duncan Noble taught at a place called North Carolina School of the Arts, and in this audition, he also had the power to choose which students received scholarships at multiple schools. The school where he taught was so prestigious, according to Mr. Rose, we shouldn't even worry about it.

When the ladies running the audition handed out numbers to pin to our leotards, most girls shied to the back of the room, while us Beckley Dance Theater gals filled in the void at the front with confidence. I took Number 3, and vowed from that point forward it would be my lucky number.

Duncan Noble walked in like his spine was a steel rod, and with more severity than I'd ever known capable in a human being. It was so quiet, you could hear a strand of hair slip out of a bun. But his voice was soft and gentle as he guided us through exercises in the makeshift studio, a school cafeteria with uneven, linoleum-tiled floors.

When the audition was over, we waited to hear the winners called out. First up, there was a scholarship to a one-week dance camp at Marshall University. I had been there the previous summer and looked forward to going back. But the scholarship went to another girl.

Next, a three-week scholarship to the School of the Lexington Ballet. One of our own was called! She was a year or two older than me, and as Mr. Rose said, the scholarships would probably go to the teenagers. I was 11 and would only be 12 by the following summer. There was only one scholarship left. The fancy one, out of our league.

"Number Three." Mr. Noble glanced at me and barely nodded. I stared at him, suddenly weighted into my seat. All of my buddies started screaming and rushing around me.

I finally asked, wide-eyed, "What is this North Carolina School of the Arts?"

The girls screeched, *"It's like FAME!!"*

THREE

SUMMER PROGRAMS ARE like bootcamps, and North Carolina School of the Arts was no different. That first summer, I had a blast. The other 12-year-olds were like me, hearts on fire to test just how fast and far our skin and bones could fly. We were the youngest girls accepted into NCSA.

We each hoped that attending a summer ballet program would put us on the radar as someone to watch. If our abilities showed promise of developing into something preternatural, we would be invited to a professional training school year-round.

Back in that day, NCSA was the only place of its kind in the United States. For children on a professional arts path, such as dancing, music or acting, NCSA was the only school that offered training, academic schooling and room and board, all in one spot.

As the babiest of baby ballerinas at NCSA, we were over the moon to have a ticket to the ball. We fed our obsession like gluttons, dancing morning, noon and night. We must have felt, even then, an underlying urgency, perhaps bordering on desperation.

While ballet was the focus, we also learned flamenco, folk dancing, jazz, and contemporary movement. Then there were the classes
and workshops on all the other behind-the-scenes knowledge required for professional performing, the hair-do's and don'ts, unusual
character makeup and how to stand out at a cattle call audition of
hundreds.

Adults did not talk to us in a manner designed to temper expectations. There was none of the "Hey, by the way, most girls don't actually make it, so just have fun and build character" sort of attitudes
that Mr. Rose promoted.

Instead, we were expected to do our best. It was understood that
the only way to survive, going forward, for each of us, was to pursue
turning professional.

We were also required to read Shakti Gawain's *Creative
Visualization* and attend meditation classes two nights a week. Kate,
our meditation leader, suggested that we visualize perfecting prob-
lematic techniques every morning before getting out of bed and
every night before falling asleep. For choreography, it was "replay the
music in your mind so often, its cadence will flow through your veins."

Turns out, in certain forums, a wild imagination isn't judged or
even merely tolerated. It can be codified into the curriculum.

Adults told us that if we couldn't physically achieve it, the fault
lay only in our lack of effort in blending the mind and body. "Light as
a feather, stiff as a board" wasn't a preteen gag for us. We gathered every evening in one of our rooms to practice, certain we could levitate
with the help of our coven.

Maybe ghosts and magical practices weren't for babies after
all. Or maybe, even better, there wasn't anything wrong with being
fiercely driven and weird.

Then there were the older teenage girls who were so awe-inspiring, we piled up outside the door of their ballet classes and gaped.

God willing and the creek didn't rise, they were the embodiment of our future.

At the end of the summer, four of us preteens were chosen for an onstage exercise for the faculty. We each had to perform the exact same choreography, one by one, and exhibit that as a solo performer, we could command a stage by ourselves and not shrink under the pressure.

Easy. Mr. Rose, back home, taught us that trick. You always dance for the person in the last row. Appear nine feet tall so that the folks in the nosebleeds shift to the edge of their seat and feel the hair raise on the back of their necks. Otherwise, the black space of a theater will swallow you whole.

I can't remember if some of us, or all four of us, were then cast to perform the choreography at the end of summer recital. I just remember taking my place in the wings, then bursting into the lights, expanding my auric field to fill the entirety of the stage and the theater, warming up the audience for the big girls, the real dancers, to follow.

We 12-year-olds giggled away our summer, our dreams coming true with astonishing ease, the entire world open to us.

The world was filled with Something More. Kate even said so in meditation. "If you can imagine it, you can achieve it."

The older girls, in their perfection, never cracked a smile. That should have been a five-alarm warning.

⚜

Secure with an invitation to return the following summer, I returned home, started junior high, and attended academic classes that were at least mildly interesting. I earned an image of she-could-make-it-in-New-York one day, so the bullies either grew up or became more sophisticated in ways to wield evil. In any event, they left me alone.

Most importantly, I could attend classes at Beckley Dance Theater five days a week, and perform at a challenging level in multiple roles in both *The Nutcracker* and the spring recital.

For the grand finale of the seventh-grade recital, we performed a chorus line routine where a line of girls roped arms and kicked our legs up to the rafters, probably not unlike Aunt Grace.

Then the girl next to me lost her balance at the height of her kick. I strengthened my grip to hold her up, but it wasn't enough. Her right leg slammed down, her heel ramming onto the top of my left arch. White hot pain seared through my foot and up my leg. The entire line nearly fell like dominoes.

Thanks to Mr. Rose's training, no one hit the ground. The music didn't stop, so neither did we. We recovered without a break in our smiles, caught up to the music, and finished the piece.

As I exited into the wings, a stagehand said, "You took a major hit out there. You okay?"

"Fine," I replied, flashing him a smile and limping as soon as I passed the audience's sight line. "Just need to shake it off." I could barely breathe.

He squinted at me as I discovered that I couldn't put any weight on my left foot. "You covered it up well. Like a true professional."

Mom thought it was a bone bruise, which would hurt like hell. Besides, we had to perform several more nights.

It never crossed my mind not to perform those next shows. Everyone knows that the show goes on. With or without you.

I returned to NCSA for another five-week bootcamp that summer, between seventh and eighth grade. When I first arrived on campus, a familiar, sun-tanned face greeted me with her mischievous grin and Carolina accent. My friend from the previous summer, Jen.

She tossed me a teasing look and said, "I can't wait to get in class tomorrow!"

I learned what she meant the next morning. We stood next to each other, just as we had every day the previous summer. We were both naturally flexible, but somewhere along the way, I became, by far, the most bendy girl in any room.

I watched Jen slowly extend her leg to the side, all the way up to her ear, until her foot was a good one inch higher than mine. What the ...?!?! I tried to hoist my leg higher. It wouldn't budge without me tumbling sideways into the barre.

At the end of the exercise, she tossed her head over her shoulder and grinned. I couldn't help but grin back. Game. On.

After class, she ran up to me. "I vowed that if we came back this summer, I'd be more flexible than you."

I was floored. For one, I felt overcome with honor that she even thought of me during the school year, and two, that I had any skill or attribute that someone wanted to emulate.

Then a truth dropped into my stomach. Why hadn't I thought of what Jen did? I spent the entire previous year driven by my addiction to dancing, coasting on natural talent, but wholly avoiding all the problem spots I really needed to work on.

I quickly dismissed such an inconvenient realization.

Jen and I spent the rest of the summer ignoring all the things we didn't do spectacularly and improving the one thing we did. We contorted ourselves, drawing out every note during *adagio* for the sake of an impossibly long, graceful line, competing to see whose leg would reach the highest before our teachers clapped, "Girls, timing! You're late." And one of us caved, brought her leg down, and moved through the next movement, grinning at each other through the mirror the entire time.

⁓⁂⁓

At some point that summer, a rumor started that some girls in our class might be asked to attend for the year. "Getting asked" meant your addiction to ballet was validated. Not to mention, career-wise, you were on track.

Robert Lindgren, the NCSA Dean of Dance who previously ran the School of American Ballet in New York, called my mother in Beckley, West Virginia. He may as well have sent a footman with a hand-engraved invitation.

Going to NCSA for the year meant living in dorms away from home to focus on a fairly grueling schedule: 90-minute technique classes in both the morning and afternoon, five days a week; rehearsals for performances in the evenings; academics sprinkled throughout. Academics were fast-paced because we wouldn't spend as much time in class as regular school.

"I don't know that we can afford this," Mom said to the dean.

"We'll work out financial aid," he promised.

Mom called Mr. Rose. "She seems awfully young to go away," she said. I was only 13. Mr. Rose agreed. His voice became more measured, uncharacteristic for him. "It's harsh for young people. Many talented dancers, who go there too early, stop dancing."

I insisted I could handle it. I had just spent the previous two summers there. I knew how "harsh" it was.

Mom called Dean Lindgren back. "I just don't think this year is the right year," she said.

"If a dancer doesn't have professional-level technique by the time she's sixteen, she'll never get a job. It could be a career-ending mistake to wait another year to bring her here," he answered.

At the very least, I thought, it seemed a given that I was going to NCSA at some point. Holy cow! I was going to NCSA, *for real!* The train was arriving at the station and my pointe shoes were my ticket onboard.

After that last call with Dean Lindgren, Mom broke rank with Mr. Rose and made a decision. We headed over to Grandma and Pops to break the news that I was leaving for the school year. We stayed with them every weekend, and overall, they felt like our shared parents, the adults in life, while Mom and I ventured out into the world to explore on our own.

Mom sat with Pops on the patio, and Pops, true to character, responded with insistent negativity to cover up that he wasn't taking the news well. "They only want your money."

Mom patiently replied, "The school is offering to pay for some of her tuition, room and board."

Grandma and I eavesdropped through the open kitchen window. She said, "All you kids need to grow, make a life of your own. I just wish it didn't have to be today."

Outside, Pops was saying, "She'll never make a living as a ballet dancer. You've worked too hard to save for her college."

I was so insulted that Pops didn't believe in my talent. Mom assured me on the way back to our house, "He's of a different generation. No one around here understands that the arts offer a career path. And we have to be okay if it doesn't. Papa only wants the best for you."

A heavy realization silenced me. I had to dance for my own survival, and I had to succeed so Mom, Gran and Pops, who did nothing but work hard their entire lives, wouldn't think their pennies were wasted on something as frivolous as a little girl's dream to be a ballerina.

"Don't get me wrong," Mom said, "I don't want you to go. I'll be lonely without you, but I will never stand in the way."

Mom waffled on her decision over the next weeks. She had a hard time discerning the right timing, whether to send me off this year or next, to a place that may have well been Oz as far as my family and our surroundings were concerned.

Finally, decision made. I started eighth grade at the local junior high, content with the certainty that I'd hop on the train to my future in ninth grade. In the meanwhile, Pops and Mr. Rose would be happy.

Dean Lindgren must have made one more call to Mom. Two weeks into junior high, Mom announced, "We're driving you down to North Carolina this weekend. Classes start there Monday."

When I told Gran and Pops goodbye, Pops gave me a thin smile and said, in a funny, higher-pitched voice than normal, "I want to pay for your pointe shoes from now on. When you buy them, tell me what I owe."

FOUR

"THIS IS THE most confusing setup I've ever seen." Mom's lips clenched into a thin line. We followed the arrows drawn with a thick, black marker onto poster boards, directing us from the financial aid office across a manicured lawn to tables marked *Academic Registration*.

I didn't understand why Mom was so overwhelmed by walking short distances across a nice campus on a sunny, warm day. Which just so happened to be THE DAY I COULD FINALLY START LIVING.

Mom forced a bright-eyed smile at the young woman behind the registration table, reaching across to her at the same time I did when the woman handed me the envelope with my class schedule inside. "Where are the teachers?" Mom asked, swiveling her head in each direction. "Can we meet the teachers?"

"I teach biology. Just helping out today with registration," answered the woman. "But," she paused, double-checking my name and grade, "Andrea won't be in my class. She'll meet all of her teachers next Monday. There will be an orientation for the students ahead of time. No worries." She smiled quickly at Mom, then leaned to gaze behind us. "Name?" she asked the next student in line.

The returning high school girls greeted each other across the lawn, comparing notes after their ventures to elite summer ballet schools in New York, San Francisco and Houston. I didn't see any adults accompanying them. These girls had poise that indicated an even higher class of existence hovered in the stratosphere, way above the older girls I watched dance on the same campus just a month ago.

I sensed I was no longer in summer ballet camp.

The under-college part of the school was exceedingly small, more so than Mom or I grasped previously. There may have only been ten of us seventh- and eighth-graders combined. All of us were the baby ballerinas — "baby bals."

I identified the newbies like me as the gawking ones, with at least one worried parent hot on their heels. Just like Mom, back in the safety of their living rooms over the past weeks, these Moms were convinced this year-round arts school idea was a good one, something that now seemed questionable.

The year-round junior and high school living area was confined to a small radius at the far end of campus, sequestered on a hill by a ring of trees. Even so, Mom seemed to notice for the first time that we were all part of one campus "with COLLEGE STUDENTS." Mom blinked rapidly in disbelief.

From registration, we scoped out the dorm. My heart leapt with reassurance when I saw Kate's friendly face in the first-floor lounge.

I didn't understand at the time how incapable a twenty-three year old might appear to a parent, so it was to my great embarrassment when Mom demanded of Kate, "Is there an adult living anywhere on this floor? Anywhere at all."

Somehow, Mom got me settled in with my sweet roommate, Tiffany. Most parents involved in the building's move-in forgot that their children needed sufficient coins on hand at any given moment to work the washers and dryers for our never-ending sweaty leotards and tights, so there was a last-minute dash to cash in twenties for rolls of quarters.

By the end of the day, each student and parent let out at least one grumpy, exhausted screech upon encountering the Palmetto bugs that resided in the bathrooms.

Palmetto bugs are ginormous flying cockroaches attracted to water, not food. Palmetto bugs existed at NCSA as one last red flag to parents debating whether to leave their children alone with them.

Every single last parent left us in favor of hotels or highways back home.

⌖

Part of the registration process included a placement class, something like an audition with less formality. Everyone from seventh to tenth grade danced together to see which ballet class we would place in. I assumed that, like in the summer, we'd all land with our grade group.

So the following day, Mom, a handful of other parents and we new students wandered through empty halls in the building that housed the dance studios. We finally found a studio where returning students gathered and stretched, with a long table and eight chairs stationed in front of the mirrors. We newbie bals inched our way inside.

A line of excessively thin women and wiry men picked their way through the parents out in the hall like tiptoeing through a yard filled with dog poop. Dean Lindgren closed the door behind the faculty members, separating us kids from our parents once and for all.

The faculty seated themselves behind the table, without introductions, and stared at us, expressionless, for the next 90 minutes. As soon as the pianist struck the first chords, my nerves melted into the joy of movement. I marveled at the ease of the older girls commanding their bodies into impossible techniques, and I could think only, *This is IT.*

When class was over, the teachers huddled. One of them asked me to come back out and repeat a combination. Confused and alone, I danced the requested routine designed to show ankle and foot strength, technical precision and speed.

All eyes were on me. The other girls hovered around the edges of the studio, brows furrowed and faces long, perhaps wishing they would be called upon next and simultaneously hoping they wouldn't.

My earlier confidence waned. I couldn't help but conclude that the faculty had doubts about my admission. I felt grateful that I wore my favorite raspberry-colored leotard, not that it would matter if I didn't prove myself worthy.

I stood sweating and out of breath by myself in the middle of the floor after the last combination, waiting to be excused once and for all. Yet, I felt that in that classroom, I danced the best I've ever performed, and I noticed that it came preternaturally easy.

And that fact, for the very first time, introduced into my dancing the element of self-consciousness.

Without any further eye contact or explanation, one of the teachers dismissed the entire class. "Thank you, ladies and gentlemen."

The faculty rose and drifted away. This time, the moms in the hall parted for them to pass.

I would come to experience that the placement audition was conducted like every other interaction with the faculty. The teachers were stoic and inaccessible, accustomed to being separated from the public as performers. The parents were the public, the wrong side of the curtain, and we students hadn't yet earned the privilege of anything more than the barest recognition.

The next day, the list went up on the bulletin board for ballet class placements. B1 was the highest, reserved for the eleventh- and twelfth-graders. I placed with girls one grade above me, in B6. The other baby bals my age were in B7.

The first week of school, our little tribe of hopefuls, clad in matching black leotards and pink tights, were marched en masse out of the studio and into the infirmary for a "health check." We chattered away until we realized the health check consisted only of a scale and a device that grabbed at skin around our stomachs and thighs.

I was one of the tallest girls in the class, and expected to weigh more than most. I stepped on the scale full of naivete.

"Too heavy," the teacher tsked. The girls peered over my shoulder, gaping along with me at what was suddenly an atrocious number for a dancer my height.

Then the nurse pulled out calipers to measure my fat percentage. The tongs pinched through my thin black leotard, and determined that my bony body had swallowed a hippopotamus.

Ballet companies expect dancers to be 15% below ideal weight for height. Essentially, an anorexic weight.

My face flushed. I stepped off the scale and tried to disappear into the sea of black leotards, but my classmates shrunk to the furthest corner of the infirmary.

"Who's next?" demanded the teacher. "Tiffany! Step it up."

I felt at once terrible and better that my sweet roommate was also deemed "chubby." Turns out, if you tumble into a reality where your body, the only tool of your trade, becomes your greatest source of shame, it's best to fall into disgrace with your whole class.

We managed to show up later in the day for pointe class, spirits crushed and shoulders slumped as each of us witnessed a foreign body reflected back to us in the mirror. Our teacher didn't help. "Ladies, a weight issue is hardly the right way to start off the year." No matter how well we danced, no matter how much our technique improved, the only thing that mattered, according to the faculty, were those dreaded numbers next to our names.

I felt betrayed. And helpless. I wasn't sure what to do, how to eat differently in the cafeteria, or whether to eat at all. Our dorm mom, Kate, might have guided us on these issues, but her door was always closed.

Two weeks later, another notice went up, indicating a change in placement for several of us. A few girls moved from B2 into B1 and vice versa or other minor shuffling. I was leapfrogged to B4. Maybe I wasn't hopelessly big after all.

However, I was two grades younger than everyone else, a difference that ensured my year in dance class would be lonely. The girls in B4 were never mean or snobby. They were just dead serious, introverted and focused. Besides, which tenth-grader wants to be friends with a kid in eighth grade?

⁕

"Sing after me, girls! Aboard, about, above, across!" The first day in Arthur Ballard's English class, we remained mute, staring at the lunatic with long white hair yodeling at us.

He had a booming, jovial voice reminiscent of Mr. Rose. So, by the second day, after much protestation that we were dancers, not vocalists, we joined in to caterwaul our prepositions in alphabetical order.

Mr. Ballard handed us a long list of books, from classic gothic literature to James Michener and Jane Austen to *The Hobbit*. "Pick nine. One book report due at the end of each month. Up to you what you read and what you want to say about it."

Our other academics were equally stimulating and fast-paced, taught by approachable teachers, many of whom had colorful personalities and humor. Compared to our dance classes, the academic building offered a welcome break in tension.

⚜

Shortly after school started, *Nutcracker* rehearsals were scheduled for most evenings. I couldn't wait to be part of the performances. When the cast list went up, I stood next to the one girl in my ballet class who regularly spoke to me, Alex, as we both desperately sought our names.

I couldn't find my name. Neither could Alex. Every single other kid in my grade was cast as soldiers or mice. The older girls, snowflakes and flowers.

Alex shrugged it off. "What I expected. Looks like I won't be back next year if I didn't get a role this year."

I wanted to feel terrible for Alex, but I was too busy blinking to hold back hot tears of disappointment. Was I too fat to be onstage?

Alex rubbed my shoulder and tried to reassure me. "Let's go ask Mr. Noble tomorrow. Make sure there's no mistake."

The following day, fate placed Mr. Noble in the hallway in my line of sight. Somehow, I found the courage to approach him. "Um, is there a mistake? My name isn't listed as a soldier. Or even a mouse." My voice squeaked, as if I were trying to prove I'd make a great mouse.

He looked down his nose at me, then tilted his chin higher. "*You want* to be a mouse or a tin toy?"

Well, yeah. It would be fun and stress-free to dance such a role, and I wanted to be part of the production, dressing up and canoodling backstage with all the other kids my age. I had never, since I could remember, *not* danced in *Nutcracker*.

Mr. Noble didn't give me time to respond. "Playing a mouse is not for you. Use this time to focus in class and practice on your own." The last thing I needed was more time alone, separated from comrades.

I dreaded telling Mom, knowing that this development might bewilder her and convince her that going to NCSA was a bad decision. Turns out, the dread dragged on for a couple of weeks.

There was only one pay phone per floor in the dorms. Mom worked regular business hours, so I had to grab the phone in the prime time of the evening when another seventh- or eighth-grader wasn't on it.

Finding the phone free had been impossible — until *Nutcracker* rehearsals ramped up. Then, everyone was in the rehearsal studio, leaving me and the phone to our lonely glory.

Mom took the news in stride and agreed wholeheartedly with Mr. Noble. I felt relieved I hadn't let her down, but sitting out *Nutrcracker* was devastating, absolutely crushing. Still, I didn't let myself even think that perhaps I would have been better off if I stayed at home and danced as a Snowflake, my favorite choreography by Mr. Rose.

The heaviness of the atmosphere began to physically incarnate into my body, pound by pound. The only area I excelled in at NCSA were academics, the one thing no one cared about.

I can attest that most of my classmates felt the same repeated, stinging failure I experienced. Yet we weren't prepared to give up on our dreams. My roommate, Tiffany, said more than once through puffy red eyes, "My dad is working three jobs so we can pay for this." One of our classmates, Charlotte, stopped speaking in the first months of school. She just went mute.

As much as our dance teachers flagellated us as "sacks of sausages," they heaped all of the blame upon our shoulders. It was no one's fault but our own that we were not performing to expectations. So we cut loose in Mr. Ballard's class, belting out our prepositions like a battle cry for our psyches.

By spring, incomprehensibly, we were hopeful to come back the following fall. We were still fed the steaming pile of dung that we were lucky to be there, we could succeed, if only we tried harder, if only we ate less, if only we stopped letting everyone down. What, pray tell, was the alternative?

"Go back home to Dolly Dinkle's Dance School and be the star in your hometown recital? You're better than this," our teacher Gina Vidal reminded us. She had a way of delivering a European-accented barb with a girlishly high-pitched voice that we mistook for silly kindness.

❦

Our heads turned sharply to the girl seated across the cafeteria, leaning heavily against the wall, an unlit cigarette in her hand. Her gaze screamed, "Fuck with me. Please. I'll rip you limb from limb."

It was breakfast during Jury Week. At the end of every year, each class performed in front of the entire faculty, who graded us, critiqued us, and determined whether we would be invited to return in the fall.

One of the older girls at the end of our table hissed under her breath, "Don't stare! That's her."

Rumor rippled through the cafeteria about the dancer, either B3 or B2, so probably 15.

"What happened?" I tried to catch the whispers going around.

With her signature straightforward compassion, Alex said, "Her roommate came in last night and found her," Alex tipped her head slightly toward the girl, "saying she was going to jump out of a window."

I then noticed both of the girl's wrists were wrapped in thick bandages.

"Her parents are coming to get her today," Alex continued.

We all shuddered. Most of us had grown into the belief that parents didn't get it, wouldn't understand our lives or us. Things had to be really bad for your parents to come pick you up before the end of the year.

"Was it drugs?" one of us whispered.

Alex shrugged.

Our table fell into heavy silence. I couldn't figure out for the life of me why, after so much distress she was in, she had to be paraded into the cafeteria. It's not like she was eating anyway.

Shouldn't she be comforted in her bed? I'm not sure who I thought would perform that task, given that none of us had seen any evidence of comfort or support on campus.

Alex must have read my thoughts. "I heard that they told her if she didn't act normal, go to bed, and come to the cafeteria this morning, on schedule, they were committing her last night."

"And now she's going where? *Home?*"

"Yes," Alex replied. "She must be feeling so much pressure." We all felt so much pressure, we accepted it as normal and grew numb to it.

The cafeteria emptied out. We left the girl sitting there, leaning defiantly against the wall. We had a Jury to get to.

FIVE

❦

ONE YEAR LATER, spring found me miraculously still enrolled at NCSA as a budding ballerina. On this particular
Sunday morning, I woke up sinking into layers of burgundy satin coverlets draped on a ginormous bed, while *Victorialand*
by the Cocteau Twins seeped into the room.

Folks wiser than me planned the entire previous night, right
down to the fabric on the bed and the choice of music at sunrise,
playing on a loop from an unseen player, such that it seemed the very
walls serenaded us.

Three of us had been up all night, roaming the streets and parks
of Winston-Salem like hippie vampires, souls hungry, senses heightened to inhuman perceptions, consumed by unshakable love for it
all. Something More still existed, even after the torture NCSA put
us through.

Melissa Hayden had it all wrong — that if it feels good, you're not
doing it right.

Rewind to fall, the start of that school year. I was placed back in B4, still younger than most of the girls in my class, but now only a year separated us. My marching orders remained the same: put your head down, work your tail off, and for the love of God, whatever other dumb things you do, don't eat.

I had no wild hopes for anything different than the previous year. But by some stroke of black cat luck, the school assigned the Grande Dame Melissa Hayden to teach our class three times a week. Melissa, as we referred to her, never taught classes below B3, perhaps because there was genuine concern on the part of the faculty that her signature tutelage of terror would send us baby bals up in flames.

Melissa Hayden was internationally famous, even though she was short and squat as far as ballerinas go. It was rumored that she loved working with dancers who had unconventional ballet bodies, particularly "big girls." Everyone assured me, therefore, that I'd be one of her favorites.

The first class with Melissa wasn't as bad as we feared. Nor was the second. By the end of the first week, we were almost lured into the sense that we were getting special treatment as her baby bals.

She frequently started class ahead of schedule, barking from the hall before she even entered the studio. She sounded like a low-rent barmaid when she spoke, coarse and grizzled. Still, she was a living legend, older than any of the other female teachers, entitled and unapologetic, the likes of which none of us had trained under on a regular basis before.

But the day she lit a cigarette in the middle of class, stood behind me with the smoldering end next to my waist and commanded,

"Spin, honey, and don't stop until I say so," we knew the honeymoon was over.

"Andrea, beautiful, honey! Show the class. No, not that way. The way you just did it. No, no. Honey, I guess it was pure dumb luck you did it right once."

For the record, none of us understood exactly how she wanted us to do an exercise differently from the way we'd just done it. We spent most of her classes flopping around, eyes wide, jaws slack, attempting to please this egomaniac.

"Who's it going to be today?" my classmate, Katrina, mused into the air one morning in September as we rolled our feet and ankles to warm up in the hall before Melissa's class.

Katrina wore her long, brown hair in an old lady fashion, parted down the middle and secured at the nape of her neck, a plain Amish look that lent her wisdom and innocence at the same time. She was perpetually positive, to the point of coming off as pollyanna-ish. So she was the perfect person to ask the simple question and cut the tension with truth.

"Honey!" Melissa's use of the term of endearment forewarned that the object of her attention was about to be stabbed with a butter knife. Melissa adjusted a girl's shoulders, arms and fingers, then abruptly turned away. "You're not worth my attention. You're not going anywhere."

Or, softening her tone, "Just give it up, honey. Save your parents' money. Go to Vegas. They'll hire anyone out there."

No matter how much you steeled yourself, it still hurt more than expected. In spite of earlier conventional wisdom that any attention is good attention, most of us secretly decided it was best to be ignored under these circumstances.

The boys' class finished up in the studio, and Katrina and I walked in, bracing for more humidity, sweat and stench than normal after a girls' class. I spotted Lucas, the aptly named teenage god taking his time leaving. I had a mad crush on him the previous year and hoped against hope that he wasn't gay.

Luscious Lucas was muscular, sultry-eyed, full-lipped, and yeppers, gay. I still found him to be a work of art.

The school did too, as he was one of the only rising eleventh-graders chosen at the end of the previous school year to perform at the prestigious Spoleto Festival in Italy over the summer. Word had it that the five or six chosen ones all got a PAID TRIP TO EUROPE TO DANCE!

My brain had exploded even learning of such possibilities. The school hummed with excitement for the trip, and Lucas had been no exception, buzzing on a cocktail of nerves and new confidence.

"How was Italy?" I asked him, bright-eyed and breathless. Katrina perked up. Both of us were dying to know any detail, and we fully expected Lucas to gush in kind.

He flipped his hair and shrugged as if jet-setting was already passe. "Fine."

Katrina persisted, her face open and expectant. "Was it cool?"

Lucas picked up his dance bag and walked away, "Yeah, it was fine."

Katrina and I both deflated. We were still nobodies, and Lucas was now an international dancer. He had no time for us.

Katrina changed the subject. "I wonder when we'll know if we're in *Nutcracker*? I have an after-school job this year, and I need to tell them my schedule in advance."

"A job? Why?" Students frequently helped with performances all over the city, ushering, handing out programs or taking tickets. We were paid a little, but mainly, we worked in order to see shows for free.

"I need to earn money to help pay," she gestured around the soaring studio. "I'm waiting tables at Shoney's."

"Shoney's?! The Big Boy?" I squawked. Wasn't Shoney's where the servers wore scratchy brown uniforms and earned a nickel an hour to pour coffee for senior citizens?

Katrina smiled, unperturbed. "It's the only place that would hire a high school student that's also within walking distance from campus."

I could see nothing positive for Katrina in hoofing it to a six-hour shift after an already busy day. I felt so bad for her that I couldn't hide my furrowed brow.

"It's okay," she said with a gentle smile, reassuring me instead of the other way around. "I can do it."

Katrina was a strong dancer with ropey muscles that became more pronounced as the fall wore on. She was rewarded for her weight loss with the role of Arabian in *Nutcracker*. Arabian requires mesmerizing grace, slow, controlled, sensuous movements and extreme flexibility, a role I was born for, according to my teachers, if I hadn't been so fat.

Dark circles appeared under her eyes every morning in class, and her skin faded to gray. More than one of us asked whether we could do anything to help and whether she felt all right. She responded with her calm, pleasant assurances that she was just a little tired sometimes. She also gained an edge to her voice that discouraged further questioning.

On the other hand, our teachers heaped her with uncommon, repeated praise. "Beautiful, Katrina. Just stunning. You've improved so much already this year." Words more nourishing than food and sleep.

The thing is, I never saw anyone's skin turn gray. How was I the only one who thought Katrina didn't look good, as a human being? Something was wrong, and whatever it was seemed glaringly obvious to me.

When the cast list went up for *Nutcracker*, and my name was once again nowhere to be found on it, some part of me fell to the ground and landed with the thud of a corpse. If Katrina's current state of being was what NCSA required, she could have it and they could shove it.

⁂

Our musician friends joked that dancers were overly serious, haughty, and self-absorbed. But they also observed how the ballet industry operated behind the curtain.

Most of the girls in my class were convinced that we were disappointments, failing. With each day ticking by, the sand in the hourglass of our youth running out, the likelihood we would reach the bare minimum of what was expected diminished.

So we resurrected each morning, schlepped our heavy bodies and spirits to class, and went through the motions like zombies marking time, sharing the experience and desperately isolated from each other at the same time.

Musicians, by contrast, seemed fun, easygoing, and eager to connect with others. They didn't care whether you looked fatter or thinner than last week. They even had taboo wonders such as Oreos laying around their dorm rooms, like care packages of cookies were normal. Without those friends that second year at school, particularly a saxophonist named Mindy, I would have drowned in loneliness and pointless self-deprivation.

Against all odds, Mindy was from my town in West Virginia, and we both had Scots-Irish roots, giving us matching reddish-blonde hair and pink skin. Mindy, however, had a more naturally athletic, thin body, so she would have made a better ballerina than yours truly, who was growing a figure better suited for an establishment with a pole.

Mindy was two years older than me, wickedly intelligent and curious, and knew everything possible to know on the entire earth without coming across as a know-it-all.

Mindy's roommate was a Barbie doll vocalist from a strict, evangelical Southern family. Doll Baby Barbie found herself in nightly demand by boyfriends off-campus who supplied her with alcohol and pot and who, from a legal perspective, were too old for her. Other than her quick trips back to the room for a change of clothes, she was never there.

More times than not, Mindy let me flop onto Barbie's bed, reading something gothic from Mr. Ballard's list, until she finished her own homework. She never shooed me away or treated me like the pest I surely was.

One Friday evening in December, I bounded into her room and saw the elusive Barbie in a frenzy. "Both of y'all shoo!" she said. She talked fast but every word packed in four syllables. "Mama's comin' tomorrow, and I need all the cigarette smoke out by then."

Mindy and Barbie's room was consistently neat as a pin, and cigarettes were the least of Barbie's escapades.

"Throw all this in the laundry." Barbie shoved her sheets and blankets at us, never mind she hadn't slept on them since her mama's last visit. She shot blue-eyed daggers at us, and we nodded to reaffirm our oath of silence.

Barbie swore her mama would beat her black and blue if she knew anything at all about our heathen lifestyles. "Ours?" Mindy asked.

Barbie lifted her hair from the back of her neck and re-clasped the delicate gold cross necklace that we hadn't seen in months and explained again, "Mama can barely stomach that I have a roommate who smokes and a friend who *dances!*"

"I'm not a stripper," I said, confused.

"Yet, according to Mama."

The black and blue beating threats were all too real and recently reminiscent for Barbie. Mindy and I swore to do backbends all the way to our grave if we had to in order to prevent Mama from finding out about Barbie's free-wheeling lifestyle.

Mindy picked up the laundry basket, and we left the room. "You could throw that flannel shirt and jeans in the wash too," I commented, nodding to Mindy's daily uniform.

She rolled her eyes. "My wardrobe is fine, Miss Priss."

I would have retorted but we noticed a handful of dancers sliding into Delia's room, eyes shifty, the door shutting quickly behind each one who entered. I glimpsed a luxurious bed, mounds of plush pillows and comforters, not like the singular thin bedspread and lumpy pillow the rest of us made do with. In the middle, Delia carefully opened a large box.

These were the B3, B2, and B1 girls. The cream of the crop. I wanted to receive an invitation to their ball, and I knew I never would.

Mindy sighed in unmistakable condemnation, and we continued down the hall. Her family, like mine, didn't have extra pennies and dollars to toss around on throw pillows and bales of fabrics.

Barbie's sheets in the wash, we hoisted ourselves to a comfy seat on top of the machine, opened the window, and lit cigarettes. Mindy inhaled, "I know you'd like to spend Friday night with the bunheads, but here you are stuck with me."

I realized there was no way in hell I'd trade solid conversation with Mindy for a vapid evening with those particular girls, as much as I admired their dancing. "I would like to see whatever luxuries Delia's mom sent in that box, though," I confessed.

Mindy wrinkled her entire face and looked at me like I said the earth was flat. "You seriously don't know what makes those girls sneak into Delia's room on Friday nights?"

"Cigarettes?"

Mindy sighed, accepting the fact that her next word murdered yet another part of my childhood. "Drugs."

"DRU—"

"SHHHHHHHH!!! Zip it!" she hissed, frantically looking around the empty laundry room.

I knew in my gut Mindy was spot on. There were whispers of Delia having pills to make her skinny and something about her mom understanding the ballet world, but I hadn't paid much attention previously.

According to Mindy, Delia's mom didn't just send pills hidden in all the glamorous clothes. She also sent pot, cocaine, heroin, the hard stuff. How else was a girl expected to survive?

I was still trying to wrap my head around a reality where parents supplied their daughter with not just beer or cigs but also hard drugs, when Jamie, a drummer, poked his head in the laundry room door. Jamie was a skateboarder, his slight build hidden under baggy clothes, and same floppy-in-the-front hair that Lucas and every other cool boy sported.

Most of the boys lived in a dorm next door, and some lived on the first floor of ours. We plopped in and out of each other's rooms like one big comfy family. We were all supposed to be snug in our own rooms at curfew, not that anyone ever checked.

"I have it. I've figured it out," Jamie said. "It's the ley lines that run through Winston-Salem and, supposedly, a few converge and cross right under campus."

This dose of weird seemed way more interesting than Delia's drug box from home.

"Like meridians on a globe?" I asked.

"Nah, man. Energy converging in certain spots. Come look."

Mindy and I jumped off the washing machine, and the three of us huddled our heads out the window. The evening had faded into night. Jamie gestured toward the field surrounding our dorm.

"Just walk out there. You'll feel currents of energy in the ground, like an electrical grid humming under our feet."

"Dude, no one's ever been able to measure ley lines," Mindy said skeptically.

Mindy knew about this phenomenon?!

"Maybe they're not using the right tools," I offered, the only thing I could think of to contribute to the conversation.

"Exactly, man," Jamie continued, unphased. "Energy can be really creative. Or all that power in one spot can turn a place upside down. It's why this place is so fucked up, man." He delivered this pronouncement with his ever-loving, peaceful acceptance.

Jamie seemed like a wizened old guide, a conscientious caretaker in a 15-year-old body. I adored and trusted him wholly, both to hang out with after hours and to give serious thought to any philosophy he proposed.

"You dancers are sensitive to it. Like, I can feel the beat, the pulsation of every living thing. But you live it in your body. You need to be aware, so it doesn't fuck y'all up so much. I mean, y'all take the brunt of this unholy institution."

In the previous five minutes, I had heard so much that opened my awareness to the shit rockin' and rollin' around me that hell's bells, Jamie's conclusion offered to make it all make sense.

He turned around and floated back out the doorway.

"Was he high?" Mindy asked.

"Probably. Kinda hard to tell with him. Does it matter?"

Mindy shrugged, then granted me the rare giggle. "Let's talk about something really important. What if I'm in love with my best friend from back home?"

"If you wanna talk about Tara AGAIN, then I get to rehash my crush on Ricky, who I'm definitely in love with for the rest of my life."

"No, you're not! I know Ricky. He's an idiot. But you don't know Tara, so let me explain."

And there went the rest of the night, gabbing about whether Mindy was gay or it was just her feelings about Tara, the difference between desire and emotions, whether Ricky from back home remembered that I existed, and mainly, luxuriating in the miracle that we weren't born to moms that Barbie and Delia were stuck with.

⚜

Mindy, Jamie, and I, along with several of our other friends, spent many nights over the next months obsessed with notions of good and evil, underworlds, above worlds, parallel dimensions, doppelgangers, free will, telepathy, anything that offered to bend generally accepted notions of reality — likely because the one we were living in wasn't up to snuff.

We agreed there were certain truths holding the fabric of our existence together. You just needed imagination and a relentless commitment to exploring it.

Therefore, it was hard to grasp why some girls were interested in drugs tailor made for shutting down one's mind, and why so many of them, like Barbie, engaged in rampant sex and idiotic keg parties with older men. In fact, that party-till-you-pass-out scene filled

Mindy, Jamie, and those of our likes with a sense of primal fear, to be avoided at all costs.

But according to Barbie's sensibilities, "Y'all are weird, sitting around, blab, blab, blabbing, all night." She rolled her big, blue eyes with a smile, gently teasing Mindy and me. "You're the boring ones." I'm sure the bals partying in Delia's room agreed.

At that point, trying to fit myself into the NCSA ballerina mold was like putting toothpaste back in the tube. I opted for expansion. So when Jamie suggested I trip on acid with him, I hopped on board and never looked back.

LSD had no addictive properties, it would be a one-and-done thing, and according to Jamie, we wouldn't black out of reality, we'd tune more in, and we wouldn't forget any moment of it afterward. Sign me up.

Also, Jamie said, the first trip is a rite of passage.

This wasn't Jamie's first rodeo, one of several requirements handed down from the Gatekeepers of The Trip.

Whoever this Gatekeeper was, Jamie had to assure him that we were "ready" or we wouldn't get the goods.

Mindy had a saxophone exam and couldn't partake, so another trusted friend of ours, Ami, joined Jamie and me. After class one spring Friday, we followed Jamie out the school gates into the wilds of the city beyond.

1. You don't trip alone.

2. You have an experienced guide to ensure physical and mental safety.

3. Never talk to people who aren't tripping.

4. Every trip is sacred.

We walked past Shoney's, where I saw Katrina inside, dressed in her drab, brown waitress uniform, quite the contrast to her shimmering, gold Arabian costume in *Nutcracker*. She smiled and chatted with diners, coffee pot in hand. I wanted to tell those customers who she was, how much talent she had, how hard she worked, and please, for the love of any ballet dreams left in the world, leave more than a dime on the table because this wasn't a frivolous after-school job for her.

Maybe it was Jamie's unwavering calm and confident nature, but other than excitement, I had no pre-game jitters arising from my ignorance of where we were headed, who would be there, or what the hell was going to happen.

We crossed over railroad tracks and into a neighborhood filled with small cottages. Many were painted indigo blue, with blue paint around the windows or other strange blue symbols painted next to the front door.

"What's with the blue?" I asked.

"Southern tradition. Wards off evil," Jamie answered, matter-of-factly.

I was impressed by these homes wearing their magic right out in the open. It's like we already walked into another world, and hadn't even taken any mind-altering substances yet.

Jamie led us into a small, white cottage and opened the door without knocking. We quietly stepped into a living area with thick, drawn curtains. A slight young man with long, straight black hair, porcelain skin, and high cheekbones emerged from the darkness. A gentle glow emanated from him.

He gave Ami and me a curious, non-judgmental once over, while Jamie introduced him as our Gatekeeper. Jamie explained that he had graduated NCSA a year prior from the visual arts department. Visual artists, meaning the painters and sculptors, were known to be the quietest but most intellectually creative of us all. It made sense that his was the home we were in.

The Gatekeeper motioned to us gracefully. We followed him into the kitchen, and he opened the freezer door. There was nothing inside but a tiny, plastic black coffin. The Gatekeeper pulled out the coffin, placed it in the palm of his long-fingered hand, opened the lid, and handed us three small squares of paper.

Hello to the rest of your life.

⸎

I do not advocate drug use, legal or non-legal, for any other person, but for me, it was the right choice, at the right time, in the right set of circumstances.

Jamie led Ami and me through a night filled with exploration of miracles as simple as blades of grass waving in the wind to as grand as watching clouds react to our thoughts.

"The cloud is answering me!" I whispered, wide-eyed. We were lying on our backs, three of us in a row, on a hillside in a park.

"Maybe your thoughts are telling your mind how to perceive the cloud," Jamie suggested. "Or maybe the cloud is a canvas. The universe is using this moment to remind us that grandeur is everywhere. It's so simple."

We danced with the cloud-universe, laughed until our faces threatened to break, and spent most of the hours throughout the night marveling at what the world looks, sounds, and feels like with vampire senses.

Jamie had insisted we stay in quiet areas, no interactions with other people. Wise counsel, given that our newly-heightened perceptions were overstimulating.

The whole night was proof of Something More. Everything I perceived wasn't the mere byproduct of brain chemicals sloshing around, even though my practical side knew that brain chemistry was, in fact, the mechanism by which I saw and heard as well as I suddenly did.

The sky lightened. Jamie said, "Time to go back to the house." I knew he meant the Gatekeeper. "He's waiting on us."

I found that confusingly generous, but sure enough, our host was asleep on his own couch. He awoke when we arrived and pointed into his bedroom. "Feel free to crash in there," he whispered. "It's ready for you."

That's how I found myself, several hours later, waking up in mounds of burgundy satin, sun glowing through the window, peacefully snuggled up with two of my closest friends. In my experience, there is way too much going on in one's awareness during an acid trip for there to be room for anything sexual — which seemed mundane anyway after a night of miraculous wonder, peace, and hope.

The Gatekeeper glided into the room. "This will be good," he said softly, hit play on the Cocteau Twins, and checked that the volume was turned down.

What we saw that night would never again be unseen or forgotten. The veil, once lifted, does not ever fully descend again.

SIX

WHEN I FINALLY saw Mom again in the spring, I did a double take. A shock of her auburn hair had gone gray. Mom had been sick all winter with a pesky upper respiratory infection. Our phone calls were cut short with fits of wet coughs and exhaustion.

Mom was tired of being sick, and even more fed up that not one single person from the dance department returned her phone calls for a simple parent-teacher check-in. She finally took off work, drove to Winston-Salem, found the faculty offices on the basement floor of the dance building, and started banging on closed doors. Unsurprisingly, no one answered.

Finally, our dance instructor, Fanchon Cordell, appeared after teaching her last Friday afternoon class. Fanchon and her husband came to teach at NCSA after dancing with American Ballet Theater. We recoiled on the rare occasion she attempted to smile, as the effort resulted in a frightfully unnatural crack across her face.

Then she took a one-eighty. She walked into our class one morning with a spiky, short haircut.

"Do you like it? The hair thing?" She looked in the mirror, self-consciously tugging at the short ends where waist-length tresses had once fallen.

Ballet Bible Rules dictate that no ballerina could have short hair, tan lines, or tattoos. One could never assume what skin a costume might not cover or what hairdo a role might demand. We froze at our places by the barre, staring at our punk rock, short-haired teacher.

"I've never been allowed to cut my hair." Then she turned to us and breathed in deeply, as if gathering conviction. "I want to try an experiment. It will probably get me in trouble." Her voice shook. "I think we, the faculty, should encourage you, be nicer to you."

Had an alien body-snatched Ms. Cordell?

"If there's anything you're having trouble with, in the dorms, with your friends, your boyfriends, I want you to feel like you can talk to me. I'm going to have open office hours."

She broke into a grin, one that seemed mischievous and real. "Call me Fanchon. No more Ms. Cordell nonsense. It makes me feel old."

We had been too berated, for too long, by too many teachers to believe this newfangled notion of support would last longer than the class itself. So we went through our exercises, sliding sideways glances at Fanchon, and waited for the inevitable barb to arise.

Lo and behold, her kindness curriculum lasted all year. Rumor had it that Fanchon divorced her hubby and was ready to live her best life.

As the year wore on, she confided in us that the dean reprimanded her for the spare-the-rod-spoil-the-child approach, while the faculty heralded Melissa Hayden's cruel and chaotic methods.

Fanchon shrugged. "What are they going to do? Fire me? Let 'em." She had an understated, low voice but smiled more and more freely.

It made sense, then, that Fanchon welcomed Mom into her office, with care and warmth that melted Mom's anxiety like a snowman in June.

"Why will no one at this school talk to me?" Mom vented. "I feel like something is wrong with my daughter and her dancing here."

"It does seem like something is going on with Andrea," Fanchon agreed. "She's less interested in pushing herself. Her weight is always an issue. But honestly, I think she's a normal teenager with a normal teenager body."

Those words were all Mom needed. Still, Mom asked, "Why is it so hard for you teachers to talk to a parent?"

"The teachers are idiots. I'm trying something different," Fanchon said.

Mom's shoddy treatment from everyone else associated with this entitled academy embarrassed me. My hardworking, single-parent mother had to traipse across three states to get someone to acknowledge her existence.

The following day, Fanchon entered class, the building manager wheeling a television and VCR into the studio behind her.

Talk class!!!! Woo hoo!! We won't have to work!

Fanchon turned off the studio lights. "Girls, I would like to stage a historical, classical ballet just for you for the spring recital. No auditions, no cast list, everyone dances. This class is neglected. You're too advanced for the children's roles in *Nutcracker* but not advanced enough for the more technical roles.

"Let's watch *Les Sylphides*." She pushed the tape into the VCR. "Here's when I danced in it." That Fanchon would stage this hauntingly beautiful piece about *ghosts*(!!!!) on us seemed like an undeserved gift.

Our perpetual anxiety over performing, not performing, succeeding to expectations, not succeeding, erupted into nervous, grateful laughter. We couldn't believe she was giving us the chance to be seen.

Mere weeks into rehearsal of *Les Sylphides*, stretching in a morning class with my leg resting on the barre behind me, upper body contorted into an impossible backbend, something pulled. I pulled my leg down to the floor, bent forward, stretched out my lower back, and kept dancing. By the end of class, I landed a big jump and my lower back went on strike. I couldn't stand up straight.

I knew enough about my body to recognize a severe muscle spasm. My left arch still endured searing bone pain, and I had started the school year on a sprained ankle. Then Christmastime brought a blister on my pinky toe that closed up but never healed.

In our last class before Christmas break, I was still complaining about how much pain a mere blister could cause, so Katrina took a look at my flaming, swollen little piggy. We noticed a red line creeping under my skin, up my foot nearly all the way to my ankle.

"You have blood poisoning!" she screeched. "If that line reaches your heart, you'll die!" I hobbled to the infirmary, and sure enough, Katrina was right that I had a nasty, internal infection.

So by spring, a pulled back didn't hurt as much as it was annoying as hell. I couldn't worm around the pervasive, thick pain, and worse, I moved like a wooden horse.

Turns out, I didn't pull a muscle. I severely sprained both sides of my sacroiliac joints. It would take months to recover. Goodbye, *Les Sylphides*. Goodbye, my ghosts.

With only a month left of school, the doctors green-lighted me to pussy-foot through class a few exercises a day at the barre. By then, I wondered, *Why bother.*

But if Katrina could work in and out of the studio like a farm horse, no matter that her skin now harbored a sickly yellow tone over the gray, I could drag myself to the barre to stand next to her.

A few weeks later, our class huddled in the hall outside the studios, warming up for the afternoon class, the chatter clipping along faster than normal. *Who was going to which summer school? Who would be invited to come back next year? Who wouldn't come back?*

"Did you hear about Parker?" Alex asked.

"Parker Posey?" Katrina replied.

Parker wore her dark hair as short as she could get away with and sported blood-red lipstick, even to the 8:30 AM class. She had the epitome of a ballerina's body with no lumps or bumps in the wrong places.

"She's not coming back," Alex announced.

"WHAT?!" we all shrieked. Parker was IT.

"Yeah, I heard that in her end-of-year conference the dean suggested she switch to drama and give up dancing. They're making an exception for her in the drama department to allow a high school student so she can finish school here."

A hush fell over the hallway. From our limited vantage point, we were mortified. Any life outside ballet meant you failed. The option the school gave Parker seemed like offering a scarlet letter.

Hey girl, you're welcome to pay tuition and finish out high school along with your classmates, but you're now an outcast from the dance world. They may as well have told her to take up typing classes.

The next time I saw Parker warming up before class, she looked bright and happy, red lipstick and all. Maybe she got the best end of the deal. Stay in school with the cool kids, without the indignity of pouring oneself into pink tights and slinking into classrooms to be ridiculed each day. I was jealous.

Melissa's office was packed with videos and yellowed magazines, all featuring her. I nearly burst into tears from stress before I crossed the threshold.

Melissa Hayden's Office Year-End Review

She cleared off a chair and patted for me to sit. There wasn't enough space to seat two people comfortably, so I shimmied my legs toward the doorway to keep from banging knee caps with her. I was still in my after-class attire, a leotard and tights, with a meager dance skirt. I felt awfully exposed.

"Talk to me about your year, honey." She pursed her hot pink, overly-lipsticked mouth, and bore holes into me with her false-lashed, beady eyes.

"Umm," my voice cracked. "It's been hard, my back injury."
"Oh," she waved her hand, "injuries are part of the game. I'm not worried about that, and don't let it worry you either. The way I see it, you're one of my big girls."

I never got used to being barked at about my weight. I blinked hard to hold back tears and gripped the edge of my chair.

"I love big, strong dancers. You just don't have confidence."
She lit a cigarette.

"Listen to me right now, honey. I'm going to make you stronger and stronger, and you know why I know I can do that?" She blew smoke over our heads, then pointed her cigarette two inches from my face. "Because I've never been able to make you cry. God knows I've tried.

"You take it and you perform so well in my classes. You've got strength of character I don't see in anyone else. You're one of my special girls. I want you in my class every single day next year. You hear me, honey?"

I stopped breathing, couldn't swallow, and nodded the best I could, considering I was staring down the barrel of a cannon.

"Go rest over the summer. It's you and me next September."

I ducked out of the office and hot-tailed it back to my room. I told myself that Melissa spewed the same muck to everyone, minus the weight business to the skinny girls.

I made it back to my room before I burst into tears and cried into my pillow for the rest of the evening. I hated being too fat for ballet. I hated walking around in shame about my body. I hated not dancing with the reckless abandon I'd always known.

Above all, I hated the idea of spending every single day with Melissa. Surely, however, that wouldn't be true.

After comparing notes, however, Melissa hadn't told anyone else what she told me.

"She legit loves you," Alex said. "You're her favorite in our class. Everyone knows that."

I hated that my only ticket forward was via a narcissistic lunatic, not a credible source of support.

I knew one thing and one thing only: Melissa was dead wrong. She made me cry a lot over the year. I didn't have it in me to put up with her ever again.

"Have you considered Broadway? Or Vegas?" Fanchon asked with such earnest consideration. Tears I didn't know I had left streamed down my cheeks. She might as well have stamped "FAILED" on my forehead.

"Now that you have solid technique, I think you'd do better in different venues. You're a big presence in the studio."

Here we go again. Too. Big.

Once again, the dreaded talk took place after class, which had me showing up vulnerable and exposed, spilling out of my leotard and tights, bracing for the fat talk.

"I don't think ballet is right for you anymore. This place," she looked around the studio where she held our conference, "isn't good for you."

Broadway. Vegas. A 15-year-old couldn't go there on her own. Might as well start planning for a trip to the moon.

SEVEN
❧

BACK TO THE ol' dining room table at Grandma and Pops' house on Sunday afternoons, parked under the cabaret chandelier with its cracked glass and dry-rotting fringe instead of performing in the theaters it promised.

"What is this?" Plump old Auntie Maude wrinkled her nose at every dish that passed by. She sat next to me in her threadbare, sleeveless floral house dress.

Grandma's mouth dropped open in exaggerated surprise. "Why, it's the same mashed carrots we have every Sunday." Grandma took care of Maude's every need, only to be met with derision and criticism. I sat wedged between the two.

"I'm sure I can't eat it." Auntie Maude leaned away from the table and refused to touch the dish.

"Well, at least pass it along so the rest of us can. I never cook anything you can't eat." Grandma nudged me. "Old sour puss," she mouthed under her breath. "She'll complain it's cold next." I could tell Gran was trying to make me laugh. It almost worked.

Grandma, Papa, Mom, Dad, my cousins, even the resident grouch, Auntie Maude, was happy for me to live back at home full-time. Everyone was happy but me. I think my family harbored hopes that I would turn into someone satisfied with high school football games or photography for the yearbook. Sleepovers and pillow fights.

Grandma had hovered around me like a flame on a candle since the moment I returned, smiling and effervescent, as always, but her eyes piercing into mine, convinced something was wrong. Grandma's sixth sense as to her family jangled as loudly as the telephone.

As a fifteen-year-old, I wanted to escape Grandma's all-knowing gaze and wallow in gloom by myself.

I took a teaspoon of carrots, then passed along the potatoes, years of habitual food deprivation kicking in. "Andrea," Grandma whined, drawing out my name, "you don't want my potatoes? I'll stop cooking since no one wants to eat anymore."

Suddenly, I realized I could eat! Glory on high, I no longer needed to chase skinny. Grandma's potatoes were decadent, with butter, salt, and who knows what else. I grabbed the bowl back, heaped a spoonful of mashed yumminess on my empty plate, then threw caution to the wind and helped myself to a homemade dinner roll too.

Once I filled my plate, Auntie Maude joined in. Next thing you know, her plate was piled higher than mine but she made a fuss over there being nothing she liked.

"Is there a draft in here? Why do I always get seated under the draft?" Auntie Maude rubbed her thick, bare arms.

Gran nudged me again. "Law's sake."

Pops pretended he couldn't hear any of the conversation and focused on the food. I started to crack a grin. Auntie Maude's grumpiness was a vibe I could get down with.

Auntie Maude pushed her chair away from the table once her plate was nearly licked clean, her lips pressed thin. "Don't waste good money on meals for me again." She lumbered to her feet and waddled toward the living room.

"I'll carry her dessert for her," I offered.

"She's not allowed to have sugar," Pops said, but Grandma was already scooping a serving of cobbler.

I knew I should stay and help with the dishes, but I was desperately worried I'd start screaming. Over nothing, for nothing. The smallness of everything.

For the first time in my life, I had nothing to daydream about, nowhere to place my obsessive focus, no fantasy sparkling in the twilight guiding me forward. My best option in that moment was to join Auntie Maude in mutual ingratitude.

Auntie Maude plopped herself in one of two reclining chairs in the living room.

"Do you want me to turn on the light?" I asked, handing her the dessert.

"The light hurts my eyes. I prefer to sit in the dark."

I agreed. She and I had always gotten along, and perhaps because we were both currently in a foul mood about our lives, I felt better in her presence.

"At least the cobbler's good," I said, sitting next to her in the adjoining recliner.

She swallowed her mouthful. "I can't taste it."

I started laughing, and she smiled, shaking her head, perhaps at herself.

⚬⚬⚬

Mindy didn't go back to NCSA either, as her scholarship ran out. So we steeled ourselves against the looming September, when we'd begin serving time in high school with people who hated weirdos, according to my lived experience in elementary school.

We had ventured into the big world, under the promise that we were special. The world of Something More spit us out, right back into the pot with everyone else who was expected not to go very far.

Unfortunately, Mindy and I lived in neighboring towns and wouldn't attend the same school. We would have to fight our battles solo.

Until then, we had the summer. Mindy's Dad gave her a car, and she spent most of the summer driving us around to spots in the woods where we could smoke cigarettes, sit on cliffs, and mourn our lost dreams and future selves. The pit of dread in my stomach eased with her.

We'd spent every waking moment for years practicing, rehearsing, pushing ourselves with relentless drive. We didn't know how to idle away all of the time we unexpectedly found on our hands.

Reliably, Mindy soon proved to be several steps ahead of me. She discovered Richard Bach, an author in the philosophy section of the library, and lo and behold, there was now a "new age" section in the bookstore at the mall, offering all of the possibilities we could imagine: past lives, alternate universes, manifesting and magic, telepathy and communicating between the realms. All the notions that would rescue us from our current realities.

We gobbled down *Illusions,* then works by Edgar Cayce, and on and on. Richard Bach was my favorite. Just as I had reread my favorite book on mediumship and ESP as a child, I read his books until they fell apart.

It was when we tried to tackle something incomprehensible by Aleister Crowley that Grandma declared she finally knew what was going on with me. I belonged to a cult.

The Satanic Panic of the 1980s was on the local or national news on a weekly basis. Grandma had started worrying about cults a few years earlier when Mom and I went vegetarian for a summer, prompting Grandma to observe at the time, "People in cults don't eat meat either."

Now that Aleister Crowley writings appeared in the house, she was convinced. "People in cults read strange books instead of the Bible."

I rolled my eyes and continued devouring books that made sense of my deep knowing and promised mental escapism to boot. Arguing with Grandma was a no-win endeavor, and it would only leave me feeling further isolated and misunderstood.

There *was* Something More. It wasn't just a bunch of teenagers in art school who imagined it.

The only problem, as I saw it, was that Something More didn't exist fully on Earth. But at least it existed Somewhere, and that knowing provided the slimmest of golden threads for me to dangle from.

⁓

Mindy was a rising senior and didn't dread school as much as she dreaded living with her dad for one more year. Mindy's dad was the monster of all monsters. Rumor had it he ran the KKK in Southern West Virginia.

In her early teens, with nothing further to lose, Mindy slugged her drunk dad across the head with a 2x4 when he tried—again—to get handy with her. She must have knocked some sense into him because after that, he turned his oppressive physical attention away from her and onto her mother.

With Mindy now living back at home, he tried to keep crawling out of his hole of guilt and shame and sought to win her over with a car. Then, oddly, with the gift of a gun.

"He's probably hoping you'll use the gun on him. Put him out of his misery, and you'll be the bad guy." I got a dark laugh out of her on that one.

I understood her anxiety at returning home to her living situation. I didn't understand mine.

I knew I would miss the unlimited, imaginative possibilities that NCSA fostered and the sense of finally belonging — at least outside the ballet studio. But I still had Mindy. At worst, I'd be bored in class and made fun of for being different and a lonely loser. At best, I was free from mean teachers and the crushing pressure to succeed. Plus, I could eat.

The rationalizations didn't work. I couldn't seem to pull myself up.

That summer, Mom moved us into a beautiful, two-story apartment on a tree-lined street that dropped into cliffs. I had a large room, decorated with the calming prints of Monets and Renoirs, my old posters of ballerinas in arabesques tossed in the trash.

Something kept tickling the edges of my brain, like, what was wrong with me that I couldn't just chill? Why did I harbor a dread so heavy that I could barely get out of bed and move around each day? Why was my brain filled with fog?

And why now, of all times, did I finally lose my stupid appetite and shrink to skinny?

"It's totally normal," Mom said. "You're in a hard adjustment period. You'll feel much better once school starts and you make new friends."

It pained me deeply that Mom, Grandma, and Pops seemed relieved and pleased to have me around, while I felt only desperation to get away again. But I had used my one ticket to Up, Up, and Away, and it wasn't good anymore.

When I whined that I didn't want to go to the local high school and couldn't see any other way forward, Mom answered, "There are all kinds of possibilities. We could move to Europe for a year. I could work as a nurse, and you could be an exchange student. Wouldn't that be fun?!"

I couldn't see it. For an unfathomable reason, I couldn't even get excited about a year in Europe, clearly a ticket OUT. All I knew is that I didn't feel safe facing the year ahead, but I didn't have the words to express it or any explanation for it.

"Or," Mom offered, "you could apply to page school. Your father was a page in D.C. for the United States Speaker of the House."

"Dad went away for high school?" I asked. "What's a page?"

"You work for Congress on Capitol Hill, running errands and such, and you go to school there," Mom said.

"Yes, but," Grandma interjected, "your dad's mother was an alcoholic, and your dad chose to leave D.C. to come home and take care of her before he graduated. Just think of the opportunities he had."

Leave it to Grandma to kill a great Dad story.

"Well," Mom reminded Grandma, "his mother used to call him while he was working on the floor of the House. She was drunk, and I think it was embarrassing."

Leave it Mom to always offer the other side of a situation, non-judgmentally.

As interesting as it was to hear about this history, I couldn't see myself shapeshifting into a perky teenager, running the halls of Congress. So that suggestion likewise fell flat.

One of Mom's best friends, Sandy, visited one day as I skulked on my bed upstairs, face down in my pillows. She knocked on my door softly and asked to come in.

"Sweetie, how are you doing?" She perched on the edge of my bed and rubbed my back. "You've always been so cheerful, and now you're withdrawn and losing too much weight." I burst out laughing, the sound erupting maniacally. Oh, the irony of now being seen as thin. I couldn't muster any words.

Sandy continued, "You have a beautiful room here, but I do miss your ballet posters. I guess you're too old for them now."

I stayed mute.

"If you ever want to talk to me, I'm here. Just know that I'm your friend." Tears rolled down my cheeks at her gentle acceptance of me being nothing more than a lump.

I didn't know what was wrong with me, other than I was miserable, and I was certain it would never end.

I finally confided in my lifelong friend, Vivi, who walked with me all through grade school and stood by my side against bullies, that I was afraid of being hit by a car, or that a tragedy was getting ready to strike. I only mentioned this secret after she confided in me something mind-shattering.

Vivi, my preppy, unfailingly loyal comrade, went to an exclusive private boarding school and was home for the summer.

"How's your school?" I asked glumly, as we strolled around the neighborhood.

"Well, I only went one semester. I spent the rest of the year in and out of a psych ward." I stopped in the middle of the street and gawked at her.

Her green eyes twinkled. She had grown confident in her mannerisms and eloquent in her speaking, something I chalked up to boarding school education. "Nope," she said, answering my thoughts. "I got all this," she gestured at herself, "from group therapy."

She explained with no minced words that her well-admired, successful grandfather had sexually assaulted her throughout childhood and that she became suicidal when she had to return home over Christmas break and face him again.

Mindy's and Vivi's stories made me wonder whether all the underground coal mining around us accidentally tore open a doorway to hell. How was it that two of my closest friends had suffered sexual abuse as kids?

Vivi continued, "I was diagnosed with depression. It's the best thing that ever happened to me. Now we have something to work with that makes sense. It's a tremendous weight off of my chest. I feel like I have a future."

"Why would *you* feel like you have no future?" I asked slowly.

"Dee-presh-un."

Depression wasn't something folks talked about or got "diagnosed" with much back then, so it took Vivi the rest of the walk to educate me that it was more than a pesky bad mood. It was super weird that she was so lighthearted about her entire experience and exhibited no shame over spending a month in a looney bin.

I felt so saddened that Vivi had to spend time in a mental hospital, but my chest burst with pride for her, for her unfathomable bravery. She was a tall but slight wisp of a girl and one of the strongest people I knew. She stuck by my side when we were kids. Now she was standing up for herself.

When we looped around to the front of my house, Vivi turned to me with an uncharacteristically serious look. "I don't know what you've been through at NCSA. I do know, one hundred percent, that you are clinically depressed. It's an illness. It's like your brain has gone sideways. You can do something about it. You can get help."

My head couldn't wrap around how her circumstances applied to me. "I don't have an abusive family. I have nothing to account for any 'depression.'"

"I thought the same thing. 'Other people have it worse,' I thought. But I've known you our whole lives. I'm pretty sure there's an explanation," Vivi suggested.

She left the topic alone for the rest of the summer, but I grew aware of another presence who moved into our friendship, into my friendship with Mindy, into my room. A shadow hovered around me everywhere I went, just out of sight.

I fully agreed with Vivi that something was wrong with me.

The difference between us was that I had secretly feared since age nine that my particular form of Being Off, of seeing and hearing things that no one else experienced, would catch up to me. There's only so much you can chalk up to imagination, LSD, and new age philosophy.

I knew, without a doubt, that when I glimpsed into a world largely unseen here, it was just as real as planet Earth. But what good is an expanded notion of reality if you're the only one living in it? What good is it if what little you know to be true makes you bat shit crazy to everyone else?

I became more certain than ever that eventually, no matter what, I would end up imprisoned in a sterile, smelly psychiatric hospital. It would be different from Vivi's stint because Vivi still seemed normal in a way I never felt.

The next time I went walking, I heard a car approach behind me. I prayed with every fiber in my being, *Swerve. Take me out. There's no way I can live fully as me, as a free person, on this planet.*

⚬~ℓ~⚬⚬⚬~ℓ~⚬

It dawned on me that my biggest dread, really, was that I would have to endure the next three years of high school in a small mountain village as an old woman subjected to fifteen-year-old-girl rules, surrounded by children who hadn't been exposed to anything, didn't know how to think big or take care of themselves, and were content with the status quo.

Misery sure does love company. Good thing there are always a number of miserable folks in high school.

Color me flabbergasted when the first person I saw in the crowded lunchroom cafeteria wore a black leather motorcycle jacket and a long mohawk. Eyes wide, I beelined my desperately relieved carcass over to the only other freak in the room and introduced myself like an old friend.

"I'm Darren. I just moved here," he explained.

"Where did you move from?"

Darren puffed out his cheeks and exhaled. "I'm a system kid. Foster care. Get tossed around a lot. Not even sure how long I'll be here. Sucks." His openness didn't match the sullen punk stereotype. "What about you?"

"Um," I hesitated, reeling from the revelation that this kid didn't even have parents. Or if he did, they were worse than Mindy's dad, and worse than the moms who sent coke to their daughters at ballet school. My last two years at NCSA suddenly seemed like an embarrassment of riches. "I was a dancer." It surprised me that those were the words that fell out of my mouth to connect with a potential friend.

I started to apologize for my weight — *I know I don't look thin enough to be a ballerina . . .*

But Darren responded, "Yeah, I get that. The way you cut through the crowd and carried yourself across the room. Or it's what you're wearing that caught my eye."

It was 1988. Darren and I were ahead of the curve on punk grunge — lots of black, combat boots, and spiky metal jewelry.

For the past months, I really wanted a long mohawk, but ballet rules die hard. I ventured out toward the edge as far as I dared, gave myself an extreme side part, and had my hair cut with the right side as short as my chin, tapering around the back to shoulder length on the left. I could still pull my hair into a ponytail and bun — just in case it were ever necessary to do so.

Darren and I were in drama class together, and soon, our teacher, Mrs. Wills, invited us and a few other distrustful misfits to spend lunch goofing around on the little wooden stage in her classroom.

"You can all help me pick the fall play," she said. "Here are some scripts. Try different roles, amongst yourselves, see what you like, just for fun," — those last words as foreign to me as Chinese.

I eventually chose our play: Noel Coward's *Blithe Spirit*, a comedy about a seance and a spiteful ghost. I played the medium. Go figure.

Walking to the drama room one beautiful September day, Darren and I opted to take the outdoor route around the building rather than through the halls.

We moseyed out the front door and meandered along one wing, enjoying the sun, on the way to the drama room at the end. Darren lit a cigarette along the way and snuffed it out before we reached the end doorway.

When we opened the door to return inside, the vice principal met us with a look so severe, we both assumed someone died. Apparently, we weren't allowed outside in the yard during school hours, and we weren't allowed to smoke cigarettes on campus.

Darren threw his hands up. "I was the one smoking. I'm sorry," and let it go.

My brain short-circuited. I cross-examined the principal six ways to Friday all the way back to his office trying to understand what was wrong with walking outside on a beautiful day.

Result: Darren and I were suspended for the rest of the day.

I found the whole thing hysterical. This school business was a joke.

Mom threw a fit when the poor assistant rang her about the so-called bad news and asked Mom to come pick me up. "I'm not taking off work for this nonsense! You're going to keep her the rest of the day and suspend her tomorrow," Mom demanded. "Or better yet, make her come back to school tomorrow."

Later, at home, Mom said, "Can you just try to conform? I know the rules don't make sense to you, but most kids need them. They are what they are. Walk the halls inside."

❦

With nothing else to do with myself after school, I returned to the only place I knew, and that still held some sense of rationality to me: the ballet studio.

Mr. Rose tried to act as if I'd never left, but it seemed that he went above and beyond to rebuild my confidence. "Look at that perfect NCSA technique! You can still turn professional!" I inwardly rolled my eyes and tried not to cry, knowing he was merely giving lip service to a ship that had long sailed.

I didn't know if I wanted to dance in *Nutcracker*, but Mr. Rose simply called me into rehearsal one evening and started choreographing a solo for me.

Something about the music in "Waltz of the Snowflakes" and dancing in spite of the bastards at NCSA briefly, but consistently, lifted some of the heaviness of my being. In those evenings in rehearsal, I never wanted to be anywhere else.

A month back into my old ballet studio and I was soaring through leaps higher than I'd jumped in years. "Who told you that you can't jump?" Mr. Rose asked.

"All the teachers at school," I stammered. *They always said I was too fat to get myself off the ground.*

Mr. Rose never bad-mouthed anyone and never cursed. But his words were snippier than normal. "Don't let anyone tell you what you can or cannot be or do ever again."

Still, outside the studio and outside lunch on Mrs. Wills' wooden stage, my spirits plummeted. School wasn't nearly as bad as I feared, and most of the students were incredibly kind. Even those who had been mean girls in grade school and junior high went out of their way to welcome me back and try to befriend me. I felt grateful, but I could not shake off the shackle of sullen hopelessness.

One Friday at the end of September, Darren said someone was hosting a movie night a few doors down the street from me and that

I should walk over. I'd be the only girl, but he didn't think the guys would mind. Mom said fine, as long as I washed the dinner dishes first.

I started to grumble about the dishes when I heard a knock on the door. I opened it to see the most stunning human being I had ever laid eyes on.

He was about my age, had bright blonde hair, arresting blue eyes, and a face chiseled by angels. Surely, he was at the wrong house.

"Andrea?" he asked, his voice luxurious as melted butterscotch.

I gaped. He looked around the hallway of our apartment building. "This is number three? Are you Andrea?"

I broke into a full body sweat. "Who are you?" I croaked.

"Jason."

I had no idea what this stranger was doing on my doorstep or what messenger of heaven sent him to me.

I swung open the door and gestured as gracefully as I could manage. "Come in." That moment changed the course of my life forever.

EIGHT

THIS ANGEL-AMONG-US called Jason hesitated in the doorway of our apartment and gestured outside. "I came to walk you to the movie down the street. I didn't want a girl walking alone in the dark."

"That's polite," I stammered.

Jason shrugged. "I just had a feeling I needed to come get you."

His elegance put me at ease — or perhaps further into a hypnotic trance. I managed to explain, "The only problem is that I have to wash dishes before I can leave, so if you need to go ahead, I understand."

I expected him to vanish into thin air, as a vision I conjured in my months-long gloom.

Instead, he crossed into the living room and took off his coat. He walked gracefully and smelled sublime. "No problem. I'll help you."

I couldn't get enough of every single thing about him. When he'd leave my house and drive his burgundy boat-of-a-car back home, he'd call and we'd stay up until midnight talking more.

Jason meditated, danced in his room, took himself on shamanic journeys, wrote poetry, and gifted me books by Khalil Gibran. He tried to teach me chess, but I didn't have the patience to sit still long enough to learn.

When I saw him in the hall between classes at school, we'd pass notes, irrepressible grins plastered across both of our faces. Rather than being misunderstood, I could barely keep up with his brilliant mind and serene, unearthly wisdom.

Most importantly, when I was with Jason, I felt fully accepted, weaknesses, failures and all. Even the shadow lumbering around me that signaled the Thing Wrong With Me seemed okay, something to understand and work with.

Yet everything about our interactions and our relationship felt inevitable, the giddiness of oh-thank-God-finally instead of tingly, teenage newness. He was the breath of my soul, and until the moment I met him, my soul had been waiting to exhale.

One evening, walking back from the cliffs at the end of my street, I looked down at our feet. I saw them in black boots with pointy toes, a style from hundreds of years earlier, not the Doc Martens we were both wearing.

His pants were dark and hit above his ankles, his coat shorter than his ever-present trench coat, and suddenly, my legs were weighted with layers of heavy skirts. I sidestepped patches of snow, moving him aside on the walking path.

But wait, wasn't it October? Or a blustery January night? Where did the snow come from?

I did a double-take and reached down to grab his leg. I felt jeans, not pants. His hands were bare, not gloved.

"What are you doing?" he laughed gently, and stopped.

"Did you see the snow? Back there. Dude, let me see your boots. What the fuck? What month is it? Did we ever live in New England together?"

Jason didn't miss a beat. "Yes. I'm sure we did."

"No, but, do you actually remember it? I'm in a memory, or a weird time mash up right now." I saw what I saw, clearly, in 3-D reality. My brain kicked in, trying to make sense of it.

I sounded disjointed, but I knew I could let my perceptions tumble out. "I used to write a lot. I wrote . . . your letters. You were a writer. I helped you. Just now, it's like we were walking down the street talking about your letters, what you were working on. It was a long time ago." Memories and present day collided.

"Sounds right. Over the last few weeks, I remember a lot about our past lives. They come back, sometimes in a tumble."

We stood in the street. It took me a moment to get my bearings. I knew where I was. I knew it was October, 1988.

Yet there was an earlier Andrea next to an earlier Jason, still whispering in my ear, as close as our shadows. The flash, the feeling, the sense of hundreds of years whooshing by in an instant was very real. It felt like a chunk of my brain fell out of the attic and into my awareness, a subtle *a-ha*, a puzzle piece dropping into place. There was nothing crazy about it.

⊱•⊰⊱•⊰

Each morning, when I arrived in English class, I could spot Jason through the window walking between buildings to his next class. Jason was a senior and only needed a few credits to graduate.

His mom's boyfriend ran a garage and taught Jason the basics of car mechanics. On busy days in the garage, Jason skipped school and helped out.

I started testing myself. Would he be in school or the garage? What was he wearing? After being right for a week, I let him in on my exercise.

"That's funny. I do the same with you with what you're wearing or whether your hair will be up or down."

Only before fifth period did our schedules converge so that we could meet in the hall between classes. He had no way of seeing me each day before that moment. He started writing down my shirt color when it came to him earlier in the day, or something about my hair, then passing the note to me in the hallway the first time we could see each other.

Jason's being had a certain essence to me. When the phone rang, I could tell through a zing of connection whether it was him calling or whether it was someone else.

Grandma had that knack. Every time the phone rang, she'd say, "That's Mary," or "Vivian." When I asked her how she did it, she said, "I can feel who's thinking of me when the phone rings."

The thing is, however, Jason supported my need to escape my current reality. His existence certainly made living rich, but both of us could barely tolerate the mundane that everyday life presented. Neither of us could see any future independently or with each other that seemed *enough*.

I don't remember the first time I felt that I was done with this Earth. I'm pretty sure it was back at NCSA. It didn't seem like despair or desperation. I just slowly grew tired of trudging forward into the Bleak and wanted to move on.

Then I had one of the most significant dreams of my life. I was with my grandparents and Mom in the backyard when a gigantic being descended from the sky, clad in thick glistening robes, threads of golds, reds, blues, and greens woven like tapestry. The Being reached to me, took my outstretched hand, and lifted me up.

At first, my family could see me ascending. But shortly, they returned to their tasks in the yard, my entire existence completely forgotten.

The Being assured me they would feel no pain in my leaving, as it would be as if I had never existed in the first place.

I was finally free to leave. The euphoria was perhaps comparable to what folks experience during times of near-death.

I awoke with the feelings of profound peace, love, and acceptance still coursing through my veins. But I also felt the grounding, crushing pain that leaving would cause my family. There was no Being who could truly promise me no consequences.

Freedom would have to wait.

⁂

Even so, I relived my dream and its feelings with the obsessive focus I tend to throw at whatever captures my attention.

The idea of dying became the only thing that gave me hope. It was as if the only way I could survive was to move on, leave the current chapter, and head into the next. I finally, finally had something to look forward to.

Jason said he'd always known he wouldn't live to reach his 18th birthday. For my part, I always knew I would live to be way older than anyone around me, outlasting everyone by decades and decades. But perhaps I was wrong about that.

So on the Wednesday before Thanksgiving, I went to Jason's house after school and didn't tell anyone my whereabouts. Jason's mom and her boyfriend had embarked on a cruise for the holiday, so we had the place to ourselves. I didn't take anything with me, didn't pack any clothes, just disappeared.

Jason's older brother-in-law had borrowed his gun for a hunting trip that weekend and was out of town. So we were left with a bottle of pills and sharp objects that damn near did the trick.

It dawned on me late in the evening that I needed to tell my grandparents that I hadn't been kidnapped and that I was safe.

For some reason, I called their house instead of Mom's. Grandma answered and gasped when she heard my voice. Pops talked over her and his voice broke when he said my name. "Just come home. No questions asked." He choked up again.

That was the first time I heard Pops cry. The sound caused a knife to twist in my gut. I hung up.

Then Jason and I did about the dumbest thing two people could do if the goal was to let the pills take effect and keep the blood flowing. We went out into the night and walked deep into the forest.

We climbed onto a flat boulder in a clearing, huddled together for warmth, lying on our backs, and watched the stars march across the sky. Jason was the one to show me the constellation of Orion a few months earlier, and Orion didn't disappoint that night, suspended over us like a guardian.

We didn't talk much. From the outside looking in, it would have been quite the boring rendezvous. From the inside out, there was nothing more intimate.

No Being came to rescue me or Jason. But no one came to insist that I stay on Earth and live to die another day either.

It seemed that the veil between this world and the Great Beyond was as close as the air on my cheek. *It would always be that close.* The magical promise of any alternate next life was never more than a breath away.

Jason and I must have realized the same thing at the same moment. He slowly sat up, wrapped me close to his chest, and said, "You're very cold. Let's go inside."

As it turns out, we had been outside for hours. It was nearly 3:00 in the morning.

I wasn't disappointed that life as I knew it wasn't quite over. Nor was Jason. Instead, both of us were filled with love and wonder at our tiptoed voyage to the edge.

I never again felt the need to escape this life on Earth. The edge of existence here is perilously close as it is.

You can always die tomorrow. Or tomorrow's tomorrow. You don't have to die today.

HOTLINE! CALL OR TEXT 988

The following morning, a police officer arrived. I didn't want to leave Jason and burst the bubble of sacred space out of time that we created. But I accompanied the officer.

I assumed that everyone who looked at me could see that I spent the night cavorting with the Grim Reaper and was a wildly different person because of it.

Nope.

The officer glanced through the rearview mirror at me in the back seat. "Your birthday's in a few months, right?"

"Yeah."

"Once you're sixteen, you can run off with your boyfriend. Until then, don't make me come looking for you again. I have to file charges against you."

Something about having "charges" against me cracked me up. I wanted to explain that I hadn't merely run off with my boyfriend, that I had almost fallen off the Earth, but I chose not to bother.

If I were a criminal for stumbling over my will to live and experiencing a truth so profound and majestic in the process, so be it. I pressed my face against the window and tried to hide that I had the giggles at the ridiculousness of my situation.

⚘

Mom soon arrived at the police station. I'm certain her feet pounded the ground so hard, there are footprints in the sidewalk still visible there today.

The night's experience crashed into the fact that no one was curious enough to even ask about it. I couldn't understand why no one said, "Hey, girl. What happened?"

For Mom's part, the poor woman was working her tail off to provide me with as many experiences as she could to set me up in life, including actively looking for jobs in Europe so we could travel the following year. At that time, this possibility didn't penetrate my dense, self-absorbed fog though.

When we got home, Mom grabbed random clothes out of my dresser and of all things, a hair dryer, and jammed everything into a suitcase. "You're going with your dad. Don't come back here until you're ready to follow some rules and be a responsible member of a household."

Dad and Drema lived about an hour away, but he must have put the pedal to the metal because he arrived on the scene right in that moment. "Stop yelling at her! For Chrissake, if I had to live in this house, I'd flee too. I don't know why you're the one mad."

Mom huffed out of the room. Dad wrinkled his nose at me, made a funny face through his bottle-thick glasses, and said, "It will be okay, kid."

Mom always said that in a crisis, Dad was his best self and the one to call, and boy, was that true.

Dad didn't tell me until years later that he got the police to never even write a report. Apparently, he told them the same thing he told Mom. "*Officer, you spend one night with her Mom's side of the family, and that pecking hen of a grandma, and you'd be running away too.*"

My unplanned stint with Dad meant I crashed his romantic holiday weekend with Drema. If Drema was disappointed that I had to unexpectedly tag along, she never let it show.

I hunkered into the back seat for the second time that day, desperately missing Jason and wishing he could go off with us. Dad told me I could talk, or not talk, or talk to Drema in private, or sprawl out and listen to my Walkman all weekend. Main thing was to just take a breather.

Drema said, "I want you to know you are welcome to come live with us. Just say the word."

"That's right, kid. The only thing I want for you in this whole wide world is to get out from your granny's talons."

Mom and I lived thirty minutes away from Grandma and Pops, but we still spent every weekend and holiday in their house. I hadn't thought one way or the other about it, aside from that I felt very close to them. They were bonus parents, in addition to Dad and Drema.

Plus, their house always had guests in and out and involved a high level of action, and Mom and I enjoyed the time with them.

But Dad used the occasion to lighten the mood and crack jokes, and along the way, let his own frustration with his former in-laws be known.

"Grandma's well meaning," I offered.

"Well meaning, my ass! She's a controlling busybody!" It felt like a betrayal to agree with Dad, but he was making me laugh.

The space Dad and Drema gave me was exactly what I needed. I was coming to realize there was no way I could explain the significance of the previous night to anyone without them judging it as something to be ashamed of.

Or worse, vilify Jason and keep me away from him. I decided to protect the sanctity of my experience with him, all the way to my eventual grave.

Dad took advantage of the weekend to walk me through a few college campuses. I couldn't imagine I'd get out of high school, much less attend an esteemed college.

On that walk, Dad said, "Did I ever tell you about my mother, Kid? She was something. She was abusive and an alcoholic."

That was the first time I heard Dad say the words, rather than them coming from Mom or Grandma.

"Depression runs in our family. You need to be aware. I've always had a proclivity for the highs and the lows. I want to ride the backs of mountains, but when I come down, it's worse than the lowest pit of hell."

At the end of the weekend, Dad asked me where I wanted him to take me, his house or back to Mom's. Two things sprung to mind: Jason and *The Nutcracker*.

I couldn't drive ninety minutes each way, every day to do the two things necessary to my existence: dance in Mr. Rose's studio and be with Jason.

I responded, "I have *Nutcracker* rehearsal tomorrow evening."

Dad said, "All right. If you change your mind, I don't care if it's in the middle of the night, call me."

Drema offered, "We can revisit it in January if you want. Just let us know."

⁂

Apparently, at one point over the weekend, Drema had spotted my gnarly, blood-encrusted wrists, wounds I was having a hard time keeping closed. The mom hotline must have been popping, because between my mother, my stepmother, and Vivi's mother, all health-care professionals, Mom got in touch over the holiday weekend with Vivi's psychiatrist.

Monday found me not in rehearsal or talking to Jason, but filling out a questionnaire with the man who ran Vivi's psych ward. Dr. Psych's demeanor didn't facilitate any vulnerable confessions or notions of healing. I had a hard time seeing how Vivi flourished in a place under his management.

He determined that I remained a heightened risk of harm to myself, because several of my answers indicated I was far too comfortable with death. Never mind that I no longer harbored any wishes to die.

I tried explaining that I simply knew firsthand that death was closer than we may like to imagine. No, that fact was not something I found upsetting.

Dr. Psych diagnosed me with Severe Clinical Depression and asked Mom to involuntarily commit me "for at least thirty days."

I would miss *Nutcracker* and the best role I'd ever had, and Jason wouldn't get to see me dance. That prospect filled me with dread. Thankfully, Mom came to the rescue.

"No," Mom told Dr. Psych. "I raised Andrea to think for herself and make her own decisions. If she says she's okay to go home, she's okay to go home."

Dr. Psych didn't pull punches. "When your daughter kills herself, it's on your shoulders."

Mom's voice grew stern to match his. "Noooooo. If Andrea chooses to die, it's on her shoulders. Period." Mom wasn't afraid to lock horns with doctors when they didn't listen, even if they did view her as merely a nurse — or a stubborn mom.

Reluctantly, the doc sent me home, with a prescription for anti-depressants and instructions to see a therapist immediately.

That Wednesday, I met Dr. Annette Zavareei in her office. On the other side of the non-descript front door lay a kingdom filled with thick Turkish rugs and lanterns, pearl inlaid tables, and plants galore.

The terrible thing about Dr. Zavareei was that she wouldn't let me spend every single Wednesday afternoon with her for the rest of my life.

NINE

❧

ON'T GET ME wrong, it wasn't like my sullen teenage self suddenly took to therapy and morphed into Suzie Sunshine. In the late 80s, the notion that you'd try to end it all was so stigmatized, no one would talk about it, much less treat an unhappy person with compassion.

Suicide schlepped around bags of guilt and shame heavier than murder. The rugged slashes across my wrists were now visible proof to the world that I had come unhinged, and might even be contagious.

Mom was so saddened for me that I may be branded for life that she took me to a plastic surgeon to see if removing scar tissue would help. The female physician handled my wrists like I was an infectious lab monkey. "There's nothing I can do, except make it worse. She'll have permanent scarring." She tsked in disapproval, making a point to address Mom and ignore me.

Mom replied, "You know, your bedside manner leaves much to be desired." Each word stepped from her mouth on the tip of a dagger. She whisked me out of the office.

"Doctors wouldn't have a profession if it weren't for patients, yet none of them lately seem to care about patients," she hissed in the car.

I felt awfully out of sorts in my skin most hours out of the day, and tried to hide my vulnerable, screeching wrists, which was incredibly difficult in ballet class. Everyone in class averted their eyes to ignore the obvious, and *Nutcracker* rehearsals went on.

Then, one night around that time, I awoke to find that my bedroom wall was missing. In its place was an infinite space filled with shimmering, golden light that appeared to have more substance than air.

Several hazy figures moved around far enough into the light that I couldn't make them out in any detail. I didn't get the sense that they were aware of me or that they felt familiar. Instead, I had the sneaky sensation that I might be glimpsing into a universe I wasn't supposed to see. I sat up slowly, fearful that any quick movement, or even breathing, would end this glorious, glowing vision, a color and consistency of which I hadn't seen on Earth.

I blinked hard a few times to make sure I was, in fact, fully awake. I squeezed my hands into fists. My fingers felt normal. The blankets on my bed had weight.

Dream? No.

Light on somewhere? No.

Fire outside? No.

Over the next moments, the figures faded further into the light, and my bedroom wall lazily solidified back into place.

The windows were dark. My room was dark. I remained upright in bed, yearning for the golden light, telepathically crying out, *Come back. Pleeeeeeaaase, come back.*

Other than Jason and Mindy, I couldn't tell anyone about the experience. Jason and Mindy were the only people who wouldn't chalk it up to a "mere dream" then get on with the mundane tasks of the day.

Any insistence on my part that the vision was *real* would be more evidence that I, the resident cuckoo, couldn't tell the difference between what's real or not.

This experience was different from Aunt Lily visiting when I was a kid, visits that, in my awareness, had gradually stopped over the years. I could wrap my head around deceased ancestors checking in on me, but I couldn't fathom why I had a vision that seemed like a tear in the fabric of the universe.

Most of us have a hard time reconciling conflicting truths, such as, This can be true, and That can also be true. My internal gremlins were no different. They chattered away, trying to convince me that my vision was only the product of a sick brain. After all, depression, in part, meant that chemicals went awry in my head. On the other hand, I *knew* I witnessed something miraculous that gave me hope.

I struggled with what to do about myself, with a (sick?) mind that could see and hear and grasp things no one else could, even with all the new age books I read. In the books, the writers had grand ideas and mental impressions that stayed tucked *inside* their minds instead of jumping out and frolicking around in the 3-D, earthly world.

A big part of me agreed with the gremlins and quietly feared that the depression diagnosis was a mere rest stop on the way to schizophrenia.

Mental illness seemed way scarier to me than death. At minimum, I had to accept that depression, particularly in the late 1980s, was a marginalized, but full-on mental illness that I would have to manage for the rest of my life.

Proof of that daily management appeared in the prehistoric antidepressants they had on the market back then. The pills made my body temperature plummet, and my mouth felt like I chewed sand.

At least once during each class period, I needed to ask permission to go to the water fountain, then some kid would shriek, "Her face is turning blue!"

Therapy was a big taboo in popular culture as well. I had a hard time even admitting to Jason where I slunk off to every Wednesday afternoon.

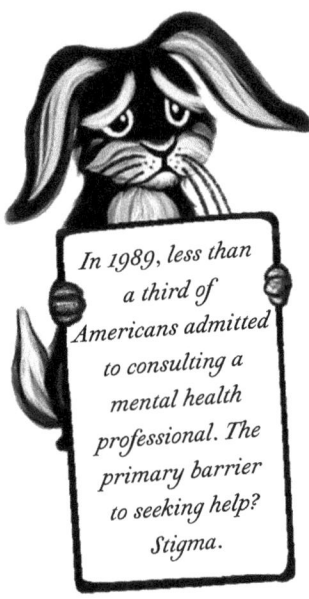

In 1989, less than a third of Americans admitted to consulting a mental health professional. The primary barrier to seeking help? Stigma.

Heading into my first visit, I wasn't sure what one was supposed to do in therapy. I assumed I would talk about hating school, hating our town, and hating my life, without divulging entirely how weird I was. I did have the good sense to leave out all mention of "visions."

In turn, I thought Dr. Z, like every other doctor, would be stony in her disdain for me, scold me for trying to commit suicide and bringing shame upon my entire lineage, both backwards and forwards. Then she'd prod me toward fitting in by faking normal behavior.

Boy, was I wrong. When Dr. Z opened the door, my eyes widened with delight. Suddenly, the last thing that mattered was me. Instead, I wanted to know about Dr. Z herself, how she got to be who she was, where she found her turquoise necklace and her flowing pants.

She didn't allow me the luxury of turning the spotlight onto her.

"What's up with your grandmother?" she asked, almost teasingly right off the bat, her large brown eyes dancing. She wasn't looking down on me as a girl who couldn't do anything right. She was the type of adult who wouldn't judge me about my weight, or my looks, or all the ways I eventually failed everyone.

"Wha —, who? My grandma's great." I thought Grandma was an odd place to start.

"Are you aware that your mother made an appointment to come see me before I saw you and that your grandmother came along?" I hadn't known that Mom already had an appointment with Dr. Z. It felt at once like a betrayal and a relief. If Dr. Z was already filled in on everything, my work was over. All I had to do was sit back and take whatever talking-to she was hired to give me. But as far as Grandma was concerned, it made sense that she had gone along with Mom for support.

"You don't find your grandmother a little controlling?" Dr. Z suggested. I cracked a smile, remembering Dad's opinion.

Apparently, there was no confidentiality attached to the appointment Mom and Grandma had, and Dr. Z spilled it. "Your mother was quite rational and wants you to have support, but your grandmother wouldn't let her finish a sentence. She was worried about a satanic cult." Dr. Z rolled her eyes.

I was so relieved that Dr. Z was turning out to be a warm, intelligent person that I almost cried.

She then pulled out the questionnaire that I'd completed with Dr. Psych, the one that landed me in her office in the first place. "Feeling sad. Check." She looked up at me. "Would you say you also feel stifled? Claustrophobic in an existential way?"

Existential? Holy cow. I nodded and barely dared to breathe.

"Well, that makes a whole lot of sense to me. Of course you feel sad and stifled. There's no opportunity for you here. Of course you're depressed! After this art school experience, and all the pressure you've been under to please everyone, something would be wrong with you if you weren't depressed."

No adult in the history of the world has ever understood teenagers like Dr. Z.

Our visits typically began with me not knowing how to start talking, Dr. Z digging out the root of things, and ended with her nudging me toward the door, our hour having passed too quickly.

She guided me through my childhood bullying, the horrible babysitter, and my NCSA experiences with a nonjudgmental but straightforward assessment and irreverent humor. She called a spade a spade about our Appalachian culture, the pervasive apathy, and the lack of artistic and intellectual opportunity at the time.

Typical, self-absorbed teenager that I actually was, it never dawned on me that certain aspects of my depressed condition might be attributable to the abusive actions of other people and the reality of where we lived.

She even had the guts to call my family "dysfunctional."

I shared that word with Mom, and we got a big kick out of it—until Mom thought about it over some time and agreed, although our family's version was more subtle than most.

I felt seen by an adult, by an authority figure, who encouraged my imagination and undirected ambition. Dr. Z gave me permission to hoist two middle fingers up to the unattainable demands of the ballet world and the permeating dreariness of life at that time in Southern West Virginia. How I had responded to both was quite reasonable, according to Dr. Z.

Most importantly, with her, a possible future on this Earth glimmered. It started as a spark in the gold thread woven into a throw pillow on her couch, representing interesting places in the world to travel, endless experiences to devour, then it appeared as flickers of magic lurking in any given shadow.

Maybe I wasn't crazy. I had a right to be happy and demand a rich, wildly imagined life. I was emerging from Depression.

                         ◦~◦⌀◦~◦

Nutcracker came, and I danced for the only person in the audience who mattered, Jason.

I knew how to command a stage, and I hoped that would be enough to mask the fact that I didn't dance with the careless abandon I once had.

But who the hell cared? I wasn't gunning to turn professional anymore. Dancing had fallen into its rightful slot as a silly hobby. I didn't need to take it — or myself — so seriously.

Sure enough, afterward, Jason's sublimely perfect face broke into an irrepressible grin, letting me know how proud of me he was. He didn't know, and wouldn't care, that I chickened out heading into a series of fast turns at the end of my solo, played it safe at the last minute, and kept all the turns singles instead of doubles.

"My dancer," he said, hugging me close. I knew that I loved him more fully than a human being normally has the capacity to love another person. It wasn't teenage thrills, contrary to what Grandma judged.

From Grandma's perspective, the fact that I spent that night alone with Jason, during my "incident over Thanksgiving," equaled sin, and worse, societal embarrassment. Good thing Grandma was never present backstage during costume changes.

In any event, Jason became persona non grata to Grandma. He was forbidden to even call me while I visited her house. It was unfathomable to me that someone like Jason, so otherworldly and wise, yet still a young person struggling with the uncertainty of his future, would not be welcomed into my family's home.

I tried secretly calling him from an upstairs phone when I visited Grandma, but she would sense what I was up to, and pick up another extension to let him know he needed to hang up. He was respectful and patient, so he always did, and without any drama or teenage blowback, to boot.

Point being, dancing for him and making him proud meant more to me than pleasing that old bat back at NCSA, Melissa Hayden.

⁂

The inevitable crash descended after the performances. There were no rehearsals, nothing but technique classes to occupy my time after school. All the seniors, like Jason, turned their gaze toward the future.

We talked about running off somewhere. I would drop out of high school and get my GED, an idea he repeatedly shut down.

From the moment I met him, it never dawned on me that I would function without him. Jason was as essential to my daily life as water, air, and Dr. Z. I could wait tables, as long as it wasn't at Shoney's like Katrina. Jason and I would figure it out.

I asked Mindy what she thought. "Don't be an idiot. You're not dropping out of high school. But I agree you shouldn't follow in Katrina's footsteps."

My ego could not sacrifice itself enough to wear the drab Shoney's uniform, even if it did mean Katrina was winning at NCSA, and securing herself a position in a world-class ballet company. For that, I was happy for her.

"Uh, noooo," Mindy corrected me. Once again, her look of

whether to destroy another aspect of my innocence flitted heavily across her face. She puckered her mouth. "Katrina's in rehab."

"Like where Vivi went?" Maybe she became depressed too and was on a psych ward for a few days.

"*Rehab*, dunce. Cocaine addiction."

Most of my essence whooshed off the nearest cliff. Not puritanical, hard-working Katrina.

Mindy didn't let up. "You remember Delia's mom and her care packages."

"Katrina refused to smoke cigarettes or pot. She wasn't part of Delia's crowd! They were spoiled bunheads with perfect bodies." I fought for the Katrina I had just seen at the end of the last school year in June, barely seven months earlier.

Mindy joked once that no one in Delia's gang had enough brain cells to do anything else with their lives, so at least they could dance, albeit without much heart and soul. Katrina was a smart and emotive dancer.

Hatred against those girls, and particularly Delia's mom, flared from my pores at the idea they ruined Katrina's promise and her future career.

Mindy continued, "I heard that Katrina was cast in Arabian again this year for *Nutcracker,* and she was so strung out in rehearsals, she couldn't dance. She got kicked out of school. Midterm. I remember you saying her aura was off."

I rolled my eyes. "It wasn't some aura thingy. I told you her eye sockets turned black, then her arms, neck, back, all of her skin was gray and yellow. How did no one else see it?"

"Her color never looked weird, Miss Dramatic, but she was definitely too thin."

Mindy was the practical one, and she liked to tease me, but she believed me when I shared with her what I saw. Grandma could read my skin color a mile away, usually the day before I came down with a cold or a fever, and she'd load me up with fluids and vitamins. Now I understood it.

"Can we write to Katrina or call her?"

Mindy pursed her lips again. "Apparently, her parents won't let anyone from that place contact her ever again. Especially her classmates."

I worried there weren't enough vitamins in the world to save Katrina from all the heartache of a crushed dream and failure I knew firsthand she was going through.

A few nights later, I had another vision. The experience with Katrina's skin colors — even though I was the only one to see them — might have tipped me toward accepting what I saw.

This vision, I believed down to my bones. I believed it so much, I didn't tell another person about it. Not Mindy. Not even Jason.

⚜

Jason thought his entire life that he would die before he turned 18. He witnessed a lot of death from a young age, including losing his beloved stepfather to a fast cancer when the man was barely 40. Jason himself had a bout with hepatitis when he was 16 that put him on life support momentarily.

Even for folks who haven't lived in close quarters with the Grim Reaper, it's not uncommon to get a number stuck in our heads about when we'll die, and it's likewise not uncommon for us to thrive well past that imaginary expiration date.

On January 25, 1989, Jason's eighteenth birthday came and went without incident. In a few months, he'd graduate. He needed to fly.

I was beginning to remember the world was, in fact, large. The future slowly crackled back to life, as if there were a promising One Day out there, after all. I'd catch up to Jason wherever he landed.

Jason always felt older than his years, and it weighed on his countenance and on his spirit. But for me, for perhaps the first time since I stepped foot on the earth, I felt my age. I had failed at everything that once mattered, which granted me permission to be merely fifteen, on the verge of sixteen, with no lofty goals.

Before all the seriousness of After High School kicked in for him, though, Jason reminded me that there was an upcoming spring prom. He didn't say it, but I sensed that attending a high school prom was beneath him. Tolerating or even enjoying an event as meaningless as prom was the first time I noticed a divide, as small as it was, in what we wanted to experience next.

And so was the state of my being during the night of February 3.

I dreamed that I walked from the street into the arched entryway of our small apartment building. I unlocked the street door and noticed Jason standing at the top of the red-carpeted staircase that led to our doorway on the second floor.

Jason wore a long army-green trench coat, an untucked, crisp white button-down shirt, jeans, and Doc Martens.

I wore black pants, a red-and-black flannel shirt over a black T-shirt, black boots, and a ton of metal jewelry.

I ran up the stairs, so excited to see him. We hugged as if we hadn't just seen each other that same day. Then a part of me separated from the moment, hovered over my right shoulder, and said, "That's not going to happen."

Instantly, I found myself hurtled to the bottom of the stairs. I ran up again, but this time, I ran and ran up the stairs with my awareness in two places — the part of me that was running, and the part of me hovering behind, up near the ceiling. The stairs grew longer and longer, and Jason, standing at the top of them, slowly faded into mist.

I could run the rest of my life and never reach him.

I jerked myself awake. I was lying on my back, my right arm flung over my head with my hand resting on something on my pillow. Sometimes, I slept with a blue stuffed bear wedged between my pillow and my headboard. My fingers didn't feel the soft plush bear though. I felt something solid, like the short, shaved hair on a hard skull, one I was familiar with. I moved my hand around and felt longer hair on top. None of this made sense.

Fortunately, there was a light on in my room. The same glowing, golden light emanating from an unknown source that I saw a few months earlier filled the entire room.

I raised myself up and flipped over to investigate. Sure enough, Jason's head was sleeping peacefully on my pillow. No gore, no blood, nothing horrific.

I thought, "I'll deal with this tomorrow," and picked up the skull. It was awfully heavy, so I had to sit fully upright and pick it up with two hands. I was very careful not to drop it.

I turned toward my nightstand and saw that two of Jason's unframed photographs had slipped from their prop against the lamp and lay face-up on the little table. It didn't seem right to place the skull right on top of them. So I cradled it in one arm, propped the pictures back up against the lamp, then carefully set the skull against them. There wasn't much space, so I scooted the lamp, pictures, and the skull more toward the wall to make sure nothing would tumble off the small table.

Then I fell back asleep.

The following morning, I woke up, facing away from the nightstand and toward my windows. With slow disappointment, I realized it was Saturday. Jason would be at work most of the day in the garage. I wouldn't be able to talk with him until mid-afternoon.

I rolled over, and to my surprise, found my blue plush bear balanced precariously on the edge of my nightstand, propping Jason's pictures against the lamp that had been pushed against the wall.

My dreams and the vision from the previous night tumbled on me like a lead blanket of doom.

TEN

EVERYONE HYPED MY upcoming sixteenth birthday, which to me, seemed much ado over nothing.

My childhood friend from down the street and now fellow Depression Survivor, Vivi, called to wish me an early happy birthday, check on me, then wondered if I would get a car. The question was absurd on so many levels. I asked, "Hi, have we met?"

We didn't have money for an extra car, which Vivi knew. In the overall scheme of things, my family valued cars just barely more than a horse and carriage.

Vivi's family had more cash flow, hence the boarding schools, Sweet 16 birthday parties at the country club, and so forth. Both of our families were practical, however, and both thought handing over car keys to a brand new teenage driver on mountain roads amounted to criminal negligence.

"It doesn't hurt to want one anyway," she teased, then added, "Seems like you're feeling better. I know I am. My psych said it's okay to start wanting things again. Even something dumb like a car."

"I want something dumber than a car. I want a triple layer, moist chocolate cake with mounds of frosting between each layer."

"That's a lot for you to ask for. You are feeling better."

Vivi and I had that conversation before the dream.

I woke up Saturday morning, February 4, 1989, wrapped in that invisible lead blanket, more like a straitjacket, really, and my plush, blue teddy bear on the nightstand. I maneuvered out of bed, feeling like I was still in a dream, yet I remembered every minute detail of the night before.

My body moved on its own accord, while my mind screamed, *Move the stupid bear, put it back on the pillow, and go back to sleep!*

I felt like I needed to start again, or at least get up on the other side of the bed. Something to change what felt to be an inevitable, looming chain of events.

My body didn't listen. It left the bear on the nightstand and walked to my closet. *Don't put those clothes on. Pick something different.* I watched my arms reach for the pants I had on in the dream. Then the same T-shirt, the flannel overshirt, then the bracelet.

I felt trapped inside a soundproof isolation tank.

I mentally tapped into Jason. He was alive. Saturday mornings meant he would be working at the garage, his mom at her beauty salon. I watched my hands dial his home phone anyway. It rang and rang.

Mom announced we were going to Grandma's for the weekend, as the family wanted to gather for my birthday on Monday. I wanted to sit, frozen by the telephone, until Jason called and let me know he was all right.

Something terrible was getting ready to happen. I didn't know what, when, or how. I only knew it would involve Jason. My anxiety was so high, I couldn't breathe. And for some reason, I couldn't break out of the odd trance I was trapped in to say anything about the dream.

So my mouth told Mom, "Okay. Sounds good. But no cake. Jason's going to make me a cake."

What?

Mom looked as surprised as I felt.

"I mentioned wanting a chocolate cake, and I think he's going to surprise me with one." This was as news to me as it was to Mom. I'm pretty sure I hadn't asked Jason for any presents other than himself, but I suddenly knew with certainty that he would bring along exactly what I told Vivi I wanted.

Mom said, "We already promised Auntie Maude a hummingbird cake. She insists she doesn't like it, but she'll be willing to eat it for you."

"It's her favorite. I guess I get two desserts."

Jason finally picked up the phone around 4:00 pm when I snuck upstairs at Grandma's to call him. I gushed a sigh of relief.

"What's the matter?" he asked gently.

"Oh, nothing." I felt gagged, forbidden to tell him the dream. "Just happy to hear your voice."

"Yeah, busy day at the garage. When will you be home? Could I see you tomorrow?"

A lump formed in my throat. "We might be home late tomorrow evening. Maybe we could skip school on Monday. I could see you then." I tried to buy myself — or maybe him — one more day. As if we could make it to Monday, my actual birthday, we'd be over the road block in the current timeline, and sail on with our lives.

Jason insisted, "I'd rather see you tomorrow too. I have a surprise for you."

Fuck. *Don't make the cake!*

My mouth betrayed me again. "Sounds great!"

For the remainder of the weekend, I sensed every event before it happened, who would say what, who would do what. Every time, I silently begged for *something* to break the chain of events, and for my jacked-up premonitory sense to be wildly wrong. Nothing did.

On Sunday morning, I again put on the same clothes I had worn in the dream. *No! You brought another shirt and jeans!*

Pops' ancient clock on the living room mantle ticked louder than ever throughout the house, clicking off each passing second and chiming the hour, a judgment of time winding down. *Tick. Tock.*

During this time, not once did I question what I had perceived. Not once did I wonder whether I merely had a bad dream and made too big a deal of it. This experience was so different from anything I'd previously witnessed, I couldn't deny it.

The relentless dread made me want to jump out of my skin. What I didn't know was how or what or when the Dread would take shape in real life.

On Sunday evening, Mom and I returned home. I tried calling Jason. No answer. My anxiety was so heavy, I could barely haul myself to my feet. But I couldn't bear to sit still another moment either. "Let's take the dog for a walk."

A mere few blocks into the walk, I sensed Jason had come to our house. "Let's turn around. What if Jason is trying to stop by?" Mom didn't argue.

Sure enough, we arrived home to a beautifully wrapped, home-made, three-layer chocolate cake at the door. "How wonderful!" Mom clapped in glee. I couldn't speak.

I calculated the time it would take for Jason to arrive back at his home, called, and he picked up. I feigned happiness over my present, and he agreed to turn around and drive back to wish me a happy birthday in person.

I *needed* to see him, even though there was nothing I could do to stop the chain of events, and even though I firmly believed in free will over rigid predestination.

Mom warned, "Jason needs to leave early. It's a school night."

"I'm not going to school. Tomorrow's my birthday. None of us are going to school tomorrow. We're going to play hooky instead." Once again, the pronouncement that fell out of my mouth was news to me.

Mom didn't even turn her head from the television. "You're going to school tomorrow. All of you kids."

When I laid eyes on Jason, my anxieties dissipated. Our visit was uneventful, other than the fact that it's not every day or even every birthday that the most beautiful being on the planet decides to bake you a decadent dessert from scratch. And it turned out to be delicious.

Right before I went to bed that night, I called him a few minutes before 10:00 pm. He said he was waiting for my call.

I burst into tears, blubbered that I had been crazy miserable all weekend, waiting, waiting for something terrible to happen, and I couldn't take being on edge anymore.

Nothing I said should have made sense to him. It certainly wasn't his fault that I had a stupid nightmare I couldn't shake. I had no reason to be mad at him over it.

He didn't ask any details. As always, he was unflappably calm and loving. I remember hearing him tell me he loved me. I don't remember whether I returned the phrase or not. But I felt calmer when I slowly placed the handset of the telephone back into the cradle, so I know that we didn't end the conversation on bad terms or with angry words.

I never told him about the dream. I still wasn't sure I physically could have, if I'd tried.

I crawled into bed, turned off the lamp, and lay on my back. Suddenly, the lead blanket binding me exploded into bits of dust, scattering into the ether. My head felt free, my chest expanded, my entire body felt so light, I could have floated.

I sensed Jason as if he were a dense cloud of ethereal substance, hovering just around my ceiling. Of its own accord, my heart gushed energy, anguish, and *I'm sorrys* up into the cloud of Jason, fresh hot tears of relief, wetting my face, hair, and pillow. I felt pure acceptance and assurance in return.

This experience was blessedly mystical. It wasn't Real Real, like the last two days of embodying horror Real.

I finally broke through the trance.

Everything was going to be all right.

⚬⸗⸎⸍⸏⸗⚬

I went to school the following morning, feeling foolish for my bizarre overreaction throughout the weekend.

Then, in my first class, I couldn't focus on our assigned busywork. Someone was coming down the hall to get me.

Sure enough, the classroom door opened, and the principal's assistant entered with a pink hall pass. The teacher read it, looked straight at me, and I began to pack my book bag before he even finished, "You're wanted in the principal's office."

On the interminable walk down the hall, the assistant didn't speak, and I didn't ask. Darren met me in the doorway of the office and ushered me back into a stairwell. "You know what I'm going to say," he ventured.

"Yeah. But I need to hear it anyway so I believe it."

"Jason shot himself last night."

I nodded, tears rolled down my face as the horrid finality that Jason was gone thudded into my bones. Darren's voice broke when he continued. "Just after 10:00 pm, his mom came home and found him. Do you want me to keep going? Because there's something else." I nodded again. Nothing could be as wretched as what had already happened.

Darren, Jason, and I had a mutual friend and classmate we hung out with nearly every day after school - John, a punk, guitar-playing poet. My grandma didn't like Jason, but Jason's grandmother *hated* John with his black leather motorcycle jacket, shaved head, and metal chains.

"Jason's grandma called John's house last night. Screaming. She wanted to let John and his parents know that she's seeking a homicide investigation into all of us."

I heard Darren's words, but they sounded like a mushy, *wanh wanh wanh wanh*. Throughout the previous few days, my body had been robotic, but my mind was all too sharp. Not anymore. If neurons were firing in my brain, they weren't connecting with anything. The inside of my skull turned into porridge.

In psychiatric shock

Next thing I knew, I stood in the hall near the front door of the school, Mom miraculously appeared next to me, the bell rang, the hallway filled with students who slowed their roll as they passed.

I realized what they witnessed: a girl convulsing with sobs, the guttural sound erupting from the depths of hell, loud enough to pierce through teenage chatter. Yikes. I turned to face the wall, not from embarrassment over my uncontrollable condition, but to protect them from it.

Mom apparently snapped into command mode when she arrived and instructed the principal that she would take custody of the few students in our friend group for the remainder of the day. Now that Jason was dead and school had always been pointless, I was in no rush to be anywhere.

I expected any reaction to tragic loss to be normal, but what happened the following day sent me ricocheting into shame so profound, I wouldn't tell anyone about it for decades.

I woke up the next morning with a blank brain.

I remembered my name. My room looked familiar.

As I stared at the ceiling, I remembered that someone died who I was very close to, as close as I was to my own arms. His name was... I scoured the interior contours of my head. Jason. *Jason who?*

I had no idea what he looked like. I had no idea what happened. I had not one single memory of this Jason.

I didn't have time to wallow in the dreadful notion that I no longer had an operational mind. Mom yanked me out of bed and instructed that I had an emergency appointment with Dr. Z. I then recalled Dr. Z.

"Why?" I had nothing to say, nothing to talk about, no emotions. I needed to stay in bed, alone, and very quietly retrieve pieces of my shattered mind and soul.

Mom, however, is a verbal processor to such an extreme, she literally can't think without talking. On a good day, if I'm talking, I'm not feeling. This was not a good day.

I silently plopped onto Dr. Z's couch.

"Looks like you were up all night?" she asked.

"I guess." I vaguely remembered a lot of people in and out of the house throughout the previous day, and a friend spending the night with me.

"You want to talk about anything?" Dr. Z asked kindly.

I shook my head. I was having a hard time remembering what there was to talk about, and I couldn't find the words to say that.

"I don't think you need to be here today. Sometimes, being forced to talk too soon is not helpful."

"Uh, duh." It sounded like I lost all of my complex vocabulary as well.

"Sometimes, when someone commits suicide, folks worry it's contagious. Like, everyone else is then also going to want to die. Do you feel like that?"

I wrinkled my face in disbelief. "No." I didn't want to die anymore. I thought that was settled. Why couldn't I just go back to bed, hug my teddy bear, and grieve my dearly departed mind? And that guy I loved?

Mom thought she was doing the right thing. After all, she was a psych nurse and talk therapy was her tool. But for me, not allowing me at least a day to simply *be* in the immediate aftermath only further shoved all of my emotions, and any last bit of my sanity, 20,000 leagues into an abyss.

As the day wore on, I got worse, not better. I kept forgetting Jason ever existed.

But there was a chocolate cake on the kitchen counter. Mom couldn't understand how I could eat it, as just looking at it made her so sad she felt sick, and I couldn't explain that it was my only tether to a reality that existed less than 48 hours earlier.

I had pictures of Jason, a striking young man who looked familiar when I looked at the photographs. For the life of me, however, I couldn't pull up a mental image of him without looking at the photos.

The following morning, I tore open the newspaper, searching for Jason's obituary, printed facts that, hopefully, I could memorize.

I grew pretty worried about how long I could carry off this zombie version of myself, when I had the idea that we should visit Jason's mother. *Win!* I remembered he had a mother, what she looked like, and her name. Carol.

I didn't remember how to get to Jason's house. But maybe Mom could figure it out, and I would find something there to jiggle my brain back to life.

"Take the pictures you have of him," Mom suggested. "His family may want them for the service."

NOOOOOOOOOOOO!!!!! I choked in horror.

I discovered that I had two copies of one photo. The rest I locked in a small cedar chest, petrified that one day, the cake would be eaten, the newspaper ink fingered off the obituary.

Oddly, no one during that time asked, *Hey, what, if anything, do you remember about what happened?* Or tried to walk me through basic questions that would illuminate that I was in shock. If I had known "shock" was a fairly normal thing under the circumstances, and that it might last a day, or that it could last forever, that alone would have saved me years worth of quiet suffering.

Three truths remained amid the ashes of my being.

First up, there was the fact that Jason chose to exit Planet Earth the night before my 16th birthday. Most people would later see that as a sign we had a fight, and that his final act was one of impulsivity, even evidence of shortsighted, teenage I'll-show-her type of revenge.

Anyone who thought that didn't know Jason with his steady, ageless wisdom.

It is true that Jason also had a singular, heavy obsession with dying, sooner rather than later. He was aware of that weight, however, and he could envision a life for me that didn't include him, one that he *wanted* me to experience. I suddenly found myself free of something I never wanted to be free of—his physical presence as a constant by my side.

Second, his love for me and mine for him was immutable, even if each memory of our time together might go in the grave with him.

Finally, his dying woke up everyone in our little band of outcast punks. A jolt of life surged through our veins. To be sure, we probably presented more like baby Frankensteins lurching around town after a lightning strike, but holy hell, we were alive and committed to remain so.

Which made it all the more confusing that Jason's grandma pressured the sheriff's office to investigate us for the satanic suicide pact she was certain we had formed.

The Satanic Panic of the 1980s–90s fueled false accusations against teenagers, despite an FBI study finding no evidence of organized satanic criminal activity.

ELEVEN

NO ONE REALLY knew how to handle this particular atrocity, so everyone collapsed into their worst selves.

Dad, of all people, called and said, "Not everything in the world is tutus and fru frus. No fairy tale like you had it in the ballet world. Sorry, kid."

What a twisted-up message of condolence. There were so many levels of wrongness about his words that I hung up on him.

Back at school, way sooner than I wanted to be, our little group was shunned, not embraced. The same kids who'd eyeballed me with concern the previous week now parted the hall as I walked by. I heard whispers, "Satan. They're in a cult." They hissed, "Witch."

It didn't help my reputation that when I heard these whispers, I felt so unsafe and misunderstood that I did the only natural thing to do when tiptoeing through snakes: I giggled. Maniacally. Once I started, I couldn't stop.

One kid had the nerve to tell me he heard I killed Jason. I was so surprised by the cruel idiocy, I nodded. "Yep. Sure."

One would think adults could offer solace, guidance, but nope. When the whispers wouldn't stop through class, my French teacher halted the lesson and addressed me, "We all know you're involved in Jason's death. Just answer now and be done with it. Did you know about it ahead of time or not?"

Every kid shuffled around in their seats to look at me. My face burned red.

I had been asked that question so many times, I knew there was no good answer. If I knew ahead of time, then why didn't I stop it? As if that would have been in my control.

On the other hand, if I hadn't known, what kind of girlfriend was I? So dumb and blind that I'd missed all the signs?

There was no way I would answer this callous question, even if my vocal chords could be persuaded to work. I dropped my eyes onto my desk and desperately wished I were, in fact, enough of a witch to summon flames from hell and burn down the whole world, or at least an invisibility cloak under which to disappear.

The teacher muttered under her breath, "You should have done something."

⬧ ⬧ ⬧

For the life of me, I couldn't understand why no one would let me simply grieve. There were no *I'm sorrys*, no sensitivity to the loss.

Jason's funeral cemented to me that most humans will choose cruelty to avoid their own sadness and helplessness. Those who don't will sit back and watch while those in power do.

Jason's grandmother took over the occasion, enlisting the preacher from her back holler church. He used the time in the pulpit to let us know that Jason's future was firmly secured as damned to hell, thanks to the suicide.

Preacher Man mentioned nothing personal about the deceased lying in the coffin in front of him.

Jason's poor mom shook uncontrollably in the front pew, while his grandma nodded her head to every word slithering out of the man's mouth.

The entire audience seemed shocked at this unholy sermon. I noticed eyes agape, brows furrowed, and jaws dropped. Surely, someone would stand up in defense of Jason's mom and tell the bully in the pulpit to go to hell, something to rescue us from this abuse.

No one said a word. We all sat there like sheep.

⁂

The following week, I had another dream.

I sat with Auntie Maude in an old fashioned sweet shop, adorned with soda fountains and bright pink wallpaper. Auntie Maude slowly dipped her spoon into a heaping hot fudge sundae and smiled sweetly to me, her entire demeanor one of innocent pleasure and peace.

I awoke, also full of peace—and knowing that her death was imminent. It felt uplifting.

It was still dark when the phone rang the next morning. "Grandma?"

Gran replied, "How did you know it was me?"

That knowing was a simple assumption. No one else had the nerve to jangle our phone at 6:00 am.

"Did Auntie Maude die?"

"No, honey, but she did go in the hospital last night. Tell your mother. Don't worry about Auntie Maude. She'll be all right." Grandma's voice sounded tired and hoarse, but she put on a false lilt.

I wasn't worried about my favorite old sour puss. Auntie Maude would be all right. Not because she would live, sick and suffering in the hospital, but because, at least in my dream, she seemed ready to pass on.

A few days later, Mom picked me up from school to cart me off to my weekly therapy session with Dr. Z. "Honey, Auntie Maude died today."

"I know." I told her about the dream. We agreed that we'd miss her, but her death seemed perfectly natural.

Her passing and its premonition, right on the heels of Jason's, was a bit much for my already overloaded mental state. I spent the two days between the dream and Auntie Maude's actual death with trepidation and unease, waiting for the inevitable. I grew pissed that my brain still couldn't remember much about Jason, yet maintained its preternatural ability to foretell death.

So I asked it to stop. I silently threw a temper tantrum on the universe. *"I can't walk around knowing someone's gonna die. If you want me down here for the next few decades, back the fuck off and let me be normal."*

Someone must have been listening. I had no visions, no dreams, no sensations of Jason or any other spirit around me. The spirit world remained very much a reality to me, with Jason an anchor on the other side. I just stopped being acutely aware of it in daily life on Earth.

Thanks to my time with Dr. Z, the curtain that fell on my memory and the steel cocoon wrapped around my grief, I didn't feel hopeless about my own life. I hated school, most people in it, and even despised the ground beneath my feet. But glimmers of a future started to beckon, as if the future were a place I needed to find. If I could just break away and get there.

Dr. Z got the memo. When she learned how my friends and I were being treated by fellow students, teachers, and other adults, her lips pressed into a firm, thin line. "All your friends are graduating this year? They're moving?"

I nodded, suddenly aware that I was stuck behind for two more centuries if I were forced to finish school, a rite of passage in which I placed zero value.

"What would you think if we got you out of here sooner than expected?"

"How?"

"You could graduate a year early."

I blinked in confusion.

Dr. Z continued, "Would you be willing to stay in school and graduate if you only had one year left, instead of two?" I looked at her sideways, scared to buy into this knight-in-shining-armor of a proposition. "I can write the school board, emphasize that you are in a mental health crisis and that your life depends on getting out of high school asap." Her eyes did the sparkly dance. "I think laying it on thick will help."

Hell yeah!

"You'll go to summer school to make up the extra needed credits, then start next school year as a senior."

There were so many times I cried in relief in her office that the pillows on her couch became permanently tear-stained.

The threatened cult investigation evaporated, I still didn't remember Jason's last name, and I couldn't feel much of anything over him. Everything about Jason splintered off and got buried with him.

Aside from that bizarre reality, I started feeling like a normal teenager. I even had a date to the prom.

By May, the school approved me to attend summer school and start the following year as a senior. Every experience the following year would be the last one of its kind in high school prison. The last first day. The last *Nutcracker*.

Only one person doubted the wisdom of me leaving the wretchedness of high school early. In a car ride on the way to ballet class, a dance friend's well-meaning mother asked me repeatedly to reconsider my plan. She looked at me through her rearview mirror and said, "Andrea, I just don't understand why you're cutting school short. These are the best years of your life."

My friend nudged me and rolled her eyes behind her mom's back. I started to retort, "If this is as good as it gets, I have a big bone to pick with Life."

But before I could get the words out, Dance Mom sighed and said, "You can't get these years back." She appeared to slip into a silent nostalgia.

I felt so sad that she peaked at 18 that I kept my mouth shut and chose to remain misunderstood.

I looked forward to an entire series of never-agains, even cherishing the last tenth-grade final exam, which happened to be with the callous French teacher. I hadn't looked her in the eye in months, throwing back my shoulders, and raising my chin haughtily every time I walked by her instead.

During that exam, I, along with 30 other students, hunched over our desks, blanketed in the thick silence of concentration. A three-foot-tall, green-haired, wrinkly orange dude poked his head into the classroom and locked eyes with me.

I jerked upright, bewildered at his presence. He took a pencil from his pocket and flicked it straight at me. The pencil twirled, lead over eraser, coming at me so fast, I ducked and cried out, "AAAAAA!"

My yip startled the class, all of whom jerked in my direction. Of course, as they careened around to gawk at me, the jaunty troll laughed and ran off.

Not surprisingly, I started to giggle. It dawned on me that, like Katrina's gray skin color, no one else could see the little man.

He had appeared only for me, and he had as little respect for this school business as I did. I felt special, and deeply appreciative of the little guy who reminded me of a long lost friend. I also sensed a message: "Lighten up."

I looked at the rest of the class, shrugged my shoulders, and mouthed, "Sorry."

I finished the test, in a state of wonderment and gratitude for my little friend, and managed to swallow the giggles that continued erupting from my belly.

Crawling out of depression and becoming mentally and emotionally stable meant I couldn't hang out as often with Dr. Z.

But by that point, two of the most meaningful relationships in my life sprung up like daffodils after a hard winter. First, a quantum-physics-type-brilliant magician, who understood time and space as if he were living in multiple realities and dimensions all at once and could lightheartedly explain the phenomenon to us peasants.

He literally walked straight from the pages of *Dr. Norell and Jonathan Strange*. I fell madly, head over heels in dizzying rom-com love with Jonathan Strange.

Second, Kathleen, an irrepressibly joyous exchange student from Norway. Kathleen and I supported each other's free spirited nature, spiking her host parents' brownies with pot, beating boys away from her with a stick (or not), and laughing til we cried on most nights.

Therefore, cognitive dissonance appeared on the daily menu. I just experienced horrific loss after depression and years of trauma. Was I allowed to feel happy and light, fall in love with a boy, and have fun with Kathleen?

A part of me worried that if I loved either of them too much, they'd die. I felt abandoned every time Kathleen chose to have a Friday night sleepover with another friend or Jonathan Strange chose to play guitar with the guys.

Don't you understand we might NEVER SEE EACH OTHER AGAIN?!

I'd like to pretend those words stayed in my head, but I'm pretty sure I vocalized a version of this desperate angst more times than I'm proud to admit.

Even so, every time I took a breath and checked some place inside of me, I came up with the same answer. Their energy didn't carry with it the heavy inevitability that Jason's did. Both seemed to have long, healthy lives in front of them.

I felt safe enough with them to trust that they wouldn't die on me, our relationships would continue or end naturally, not tragically. They felt safe enough with me and the world to assume we'd see each other again the very next day.

Or, more likely, they needed breaks from my relentless intensity.

On one of our last visits during my senior year, Dr. Z asked what I might be interested in pursuing in the future.

Duh. I wanted to be exactly like her. "I was thinking psychology."

She wrinkled her nose. "You'd get bored. I think you'd make a good lawyer."

It was my turn to scrunch up my face. Dad was born to be a criminal defense lawyer, and I didn't have his passion for keeping bad actors out of jail.

But Dr. Z said, "There's a lot you can do with a law degree. Also, consider Charleston, South Carolina. It's beautiful, artistic, and there's a wonderful liberal arts college there."

All of Dr. Z's suggestions served me well, elevating my expectations of myself and the world. But for some reason, I couldn't make up my mind on where to go to college, and more importantly, why. So I didn't listen to her — at least not right away.

Spring found my Advanced Placement classmates accepting invitations to various universities and comparing notes. We sat in AP English one March, breezing through a reading list nearly identical to the one Mr. Ballard issued us baby dancers back in eighth grade at NCSA, and the girl behind me asked, "So, what are you doing next year?"

I shrugged.

She looked confused. "You're not dancing?"

"No, no. I'm not good enough. That's done after the spring recital."

All the kids around us turned to look at me, even boys on the sports teams who had never attended a dance recital. They all chattered at once. "You *have* to pursue your dancing." "You're so talented."

"We all look up to you." "Girl, you can go to college later." And one particular jock, "Listen, my girlfriend talks nonstop about how good you are. You have to at least try."

I was stunned at my classmates' unsolicited support. Maybe we had all grown up enough to be kind to one another again, or maybe I had earned their respect.

My cousin Shaun hopped on the same bandwagon. He had a new video camera and filmed my final high school spring recital. He begged me to come watch the video with him, swearing the quality of Mr. Rose's choreography and the dancers were way better than small-town average. "You might appreciate your talent a little more if you come over and watch yourself."

My boundary of resistance still kept me from fully engaging with Shaun, even though he was the one to call and check on me on a regular basis, and he prioritized family gatherings more than the rest of us did.

I finally spent an afternoon at his house, amidst the Star Trek models he'd built, surrounded by the latest video and sound technology and a large screen TV. He'd never outgrown his love of mechanics and electronics, and always had a sports car or motorcycle he tinkered with in the driveway.

He didn't ask me about all my troubles the previous couple of years, though he made it clear he was there if I needed him. He just slyly mentioned, "Looks like we have matching scars," referring to the chemical burns splotched up his arm.

"Almost," I said, not inviting further conversation on the topic.

Shaun was 26 at the time, earnest and upfront about his faults, as always. I plopped on the couch between him and two large rescued mutts and asked how he was doing.

"Remember Libby?"

Libby was his girlfriend, then wife, for a few long years. She was a mess and nowhere near as attractive as Shaun, who was lanky and tall with a perpetual lopsided smile.

She left him on and off, and when they had a baby, she left him with the little girl too.

The family thought the whole baby idea was disastrous. They encouraged him to give up the child for adoption, and after a heart-wrenching period of time, he listened. He wanted the best for his child, and didn't believe he could provide that.

"You know," Shaun said to me, "everyone in the family treated Libby like a mooch. You were the only person who was ever nice to her. Clearly, your judgment is piss poor." He chuckled, his voice and his laughter originating deep in his throat.

I laughed with him. "Please tell me she's not back in your life."

"She showed up the other day begging for money, but no."

He continued, "She's working at a titty bar, but not even as a dancer." He gestured with the remote control at the TV, where the opening scenes of the recital started to play. I appreciated his dark sense of humor and grinned at him.

We watched the video of the recital, and Shaun was right, it looked more professional than I expected. "So are you going to keep dancing or not?" he asked.

"Where am I going to go dance? At Libby's titty bar?"

Shaun rolled his eyes. "What did I just say about your piss poor judgment? You need to use your talent while you're still young."

His belief in my ability suddenly swayed me.

Kathleen would be returning to Norway. My boyfriend, Jonathan Strange, was already off exploring other ways to exist in the multiverse.

I missed Mr. Strange so much when he was gone, I could barely breathe, and thinking of Kathleen not being reachable on the daily sent waterfalls of tears down my cheeks and into my lap.

Without my human crutches, what did I have left? I once again chose ballet.

⚜

Mom was the one who saved for 17 years for my college, though, and she refused to use college funds to pay for extra ballet training alone.

Fortunately, there was one remaining audition for the upcoming school year at the Cincinnati Conservatory of Music, which had an excellent dance program with college credits. Promising dancers fed into Cincinnati Ballet, a highly respected contemporary ballet company.

I determined it would be a waste to earn a college degree in dance, though. If I couldn't turn professional within two years, I'd resign myself to an academic degree or another life path altogether.

I showed up for the audition in Cincinnati a few weeks later in early May, even after being told that most spots had already been filled. Lo and behold, the teachers conducting the audition were *nice*. They reminded me of Mr. Rose. They talked to us as if we were human beings, worthy of their consideration. Perhaps for that reason alone, I wasn't nervous. I just danced and enjoyed myself. And I got in.

Dancing in Cincinnati was one of my best years in ballet. I danced well, we had performance opportunities throughout the year, the dancers wanted the best for each other, all of our teachers had had illustrious careers and turned out to be fine human beings.

Crazy, but most of us thrived under the support instead of cracking under the pressure that NCSA placed on us.

Nearly two-and-a-half years after Jason died, I must have been safe enough to start falling apart.

First to go: Jonathan Strange.

Mr. Strange, being the magical free person he was, enjoyed conducting extreme lab tests on himself, such as staying awake for three solid weeks on experimental chemical cocktails, just to see what would happen, while still enrolled in the study of quantum physics at Carnegie Mellon.

He called from payphones in various cities at all hours, but not often enough to punctuate large-to-me blocks of silence or alleviate my mushrooming anxiety.

I thought I was fine with this status, but one night, I heard myself crying into the phone, "I can't do this anymore. I can't stand not knowing whether you're alive or dead or where you are."

Those words felt frighteningly honest. Apparently, the feeling had been lurking under the surface until it gushed out, catching us both off guard.

"I'm not going to *die*," he cried back, in agony.

I didn't know how I was going to put one foot in front of the other without him, or why I would willingly shred both of our hearts.

But I was back in the disciplined lifestyle of ballet, where I controlled how many pieces of unbuttered popcorn or unsalted sunflower seeds I allowed myself to consume — the air-sucking type of discipline that doesn't allow space to accommodate another person or another way of living.

Shortly afterward, one evening toward the end of the school year, hanging out with a friend, I suddenly felt like something was chasing me—*in my mind*. I wasn't sure what It was or what would happen if It ever caught me, but I was convinced that the Me I knew would not survive.

My unawareness of what lurked just beneath my own surface was becoming an unwelcome, annoying habit. But there It was.

And this monster in the shadow felt waaaayyyyy bigger than the surprising break-up with Jonathan Strange. Visions of a permanently-locked psych ward loomed as certain as the next sunrise.

I told a friend, "Start talking, say anything, babble, I don't care, just talk and don't stop." My mind had to stay one step ahead of the shadow.

Just when I thought I couldn't take the internal tension one more minute, the thing in my head caught up. The sarcophagus that held my memories of Jason had arrived. It burst open, and a torrent of emotions surged out like a caged tiger unleashed into the wild at night.

My physical veneer broke. I couldn't speak. I could only sob and sob, my poor friend having no idea what was happening. The more I cried, the more I felt whole, and the more I felt my mind reintegrating pieces and parts of itself.

It must have appeared like I was in the midst of a mental breakdown. Instead, I instinctively knew that I was going through a massive retrieval of all the pieces of my broken brain. I could see Jason in my mind's eye as clearly as if I'd only seen him yesterday. I finally remembered what he looked like. I remembered his last name. I even remembered some activities we did together — not all, but snippets trickled in.

Synapses connected neurons in my brain that hadn't talked to each other in over two years. I had my memory back.

Which... brought with it all the grief. My body flooded with the deep love I'd once felt with Jason, and the yearning for his presence.

If this was what going crazy felt like, bring it. Lock me up and throw away the key if it meant I could remember the feeling of him, of being with him, car rides, hikes, conversations, and decorating the Christmas tree.

I blubbered to my friend through tears, "I'm better than I have been in years. I'm finally crying!" I giggled. Even to my own ears, I sounded like a lunatic. Lord, it felt good.

Complicated bereavement or disruptive grief can freeze memories and emotions for years after trauma, affecting roughly 7% of those experiencing loss.

I pulled an all-nighter just in case my memories fell back to oblivion in the River Lethe, then made the executive decision that I would skip school and rehearsals the next day.

Responsible to a fault, I reported in with my ballet teacher. When I caught her in her office before class, I didn't hesitate to spill who Jason was, what had happened, and that the dam had finally burst the previous evening. She rubbed my arm, "Oh, sweetie, you need to take a few days and cry."

It's miraculous how far a few moments of compassion will carry a person. She didn't treat me like a whack-a-doodle or send me to the counselor. Maybe because she was a retired ballerina, and dancers spend an inordinate amount of time not talking, she innately understood that I needed time to emote in private.

For the immediate future, I had no one to take care of, to report to, or please. I returned to my room, guiltily bought a small bag of M&Ms from the vending machine along the way, crawled into bed, and allowed myself the full break I had needed for years.

When you finally fall all the way to the bottom of the Grief Well, turns out you don't need to wallow there for long. The tears slowed, I grew bored of my room, and by the next morning, I was back in ballet class — my brain and memories still intact.

The same friend who sat with me as my brain stitched itself back together was a budding choreographer. The conservatory allowed him to create a number for the spring recital, and he gave each dancer a word to embody. While other girls had "compassion," "buoyant," and so forth, my word was "catharsis."

I burst into tears all over again. Ugly, body-wracking sobs in the studio in front of everyone. Cold-plunged right back into the Grief Well. Splat.

The other dancers didn't know whether to hug me or escort me away. My friend was mortified that he had hurt me.

"It's. Not. Your. Fault." I managed to stammer through heaves.

"What does 'catharsis' mean?" Buoyant asked.

My friend explained, "An intense experience that leads to a profound, greater understanding or wisdom, like an awakening."

I didn't want to be the weirdo that would forever bear this pain, from multiple intense experiences, only some of which carried "Jason" on the origin label. It was pain that aged me a gazillion times faster than everyone else around and seemed to separate me from my peers.

"You are catharsis in and of yourself, and therefore, you are cathartic to those around you," my friend said gently. "It's like you see the cracks. You can point them out or burst them open wider. We all value you for that." He gestured around the room.

The girls nodded, and Buoyant leaned toward me and rubbed my back. She said, "We all got the perfect word for who we are. You're intense like a lightning bolt in the dark. It makes you a natural, effective performer because of it. I'm totally jealous."

I thought about Jonathan Strange and the pain I inflicted on us both when I gave up on our relationship. I worried that I caused the ground to break under the feet of anyone standing too close. "I'd rather be buoyant," I cried.

For the next months, tears spilled over everything. Spring flowers, a chord of music, a curtain billowing in an open window. I had been holding my breath for two years solid, and I finally exhaled freely.

During that time, Dayton Ballet premiered a version of *Dracula* that I felt compelled to see. I saved all of my pennies and bought a seat in the last row of the balcony.

The music and choreography were unflinchingly evocative. By Dracula's death scene, the dancer playing the role dropped heavily on the last note, his head and shoulders dangling precariously over the edge of the stage into the orchestra pit.

The curtain fell. House lights came up. Theater emptied.

I found myself still perched on the edge of my seat, clinging to the armrests, one droplet of sweat trickling down the back of my neck, unable to breathe. *That* was how to command a stage.

That was spectacularly, extraordinarily cathartic.

❦

Fast forward — I secured a position with the Louisville Ballet the following year, a full-time, respectable professional gig with a dazzling costume shop, on-site designers, and a state-of-the-art home theater. They even supplied all of our pointe shoes, with the caveat that when they wore out, we autographed and returned them to be sold in the theater's gift shop. Heady stuff.

I also learned that three older girls I looked up to back in school at NCSA were currently working in the company's corp de ballet. Holy cow.

NCSA considered these girls part of the cream of the crop. NCSA kicked me out. The universe executed a sleight of hand, and all of us ended up in the same place after all.

So I dropped out of the conservatory a full year sooner than my self-imposed two-year deadline.

Dad looked over the contract with a fine tooth comb, not that any term in it was negotiable. I was over the moon to have a legal document that characterized me as a professional dancer, and Dad was so proud, he offered to help me pay rent.

Eighteen years old, and I might as well have driven into Kentucky with a bullhorn. *"Louisville, look out! I'm comin' atcha!"*

In turn, the ballet company lowered her old-lady librarian glasses down her nose, glared at me disapprovingly, and replied, *shhhhhh.* Louisville Ballet, a stuffy, old-fashioned classical company with its recycled swans and sylphs, turned out to be a horrid fit. And over the course of the year, most of Dad's rent checks bounced.

The company's prima ballerina was married to the company's director, my boss. Though Prima was a remarkable dancer, she refused to retire, resulting in her sixty-year-old self performing the roles of fourteen-year-old Juliet in *Romeo and Juliet,* and the maiden bride in *Sleeping Beauty.* Donors and Boss Man allowed Prima to carry on, so everyone acted as if Shakespeare originally envisioned Juliet as a grandmother cougaring after an underaged Romeo.

Meanwhile, the rest of the up-and-coming dancers, who should have already been headliners in their own right, got squished into roles beneath their capability. The atmosphere seethed with resentment and repressed desire, packaged in polite, thin-lipped smiles that made me suspicious.

My former NCSA classmates were a mild exception. Like me, they were the youngest of the ballerinas in the company and still had years of dancing ahead. They welcomed me like a little sister.

They didn't seem harmed by the abusive atmosphere at NCSA that crushed me and others. And not one of them had a dead boyfriend or a painful breakup. Or a brain susceptible to clinical depression and visions.

For these reasons, I adored them, and let them take me under their wing. I tried to absorb what life was like for folks I perceived as normal and uncomplicated. With every cell in my body, I wanted to be like them.

Those weren't the cards the universe dealt this round.

I couldn't fit into the mold of my classmates any more than I fit into any of the teeny costumes that appeared in my dressing room before each performance.

"You again?" The designers rolled their eyes when I stomped into the costume shop before every single dress rehearsal of a new show and dared to ask for a tutu and bodice that closed in the back.

In the last show of the season, I danced the role of one of three demons in *Firebird*. On the day of dress rehearsal, I once again found that the costume hanging in front of my dressing table was too small.

Somehow, I managed to squeeze into the wretched fabric without busting the seams. But I discovered that if I raised my arms or jumped, an X-rated wardrobe malfunction would ensue.

Back to the costume shop I headed, where Boss Man wrinkled his nose at my exposed rolls of flesh. The lead designer tsked, "Honey, I never trust my own measurements with you. We've never had a ballerina so big here at the company."

Boss Man observed, "Girl, you got it, flaunt it! You should go to Vegas."

For fuck's sake. Boss Man typically displayed the sensitivity of a hammer, but it sure sounded like he made extra effort in that moment to spit the words as an insult rather than pose a career suggestion.

I glared at him and weighed my options. I couldn't unleash the temper tantrum I felt brewing, and I bet Boss Man counted on that.

I could storm out of the company right then, toss my costume to a skinny understudy, and quit.

Then again, the role I danced in *Firebird* had me front and center, in a demi-soloist role. I could step on stage and improvise my own choreography throughout the entire ballet to ensure I stayed clothed. I was so full of spite that I chose the latter.

I risked a brutal tongue lashing, a hefty fine, or an outright dismissal the instant the ballet was over. Instead, not one person in the company said a word about my disobedience, which I found disturbing and odd.

The ballet ran for five shows over a long weekend. There was plenty of time for the designers to alter my costume between performances.

My costume stayed unfixed, and I improvised my way through every single show, barely daring to breathe, lest I pop all of the dainty hooks and clasps. Not surprisingly, the company didn't renew my contract.

TWELVE

ꙮ

L OUISVILLE BALLET'S SEASON ended in May, and I headed to
Europe with friends.
Everything went as planned until we hit the Mediterranean
coast of Italy at sunset, when we drove out of local time and space
and into a paradise I always hoped existed. The dusky rose atmosphere twinkled, then dense fog rolled in as we crossed into France.
It seemed as if seconds melted into one everlasting moment.

I had a hard time falling asleep that night in the chain hotel in
Nice, France. The nightlife chatter out on the street buzzed louder as
the night wore on. But something shifted toward the mystical during
our drive and hadn't slid back to Normalville.

I flipped and flopped around in the bed, and finally heaved
onto my side and stared at the window in annoyance. Fluorescent
street lights flooded the room, but the sense of Something More remained.

I closed my eyes and instantly saw a very old woman, clear as day
in my mind's eye. White grey hair swept away from her face, and her

eyes and smile glittered like the costume gemstones hanging in her ears and encircling her neck. She appeared in my thoughts, though I sensed her standing by the window.

Great-grandma? No. This woman was more familiar.

This woman was *me*. She was a future me.

Her mouth moved. She talked fast and with ease, but the noise on the street was so loud, I couldn't hear her. I was desperate for any droplets of advice this woman could give her younger self, a struggling girl with no job, but still stuffed with dancing dreams as big as her oversized body.

I settled for sensing what she said. I assumed my subconscious would take in every word. She didn't look like she'd spent a lifetime starving herself to fit in tutus. She lived a life full of love and meaningful experiences.

I blinked. I was still awake. I hadn't been dreaming.

It dawned on me that no friends, colleagues, or dates in my current life meant a single thing to me, including the ones on the Europe trip. Time to say goodbye to the whole lot. *That* old lady didn't have a lasting relationship with any of these people. Lovely as they were, our connection wasn't meaningful enough.

⁂

After my improvisational stunt at Louisville Ballet, I was fairly certain to be blackballed in the industry as fat and stubborn. However, the renegade little company, Charleston Ballet Theater in South Carolina, offered me a position starting in late August. I recalled Dr. Z's foreshadowing that I might love Charleston, that charming city by the sea.

Everyone in the ballet world warned me not to go. I would be going backward to a smaller market in terms of my career, and word on the street was that the management was bat-shit crazy.

Then, Jill Bahr called. She was the resident choreographer of Charleston Ballet and was becoming quite renowned. She said, "I have this burning desire to create a ballet based on the story of *Dracula*."

My breath caught.

"If you join us, I will cast you as one of Dracula's three wives. I'll choreograph it based on how you move and your body types. It will be stunning."

I was too awestruck to speak.

Jill continued, her manner of speaking to the point, with no breaks for air. "Check out the music. Estonian composer, Arvo Pärt. *Tabula Rasa*. His *Cantus for Benjamin Brittain* will be what you dance to in the wives' section.

"In addition to a full season, we do an extensive *Nutcracker* tour at Christmas, and perform throughout the Spoleto Festival here at the end of May."

She had me at *Dracula*. I immediately planned to head to the record store in the mall and snatch up the Arvo Pärt CD.

I started to say yes, when Jill interjected. "And your classmate Perry dances with us. Didn't you guys go to school together at NCSA?"

Shut the front door! Perry graduated in the same class as the three girls at Louisville Ballet. But Perry was an early iteration of Lady Gaga, with her platinum blonde hair, ahead-of-her-time style, and expressive voice.

The riches offered by Charleston Ballet kept piling up. The universe didn't need a sleight of hand to pull off this one. My only question to Jill was whether I could start early.

On my first day, Perry welcomed me to stand next to her at the barre, and for the next year, we roomed together on tour, went to art house movies at the Roxy, and she supplied the liquor for our weekend sleepovers, lent me dresses fringed with feathers, and snuck me into nightclubs.

Starting dance class next to her, every single morning, also encouraged in me an expansive freedom of movement I hadn't felt since I was onstage as a kid. So I had no desire to be like her when I grew up. When I was with Perry, it was okay to explore what it might mean to be the biggest version of myself.

The company's management consisted of Jill and Patty, the company's director. They were creative, boisterous, and emotional. Through classes, rehearsals, and shows, they met us with a list of what could have been better, while complimenting us for every small win, a balance held, an arabesque extended, a leap soared — executions each of us may have taken for granted.

If they were crazy, they were my kind of cray.

Every dancer had wildly varying body types, and although the costume department was staffed solely by Patty's husband, Don, our costumes fit.

Jill ensured that her choreography suited the dancer, such that each dancer bloomed in any given role. As a result, when we weren't onstage ourselves, we stood in the wings, enjoying our colleagues' feats.

We dancers did everything together, slept on cramped tour bus seats, smoked cigarettes, starved, and gorged. So we all noticed when my roommate, Annie, became too thin.

Patty had already gently mentioned to Annie that she was concerned about her, so I confided in Patty that Annie was barely eating at all. Patty said to me, "You know, anorexia is a mental condition, not just an eating disorder."

"Is that why she's yellow? And gray underneath?" All of the other dancers noticed her waning strength but not her skin tone. "Do you see it? Or is it just me?"

Patty peered into the studio where Annie stretched. "Yes. Her color indicates that she's both physically and mentally unhealthy."

Patty and Jill gave Annie a heads-up that she was losing strength and offered to talk with her parents or find her help. Annie stormed out of the studio, and displaying a remarkable muster of energy, yelled at them for intruding in her business and yelled at me for snitching. She didn't return after *Nutcracker* tour.

Apparently, that year at Charleston Ballet checked off a gigantic box on my life list of Things to Experience and Prove to Yourself. It also checked off the Middle Fingers Up box to everyone who told me I was too big, too fat, Too This, Not Enough That to ever dance professionally.

One day, during a dress rehearsal before the start of the Spoleto Festival, I rested on the studio floor in a beautiful, royal blue costume, handmade by Don himself, and heard the words inside my head, "I'm done."

My eyes widened. I looked around the studio to see if anyone else heard the blasphemy. I waited on an internal rebellion to argue with the voice. None came. I had the sinking feeling that the words were right. I was done with ballet.

I eyeballed the soloists in the studio and discovered that I didn't care to follow further in their footsteps or to keep forging ahead in the ballet world. I had danced my heart out all season in the best ballets of my experience. The boxes were checked, and there was no underlying desire to continue.

Immediately on the heels of that revelation, I felt free. I could eat all the M&Ms I ever wanted! I could make money!

It is possible that the constant, searing pain in my left arch factored into this decision. The ol' bone bruise back from seventh grade turned out to be a broken foot, on which I danced for years.

There were times by the end of a performance or rehearsal that my arch bulged grotesquely over my pointe shoe. God bless those torture devices, though. Jamming your foot into such a tightly-fit contraption stabilizes all of those little foot bones.

During one performance in the grueling Spoleto Festival, I leapt into the air at the climax of the show's finale and felt something in my left arch pop. I hung in the air, thinking, when I land, bones in this foot will shatter. I will collapse in a heap. Every dancer in this company is onstage right now. They will trip over me and injure themselves. The audience will be mortified, and we'll have to stop the show.

Not an option.

Somehow, mid-leap, I switched up the choreography, landed on my right foot only, and hobbled through the rest of the ballet, and the remaining performances of Spoleto. The show must go on.

⚜

In the middle of Spoleto, Grandma called, catching me at home between the afternoon and evening performances. "Honey." Her voice was heavy. "Your dad's okay, but —"

Never a great way to start off a conversation.

I froze.

Grandma continued, "He was jumped and mugged yesterday coming out of his law office. Some young thugs knocked him down, beat him up, and stole his wallet. He's in the hospital. It's on all the news today. I called the hospital, but he wasn't awake."

The *news?!*

I could hear in her voice that Grandma was aghast and worried about Dad. She was the eternal caretaker of everyone in the family, even the former son-in-law she enjoyed disparaging.

Rage spread throughout my chest. Who were these idiots? Dad represented criminals like them in his defense practice, giving them dignity in court and hopes of rehabilitation and a second chance.

I pictured Dad, good suit, gold watch, and shined leather loafers, chewing on the end of a cigar, rehearsing an argument he would make the next day as he walked the brick alleyway from his office to the main thoroughfare. Feeling safe enough to be lost in thought.

No matter where Dad lived, he knew everyone, and he treated everyone like they were special.

Judge Hallanan, who lived across the hall from Mom and me when I was in high school, told me that Dad was the best trial lawyer she ever had in her courtroom, high praise coming from a federal court judge. "Juries and judges love your dad," she said.

For the community and his profession, Dad showed up as his best self, predictably and reliably. As a dad, he had demonstrated that when the shit truly hit the fan and he needed to swoop in to rescue me, he would. But short of facing prison or a life-on-the-line crisis, he was reliably unpredictable.

Because my grandfather was a solid father to me, and Drema was a godsend to Dad, I had the luxury of appreciating Dad for what he was and mostly not bothering with the rest.

I called Dad in the hospital, but the phone rang and rang. I couldn't stand to think of Dad as vulnerable and unappreciated by the very type of person he bent over backwards for.

My anger boiled at the injustice. It's a good thing I lived three states away, had a stage on which to vent, and a contract to finish out, because I considered stomping up to Charleston, West Virginia, finding the criminals, and wringing their necks.

The next day, as my roommates and I were headed out the door to report at the theater, Dad called. He had a pretty bad concussion, maybe some broken ribs. "They got my wallet and my watch," he said, "but when they knocked me down, I put my hand in my pocket, found my car keys, and latched a finger around my key ring."

It's not like his dented-up, two-door compact Chevy was a fancy ride. "They took me by surprise. I couldn't fight back. But they didn't get my car."

My roommates stood in the doorway giving me the *let's gooooooooo* eye. I couldn't hang up on Dad just then.

"I'm pissed as hell, most of all." While he hadn't tried to fend off three attackers, as far as he was concerned, he got off pretty good. "And you know what else?" Dad laughed, his tone lightening. "Poor Drema called the house and the office, looking for me for two days before she found me in here. She figured I'd fallen off the wagon and was laid up drunk somewhere."

Drema traveled for work, and for a few, nerve-wracking days, she couldn't reach Dad. Later, she felt horrible for doubting him, not finding him sooner and rushing home. Dad never indicated he blamed her, but I'm sure he used it as a weapon when he needed to, never letting her forget it.

"I have a buddy in the sheriff's office, and they found the kids right away. Stuck 'em in jail. So get on with your show. Break a leg and all that. Don't worry about me, kid."

Dad never mentioned the emotional toll his attack must have taken. Then again, it was a good long while before he called again or answered the phone.

One of my roommates came to Charleston Ballet from Vegas. When he heard I was done dancing at the season's end, he was all, "Not yet, Boots! Let's go back to Nevada together! Trade the pink tights for fishnets!"

His favorite role was the princely and catty, Puss in Boots. He was Puss, and because of my dangerously high arches, he called me Boots.

I loved the performing schedule Spoleto offered, pain-in-the-arch be damned. Puss promised that the Vegas show schedule was similar, and that I'd be fabulous in a classic Strip show.

"Not stripping," Puss rolled his eyes. "The Vegas Strip. Showgirls are the topless ones in the headdresses. Their legs are, like, nine feet long, and they have the bone structure of birds. Then there are the chorus girls. Their legs are only eight feet long and they don't have tits."

There aren't that many women in the world with these body types, so the shows shoved them all together in a line and ran that line with the precision of a Swiss clock.

"Next to them," Puss warned, "you'd look like the troll who busted through security and crashed the stage. But I have an idea."

We concocted a plan where I'd outdance everyone enough to be a soloist, downstage, front and center, far enough away from the Birds flanking the rear that the audience wouldn't notice I wasn't even five-foot-seven.

Puss and I staged a photo shoot in the courtyard of our apartment complex with a disposable Kodak camera and floor lamps for extra lighting. I wore a skimpy black leotard, high heels, and a black feathered boa.

I threw my leg over my head forwards, sideways, and backwards, tossed in backbends, splits, and a short demo video, grinned at the camera, and got the soloist contract.

Seriously.

$1,150 a week, two back-to-back shows per day, six days per week. Additional pay for rehearsal time, photo shoots, and publicity appearances.

That was more money than I knew existed on Earth. Just to entertain an audience and not be shamed into ill-fitting, corseted tutus and pointe shoes?! BAM.

I flipped the script on the pervasive Vegas insult that had dogged me for years. Another box checked.

※

The orthopedic sports medicine surgeon pointed to the X-ray on the screen. "You have the foot of a very active and highly injured eighty-year-old." He started counting possible stress fractures in the numerous bones that made up my left foot and gave up after number twenty-three.

"The arch in our foot is actually an immovable joint. You've worn down all of the cartilage between your bones. For a long time now, apparently, there's been nothing but bone on bone clacking against each other which has caused severe deterioration. There's too much space between each bone. An immovable joint has become a moving one."

"Can this heal over the summer?"

He cackled. "It will never heal. You need to strengthen the soft tissue around your foot and ankle so they compensate for your degenerating bones."

"I have a contract that starts in September."

※

> **WANTED**
> *Full-time clerk.*
> *Busy Shoppe in*
> *the Market. Start*
> *immediately.*

It wasn't Vegas. But it was a full-time summer job in a delightful store that looked like a contemporary apothecary with its tiny bottles filled with perfumes, sprays, and oils stacked from floor to ceiling in dark wooden cabinets.

Historically, the Market area in downtown Charleston sold all of the vegetables, meats, fish, dairy, and seasonings the town would need. In modern times, the row of open-sided warehouses from Meeting Street down to the wharves and harbor sold tourist items, local handcrafts, and sweetgrass baskets, and housed root doctors selling herbal remedies for anything that ailed you. Both sides of Market Street were lined with restaurants, bars, and other shops.

Right at the beginning of summer, the air conditioner broke in the old Honda Mom had given me. I learned to love extreme heat and humidity pretty fast.

Also that summer, I realized my foot wasn't going to heal enough to dance by September. A part of me knew it might never fully heal, like Doc said, but I lied to myself and decided that for one year only, I'd enjoy Charleston, work an easy sales girl job, attend college, and try out the role of Normal Youngster.

Then Dad called.

He said he needed someone to talk to and didn't trust anyone but me. I never heard him sound so dejected. On this call, Dad confessed he was terribly depressed.

There were problems with Drema, he said, but she wasn't the cause. "She's flying high with opportunities. She needs to go out into the world. I'm left here in this city, that's never been my city, by myself for far too long, and I can't take care of myself. I need people. I'm in a bad place." Dad's baritone voice was so rich, you could drown in it. It took a moment for the severity of what he said to sink in.

He continued, "I want to go back home to Fayetteville, back to my people, get back in the game of politics, feel like I'm worth something. Don't worry, kid. I'm seeing a therapist. I just needed to talk to someone right now."

For some reason, I sought privacy from my roommate, walked out of the apartment and onto our small deck.

Dad said, "It's a good thing you answered the phone. I really appreciate it. I was ready to take a bullet and put it in my head. Just end it all."

I stopped breathing.

There was no fucking way I was on the phone with another human being, let alone my father, who, like Jason, was ready to exit the planet.

What the fuckety-fuck.

"Dad."

My heart bled into a million pieces, and I started sobbing for the pain Dad carried, and the sympathy and compassion for other people that Dad always embodied and unleashed into his practice.

But I couldn't stand to lose Dad the same way I lost Jason. I really couldn't stand to lose him at all. He was still a pillar in the infrastructure of my life, which suddenly felt fragile.

"Dad, I can't do this."

WHAT? That's what I said?

My brain went blank, and my mouth kept going, tears flooding down my cheeks. "I didn't save Jason. I can't save someone. I'm the worst person to turn to." Stand too close to me, and the ground under your feet will crack.

I hated the words coming out of me, so I covered the phone and my mouth with my hand.

"Oh, kid. I'm so sorry. I forgot about your boy who offed himself. I'm okay now. I really am. I just appreciate you picking up the phone."

"*Daddy, don't leeeeave,*" I full on wailed.

I was fine with Dad being the type of dad he'd been up to that point, but leaving me by suicide was something I might not be able to endure.

"I won't, baby girl. I love you." As if the whole matter of dying was now resolved.

That easy? All I had to do was scream and wail and beg, and allow his words to rip me limb from limb? I couldn't brush it off. I was furious and shattered, on a lousy apartment complex porch deck, all my neighbors within hearing range.

I momentarily swallowed my rage, told him I loved him, and made him promise to call me if he felt this bad ever again, even though I didn't mean it. He needed to call someone else. I was the last person capable of keeping anyone alive.

After the call ended, my pot boiled over. I called Mom and filled her in. "Mom, why am I so freaking mad at him? He's the one who needs help."

"Maybe you feel manipulated." Mom's words were tight, and I could tell the fire was lighting under her too. "Listen here. Your dad did the same thing to me when I tried to leave him. We had to admit him to the hospital under a suicide watch, where the nurses just loved him."

"Of course," I guffawed and coughed at the same time. By this point, I had collapsed to my hands and knees, staring at the deck boards.

"They told me he would die if I didn't come back to him. I told them he was fine without me, and whether he lived or died was up to him, not me. If he's in a state, it's not your responsibility. He's your parent, not your ward. If you feel like he's truly in danger, call 911 and tell him to go to the ER. But truly, I don't think he will ever get to that point."

Mom's words were such a relief, I found the strength to stand up. Mom was unfailingly honest about Dad. The good, the bad, and the ugly. Her words were an elixir, even while Dad expressed how low he felt.

For the next few months after that call, Dad was solid as a rock, as far as Dad went. We only talked occasionally, but on those occasions, he picked up the phone when I called, he wasn't drinking, he was seeing a therapist, he assured me he felt more stable, and he called to check in on me.

I didn't rebound as easily as Dad seemed to. I knew Dad had a flair for the dramatic, and to my trauma-addled brain, that meant he had the propensity to die tragically, by his own hand or someone else's.

I spent the next decades waiting for the grim reaper to strike Dad.

ACT TWO

The Curious Mind:
Dissonance & Disconnection

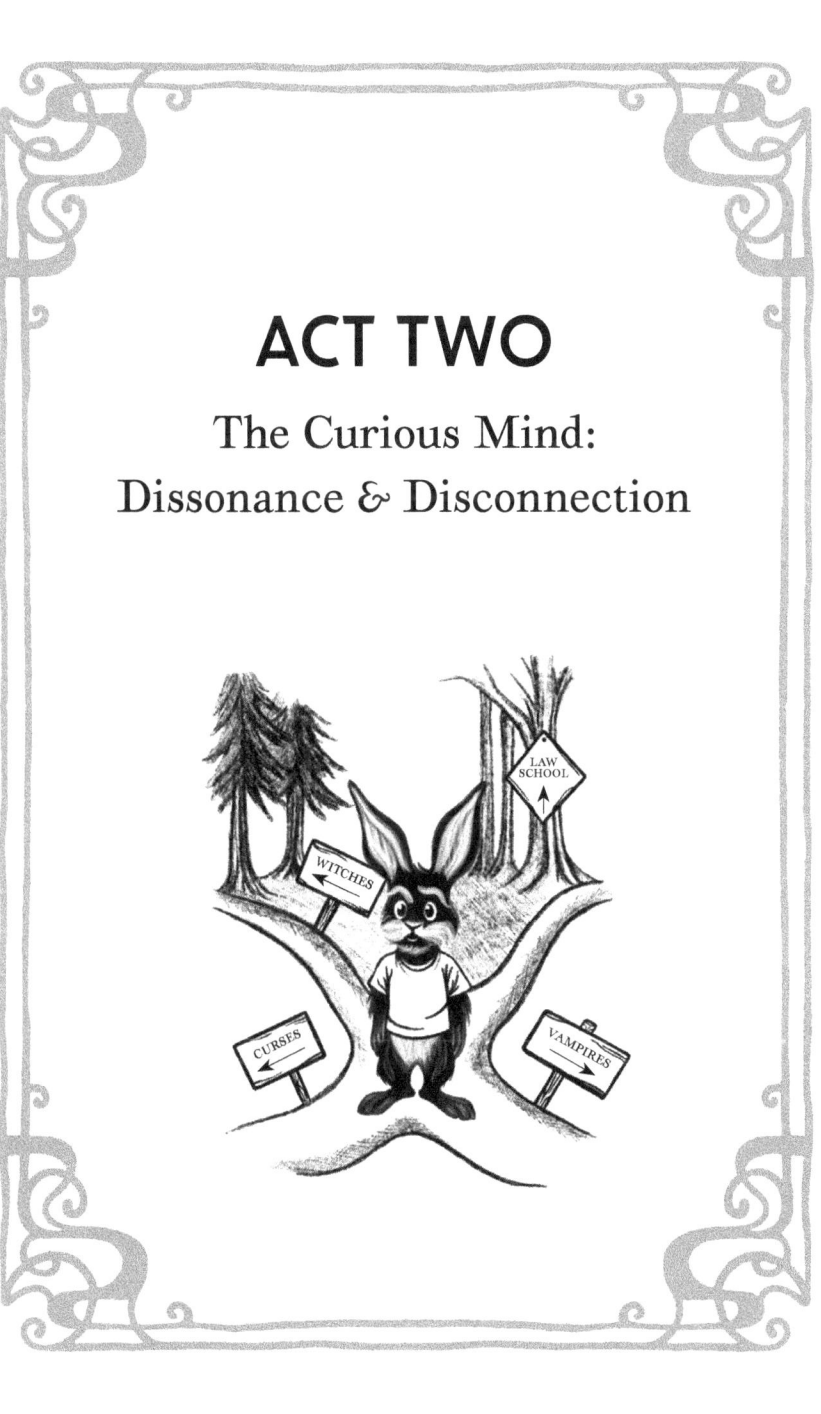

THIRTEEN

ONE ROWDY WEEKEND night, when the shops in the Market were closing and the bars were opening, a bona fide creep sauntered in. Leather jacket, sunglasses at night, stringy, dingy blonde hair, fingers wrapped in rings of skulls and pentacles. He introduced himself as a photographer.

The customer is always right, so I tried my best to swallow laughter. But I didn't want to humor this weirdo either. "Looks like you'd make a better warlock."

The guy dropped all pretense of trying to be cool. "I'm sorry! I am actually a photographer, but witchcraft is my passion." His face broke open, the sunglasses came off. "You interested in talking about witchcraft?"

Warlock came by the store on slow evenings and unintentionally revealed several significant things about himself: 1) he was deeply knowledgeable about witchcraft, rituals, and spell-casting; 2) he was so nerdy that he vacuumed the magic right out of the mysterious; and 3) he seemed fairly harmless.

Then one evening, a friend joined him. That's when I understood that Warlock had entered my life as a conduit to Mason.

Mason was a beautiful young man with ruddy cheeks, dark hair, and an outsized writing and singing talent. He could pass as straight, but he was, sadly, thoroughly gay.

That fact didn't stop us from spending every moment with each other for a season. His southern family ignored his sexuality, and I provided an elaborate mask for him.

Mason and I agreed that Warlock's version of witchcraft required too many uptight rules for our tastes. Both of us were more drawn to ideas about hearing voices of the dead and parallel lives in alternate dimensions, which we discussed over bottles of red wine and vodka until the sun rose.

He encouraged me to channel characters for his short stories and to sing with him. So we made up stories of haunted women in the Deep South, he sang, and I drunkenly caterwauled.

Mason didn't care that I had been a dancer or that, once again, without dancing, I didn't know who I was or where I was headed. He was happy to float with me on the journey one day at a time, with no destination other than the present presence.

I reverted to my other first love. Ghosts and goblins, monsters, and vampires. The English Department at the college offered courses in Gothic Literature, as if ghost stories were a respectable literary genre. So I buried myself in books, time with Mason, and gave up the Vegas contract for good.

My roommate and co-worker from the Shoppe, Daisy ReBelle, wasn't so keen on Mason. Over the next year, I discovered she wasn't keen on anyone who wasn't a white good ol' boy, a breed of human I found instinctively threatening.

The first time I noticed that red light flashing in my mind around Daisy's aura, I should have searched for a different roommate. But my dancing friends were drifting away, disinterested in my new mundane life. I was slightly older than the first-time-out-of-the-house college kids around me, and their keg parties struck me as pointless.

So I signed a lease with Daisy, her over-the-top, rural Southern ways at once drawing me in and repelling me like a carnival curiosity.

Daisy ever-so-slightly reminded me of Mindy's wild roommate, Barbie, back at NCSA. But where Barbie had a natural sweetness, Daisy ReBelle had grit. Under her quick smile, Daisy wielded a sharp tongue and a hair-trigger temper. She wouldn't hesitate to punch the lights out of a man or a woman.

Most of the time, her conflicts were hilarious. But Daisy and I had verbal knock-down drag-outs when we bumped into each other's realities.

When our friend Ben called the house with nowhere to spend the night because his girlfriend kicked him out, I didn't hesitate to offer our couch. Daisy blanched.

"I never had a black man sleep under my roof! Mama and Daddy would kill me if they knew."

"Helping a friend in an emergency is worth dying over," I said.

Ben could stay as long as he wanted and I'd invite Mason too, just to spite Daisy's parents and push her buttons.

She usually came around. "Girl, we don't know what we don't know," she confessed once. "Before I came to Charleston for college, I thought everyone grew up in segregated schools and lived in fear of the devil."

Daisy's mama controlled her daughter through childhood by telling her that she would go to hell for any minor infraction, like eating chocolate before dinner, and referring to Daisy as "the Devil's child."

Daisy would retort, "I'm going to hell anyway, Mama. Why stop sinning now?"

Daisy waged full-on war against her mama's religion, a conflict I could get behind. After Jason's funeral, folks who used threats of hell to control people made my blood pressure spike.

Still, Daisy lit candles, carried a rabbit's foot on her key chain and stuffed amulets in her purse, believing that she did, in fact, need all the good luck she could attract.

❦

"We're going to my card reader," she announced one day after classes ended. Daisy was scheduled to graduate at the end of the year and didn't know what the future held. "But Lord, don't tell Mama."

Daisy grabbed her trusty plastic cup — "Plantation Golf" emblazoned on the side — filled it with vodka, then topped it off with a splash of lemonade and two cubes of ice. She lit a cigarette. "I feel jittery." She flailed her body and arms about, like a dog shaking off water.

Daisy's card reader was a lady in her seventies, out on the highway, with a neon palm in the window, and a hand-painted sign in the yard that yelled, "FORTUNE TELLER." She read a regular deck of playing cards, not the tarot that Daisy and I taught ourselves.

When we arrived, Daisy was so nervous, she paced outside, chain smoking. "You go in first. I feel like something's wrong. I can't find my rabbit's foot."

To my surprise, there were no candles or crystal balls, and the fortune teller wore slacks and a floral top, like she was headed to the grocery store. According to my reading, I had a lot of travel in my future, and the King of Hearts figured prominently.

Interesting, but not life shattering. Then again, at that moment, I didn't need any more of my life shattering.

Daisy was more amped up after her reading than when we'd arrived, blowing cigarette smoke out her car window. "I swear something terrible was in the cards, and she wouldn't tell me what she saw."

"What are you worried about?"

She swerved the car into the parking lot of a liquor store, then turned to look at me. "Don't think I'm crazy or try to talk me out of what I'm going to say."

I reached for the Plantation sippy cup and found it empty.

Daisy took a deep breath. "I think something's wrong with me. Like, there's something evil inside my stomach. It feels like I'm cursed. There, I said it."

Daisy never wanted to listen when I suggested that she deal with the ex who broke her nose, or that perhaps her Mama's manipulations had wormed their way into her psyche after all. I kept my mouth shut, even though it seemed obvious to me that the evil she sensed came from the cauldron of unresolved abuse simmering in her gut and her hatred of her upbringing.

"We learned about curses in one of my psych classes," she continued. "It comes down to mindset. If you think you're cursed, then you are. I can't talk myself out of it though. All I see is something evil." She shuddered.

I grew angry again, not at poor Daisy, but at her Mama. So I suggested something her Mama would hate. "Let's go see a witch doctor. If there's a problem, there has to be a remedy."

Daisy's face melted with relief. "You'll go with me?"

Two options came to mind: Warlock or the hoodoo practitioners in the Market.

The latter seemed the most legit place to start. The hoodoo ladies would understand hexes and vexes because they offered potions for sale to cure them.

When we arrived at the Market—the Plantation Golf cup re-filled—Daisy nudged me forward to the stalls that offered herbal remedies for pesky exes, headaches, love potions, you name it. From what I knew about Daisy, I was tempted to tell each proprietor that we needed one of everything they had in stock.

My eyes landed on a middle-aged, heavyset black woman. She stared back at me, unblinking. Like the fortune teller, she wasn't wearing any mystical garb or scarves. I instantly trusted this stranger and beelined it to her. I noticed that Daisy seemed suddenly apprehensive and lingered far back in the Market halls.

I told the woman in a low voice, "My friend over there says she's cursed."

The woman glanced at Daisy. "She cursed herself," she judged, also in a quiet voice.

She sighed, indicating that trying to help two white girls who had no knowledge of hoodoo might be futile. Then she stood up, hands on her hips, her back toward Daisy. Her voice softened. "She needs to love herself, feel good about herself. She has to stop hating herself. It will eat away at her." She patted her stomach, "Here."

Chills cascaded down my arms and back at the accuracy and depth of the woman's instant assessment.

She continued, "But she has to want to fix it. If she don't," the woman shrugged, "nothing anyone can do. Take this."

I paid for the jar labeled Curse Removal, thanked the woman profusely, and rejoined Daisy. We walked quickly out of the Market, away from the bustling shops and bars, then pulled out the bottle.

There were instructions regarding candles, mixing the herbs with the wax, setting an intent, saying a prayer, and so forth. We had our night cut out for us.

"Let's grab tequila shots first," Daisy suggested, swallowing the remaining vodka in her cup.

I pointed down a quiet street lined with flickering gas lamps in the French Quarter. "We're headed toward the Tiger."

The Blind Tiger was a leftover from speakeasy days, right down to the pressed tin ceiling tiles and the painted black windows. There were no large screen TVs, and no frat boys hollering over each other. Only the most unsuspecting tourists could find it, and only edgy locals visited.

Daisy agreed to the Tiger, I'm guessing because she didn't want anyone in her regular stable of bar mates to catch her with the hoodoo jar.

Along the walk, I told Daisy what the woman said about needing to love herself. I cringed and waited for an argument.

Instead, she pondered it, falling silent as we swung open the heavy door to the little establishment.

Daisy ordered our drinks from the bar, just in case that was the night anyone in Charleston decided to card me. I was almost 21, but not close enough to argue about it.

I reread the Curse Removal instructions by candlelight and prepared to go about the business of saving Daisy's soul, when a handsome gentleman twice our age strolled in. He sported cropped hair and a leather bomber jacket, as if he'd just walked off the movie set of *Top Gun*.

He was, in fact, a pilot, visiting the Air Force Base. Daisy sniffed an opportunity for free booze and oblivion and dropped me like yesterday's fish.

⊕·⧉·⊷⧉⊶·⧉·⊕

The following day, Daisy's whole face mashed up in aversion when she read the instructions for the Curse Removal. "You believe this shit? It sounds like a demon working in disguise." As much as Daisy rebelled against her Mama's religion, she also bought into it hook, line, and sinker.

Then it hit me. "Are you not willing to try this, for fun, because this bottle of herbs was filled by black people instead of white people?"

Daisy drew back and grabbed the bottle from me. I glared at her, waiting for her to hit me with it.

I was so ready to give up on her altogether. The vigilance required from both of us as we banged into each other's edges was exhausting. But she was one of only two buddies I had at that moment.

Lo and behold, that very evening, Daisy's savior walked into the Shoppe while she was working. Warlock.

He laid his witchcraft jargon on thick. He could see she was cursed, plain as day, and yes, ma'am, absolutely, he could lift it.

The following evening, Daisy had to go to a safe house with him where other witch dudes gathered. They had erected all of the protection spheres around the house available on Earth. A guardian angel, nine rings of ultraviolet light, and their own gargoyles.

That part sounded cool, if for no other reason than the sheer imagination of it. I remained leery of Warlock though. An entire evening stuck with him droning on were hours of your life you'd never get back.

As an alternative, the hoodoo lady had already nailed Daisy's issue and offered a sensible solution. Daisy could work on self-acceptance from the comfort of our couch.

I clarified, "I'm not *friends* with Warlock."

"You said he was harmless," Daisy said, once again sounding like she wanted to be on the front edge of an argument.

"Harmless-ish. He's creepy."

"The only reason I let him talk to me in the Shoppe about witchcraft is because you thought it was interesting," she spat. Then, warring with herself, continued, "Besides, I can handle myself. I'm sick of you acting like you always know more about everything."

"Well, go try it then," I spat back.

Daisy wasn't innocent, but I didn't trust that she could hang out with icky warlocks, dabble in witchcraft, and come out unscathed. I didn't throw myself in front of her car to stop her either.

She came home late that night, stayed in the shower for hours, groaning, maybe coughing up demons. She acted as if she had been existentially raped, with her full consent. I felt sick for her, but she wouldn't tell me anything.

She avoided me for weeks. Finally, passing me in the hallway of our apartment, she confided that she felt physically ill over the whole Warlock-curse-lifting incident, and not just the Warlock part, but also the hoodoo part.

"What happened?" I asked gently, as she pushed past me toward the bathroom. I hovered in the doorway, intentionally invading her privacy.

She plopped down on the closed lid of the toilet. After much cajoling on my part, she confided, "There was a bunch of gobbeldy-gook muttering, then he asked me to take off my shirt." I noted she didn't use his name. "He painted symbols over my chest and stomach."

"Like he was casting a spell?" I asked.

Her next words tumbled out in a whoosh. "He was careful to not touch me inappropriately. He asked if it was okay. I sat there for *hours* with these *devil* symbols painted all over me in red. I had to chant." She took a breath. "I was so cold."

I could see how violated she felt. Worse, she agreed to every step.

Daisy would have taken off her shirt in a bar on any given night, no problem. The amount of times men painted her chest and stomach with saliva, beer, and other bodily fluids were too great to count.

In this instance, in her mind, she had grown from the devil's child into his concubine, as her Mama always said she would.

"Did anything like this ever happen to you?" Those round, blue eyes turned on me with hope that she wasn't alone in this experience.

I struggled with how to respond. Theoretically, I had no problem with someone painting a sigil on my naked body during an elaborate ritual. But no one had ever offered, or even told me it was a thing. Not even Warlock in all his explaining about witchcraft.

That was the last heartfelt conversation we had.

Daisy went back to the "safe house" to meet Warlock two more times that I know of.

After that, she escaped more and more often into the college bars that I wouldn't feel safe in, even with a bodyguard.

She blamed me for tempting her into exploring dark forces and swore she never should have trusted me and my "open" ideas. I donned on a heavy cape of guilt because I hadn't fought with her and physically prevented her from going to Warlock's in the first place.

⚜

On the next full moon, Perry from the ballet company called out of the blue. "No rehearsals for me tomorrow, and you need to get your head out of the books. Let's go out!"

The few times I met up with my former ballet friends, we didn't have much to talk about anymore. Perry surprised me though. "Meet me at the abandoned mansion on Wentworth Street. We're going to cast a spell."

My stomach tingled with excitement. All of Daisy's ick I still carried around on her behalf dissipated instantly. Warlock was gross, but magic wasn't.

Just before midnight, Perry and I met in front of the mansion, next to gas lanterns flanking an iron entrance gate where a pentagram was carved into the sidewalk. The mansion had previously housed the Freemasons, and there were a variety of intricate occult symbols in front of the entrance gate.

Perry threw her arms into the air and belted out, "I now call all the witches in Charleston."

We looked up and down the street and giggled. I observed, "I don't see anyone swooping in on their broom."

"Maybe we should step into the circle of the pentagram?" Perry suggested. She started toward the carving of the star surrounded by a circle.

"Wait!" I grabbed her arm, remembering the instructions on the Curse Removal jar. "We have to know what we're asking for first. We don't want random flying monkeys crashing in and plucking out our eyeballs."

Perry thought for a moment, then shouted, "Let's ask for our magical powers to ignite!"

We made up a chant, spun around inside the pentagram, arms outstretched, and heads thrown back. We cackled until the moon slipped behind a cloud.

Satisfied that our ritual was complete and our request logged in the grimoire of our souls, we headed toward a dance club.

The sizzling atmosphere reminded me of the moments driving on the west coast of Italy and into France two years earlier. Perry and I might have been amateurs who didn't know how to cast a spell any more than we could cast a shrimp net, but our midnight rendezvous felt like we called in a more mystical future than what may have otherwise come down the track.

Maybe asking for magical powers was all we needed to do to unlock them.

Perry and I frequented the Treehouse, a fringe nightclub whose entrance required turning down not one, but two cobblestoned alleys, then climbing up a metal staircase. Before we reached the alleys, we ran into Daisy.

Even if Daisy and I had still been on good terms, she knew better than to invite me to a beer joint on Market Street, and I knew Daisy wasn't comfortable with the idea of rainbow skin tones and an all-persuasions-welcome sort of dance hall.

But Perry didn't know better.

Daisy jerked her hands up and backed away. "Y'all go have fun with your weird shit and your fucked up, artsy friends. Good luck getting on in the world," she waved her hand at my gothic nightclub attire, "like *that*."

She headed toward the Market. Perry shrugged her off, and we ducked into the alley.

I worried Daisy was right though. At some point, if I wanted to make a life and a career in Charleston, I might have to crawl out of alleys, like a rat peeking out of the gutter in daylight, and fit into Daisy's crappy world.

Fridays meant trekking out to Mason's cottage on Folly Beach. I needed to get away from Daisy, and Mason insisted that if I had to do homework, we could write together at his vintage, formica-topped kitchen table.

Increasingly, however, Mason was already wasted by the time I arrived, which diluted our soul-searching adventures. For a few weeks, I ignored it and caught up with him, all the while fearing I'd grow bored of the new routine sooner rather than later.

This time, I headed to Mason's with the novel *Dracula* by Bram Stoker. I had gobbled up all of the pop culture novels and movies about vampires and Dracula, but never read the original book until it was required reading in one of my classes.

Most of the characters in *Dracula* question whether they're making him up. Was this monster real? Or were they all sucked into a mass hallucination, induced by suggestions and shadows? I could get down with this struggle.

Then I hit the end of the book.

Count Dracula is made of flesh and bones after all.

The band of heroes kill him.

Everyone returns to their comfy homes and lives happily ever after.

I turned the page, looking for "The End." Instead, I found five more paragraphs under the simple heading "Note," written directly to the reader as an epilogue, explaining that the band of heroes, who risked their lives to kill a monster, went back to Transylvania to the scene of the murder SEVEN YEARS LATER!

It makes no sense to trek across the Carpathian mountain range in horse-drawn wagons, with wolves circling and rings of blue fire erupting, to return to the scene of such extraordinary trauma, on "holiday," unless...

THEY MISSED DRACULA!

What?!

This discovery required a midweek phone call to Mason to start brainstorming. I told him I'd bring over a special bottle of wine the following Friday in hopes that he'd hold off on the vodka until I arrived.

He didn't, and I swallowed my letdown. We were still able to determine that through fighting Dracula, each of the characters experienced an aspect of themselves they couldn't express in the world at the time.

"He's the perfect monster," Mason slurred, his face lit by a candle flame, his eyes drowsy. "He forced out the hidden best in everyone."

"Then they go and kill the very thing they want and need," I observed.

"As do we all."

When Mason passed out, I wondered how Dracula would seduce me.

I didn't miss the ballet world, that was certain. My foot was still too injured to dream about a performing life in Vegas. I enjoyed my studies, but I couldn't see a future in ghost stories.

Vampires touch something primal within us, reflecting our repressed desires and fears.

I had no single-focused desire to identify with. No meaningful friendship outside of Mason, and that was dwindling into the bottle. There were no straight boys around that offered even a sliver of the connection I had with Jason or Mr. Strange.

I searched around in myself and couldn't find any hidden hooks for Dracula to latch onto.

On the flip side, I could only get hurt by failure and disappointment to the extent that I cared. Maybe my heart didn't want all-consuming, ambitious desire anymore.

Given that I'd spent the last year with Daisy ReBelle as my sole buddy, and a gay man as my weekend date, apparently I didn't want much intimacy with another person either.

I thought of Perry and I summoning our magical powers in the pentagram. If I had such powers, what would I want to do with them anyway? The memory of that evening suddenly fizzled, diminished to mere fancy, the byproduct of our pre-disco cocktails.

If Dracula knocked on my door, he'd probably give me the once over and walk away.

How disheartening.

⚜

The following Monday, I carted my literary thoughts on *Dracula* to Professor Carolyn's office to discuss my final paper. Professor Carolyn was young, pretty, yet unassuming with her thick, dark hair held back by thin headbands. She wore a mysterious half-smile to goad us students into thinking more deeply about any issue.

Through her classes, she offered a framework that legitimized my love of supernatural stories and lifelong pull toward the unknowable — and she made a career out of her similar love.

She approved my theory that the characters in *Dracula* actually longed for the vile thing they were supposed to reject. Then she dropped a bomb. "I won't be teaching here next year. No more gothic literature classes."

All I heard was, *"Our silly fun with ghosties and vampires is over."*

With that, my imaginary Dracula tickled my secret desire. I didn't want exploration into the supernatural to be silly or fun. I wanted it to have rich meaning. I definitely didn't want the explorations into gothic literature that Carolyn facilitated to be done with.

"I'm heading to law school," she said. "It might be something you could consider? It's a way to put to use your writing and analytical skills and make a good living."

I frowned, considering her question. Maybe she was right. I would graduate the following year.

An engine in my brain fired to life, and I saw a path before me as clear and stable as railroad tracks leading into Big Girl Adulthood.

With that vision, I also noticed that all remaining bubbles of longing in my wild imagination, my heart, and my gut audibly deflated.

Dracula sighed and turned away from my threshold without even ringing the doorbell.

FOURTEEN

❧

HEN TWO UNEXPECTED twists arrived.

The first was a fiercely driven businessman with a dynamic personality. I should have remembered all the cautionary tales of women saying yes to the first charmer who sweeps through town in a famine.

Instead, I fell for him as much as my weary heart could at the time, convincing myself that he was the King who Daisy's card reader saw in her spread.

Mr. Dynamic was thirteen years older than me, which gave me the illusion that he offered security, something I must have felt I needed. He also had a house, which meant I could move away from Daisy, something I definitely needed. He supported anything I wanted to do after college, the bigger idea, the better.

He also came with an explosive temper, yet he had little tolerance of others' emotional states. To that end, he had no patience for Dad. His own father hung the moon, and after meeting Senior Dynamic, I agreed. Senior wore a sunny smile, reflecting a deeper, gentle character with a good job in the industrial Midwest.

Mr. Dynamic said, "When *my* dad wasn't around, it was because he was working his fingers to the bone to feed his four kids."

Mr. Dynamic likewise had no patience for me when I attempted the slog of filling in the emotional side of my history. "All of that was a long time ago. Get over it. Move on."

I thought, "That's not actually bad advice. All the sludge of the past can get packed up into the attic and not fussed over again."

So that's what I did.

And that's when I started having nightmares about alligators. I knew the dreams were trying to tell me something, but I chucked that knowing in the attic and chose to loathe real life alligators instead.

Grandma subscribed to Mr. Dynamic's philosophy, frequently espousing, "The past is the past." She adored Mr. Dynamic, saving her best smiles for him. Mom wasn't so sure, but kept her reserve to herself.

Then the second unexpected twist arrived, and Mom got whip-sawed.

Mom had solid boyfriends throughout the years, but they were like wallpaper. No one knocked her socks off. The spring before college graduation, Mom called, breathless. Then she started to giggle, which was contagious, so I giggled with her.

"I just don't know what to say," she stammered.

"Sounds like you met someone special?" I asked, hoping this was true.

"He's an interim administrator at the hospital. He's never been in Southern West Virginia before. I don't know what came over me, but as soon as we were introduced, I asked him out on a date! Can you believe I did that?"

John Farrar was handsome and smart, both emotionally and intellectually. He was interested in people, slow to anger, well traveled, kind, and elegant, an all around Renaissance man.

Six months later, my Miss Independent mother married John. John was a true knight in shining armor, plucking Mom out of West Virginia once and for all, and showing her a life she'd never experienced. As far as stepparents went, I hit the jackpot with both John and Drema, even though Drema and Dad were headed for divorce.

Confusingly though, John, like Mr. Dynamic, couldn't accept Dad for who he was. Mom and I always figured we were better off with Dad sort of around, but not on the daily.

John was a good bit older than Dad, but John stood straight and tall, where the next time I saw Dad, he appeared to be shrinking, shoulders slumping forward, unable to lift himself from his grief over Drema and the idea that his life was a failure.

⚜

On a Super Bowl Sunday in the late 90s, I watched a pregame show that highlighted interviews with former Super Bowl players, a where-are-they-now type of segment. One man stood out, amidst the high energy, charismatic players who'd become coaches, announcers, entrepreneurs.

For this guy, he never found his next Thing. It was like nothing would be enough ever again.

His skin tone stood out to me more than his words. The man looked gray, a marked contrast to every other former player on the screen. I had come to understand in my own world of symbology that gray skin meant depression, or a lack of zest for life, plus an inability or unwillingness to fix it.

I vowed, standing in my living room in that moment, to never be the man on the screen, elevating nostalgia and stagnating in the present, rather than pushing forward, even into the scary unknown.

This vow struck me with the force of an irrevocable mental decision, not a heart-led one. I noticed my entire heart was packed up in the attic. I didn't care, and it didn't matter.

I also noticed I was done with lack-of-money constraints.

It wasn't that I wanted money for the sake of showing off new cars or designer clothes. Instead, I wanted a flow for the sake of the flow itself. I wanted to travel, I wanted to eat the world. At the very least, I wanted the *option* to do so.

I dedicated myself to the law school application process, though I didn't have Dad's passion for the law or justice and had no desire to be a courtroom lawyer. Dad assured me, "Kid, law school will only open doors for you, not close them."

I set my sights on the University of South Carolina, two hours away, in Columbia. At the time, it was the only law school in the state. I couldn't stand the thought of not living in my beloved Charleston for three years, but at least I'd be right up the road.

I aimed for a precise score on the LSAT's, using every creative visualization technique I'd ever learned and made up a few. I never made that score on the practice tests, but walked into the exam confident.

I earned the exact score I visualized. Maybe I was on the right path to my next Thing.

⌖

When a friend's father suggested I apply to top-tier schools, I laughed like he asked me to lasso the moon.

On a whim, I borrowed a book from the library that gave admission statistics of every law school in the country. Harvard, Yale, Chicago, and Michigan all sounded like they existed for students who may have been born on Planet Earth, but clearly lived in a parallel dimension.

The author's description of the University of Chicago stated that because of the school's intellectual rigor and reputation for innovative thought, once you got accepted, your address from there on out was Easy Street. After all, no university *in the world* boasted as many professors with Nobel Prizes as the University of Chicago.

Shew! Not me. I had no interest in writing legal treatises or gunning for a job on the Supreme Court. I looked forward to doing the law school bit, then returning to a practice in Charleston as fast as I could.

To my relief, the University of South Carolina accepted me and invited me to interview for a scholarship.

I'd never been so happy to make the drive up to Columbia. I wore a Ralph Lauren blue and green tartan blazer I found at Goodwill, in hopes of coming across as less freaky-artsy.

Two women were present in the interview. One took the lead, the one with perfect honey-blonde hair and a smile, while the other took notes. I expected questions about why I wanted to go to law school and so forth.

Instead, Honey Blonde asked, "Why do you want to attend South Carolina? Why not go back to West Virginia?"

"Um…" I could never think fast on my feet, and this question took me aback. "South Carolina is my home? I've worked here, went to college here. I want to practice in Charleston."

"But you don't know anyone here."

"Uh —." I had references from long-term Charlestonian lawyers and professors and pointed her to those letters.

"Are you a Gamecock fan?"

My blank face must have indicated I didn't know what the hell a gamecock was. Surely she wasn't talking about rooster fighting.

"College football?" Honey Blonde offered, raising her eyebrows. "Here in South Carolina, you grow up rooting for either the Gamecocks, which is us, or for the Clemson Tigers. Fans sure are rabid around these parts."

I blinked. It didn't dawn on me to just lie, "*Go, Gamecocks!*"

Not for the first time, I cursed myself for not knowing how to indulge in clever banter. Worse, when I was caught off guard or intimidated, my brain whited out, and I couldn't think of a single thing to say. Which, of course, happened in that moment.

Daisy would have known a good comeback through all her experience with bar chatter. Then I remembered Daisy saying the college party scene was way better at the University of South Carolina than in Charleston, but that Columbia had been too close to her hometown.

My heart dropped into my feet. I assumed law school would provide an expansive experience, not a contracting one. I suddenly worried that I might have to spend three years in Daisy's rotten reality, attending college football games, surrounded by drunk frat boys, just to prove I was southern and sociable enough to get through law school.

My blazer started to feel scratchy. I stared at Honey Blonde and silently wondered how much more of myself I'd need to stuff up in the attic for the next three years.

My fear wasn't limited to a possible future at the University of South Carolina. I had applied to other schools under the Why Not Theory.

Duke, a southern stalwart, sent a postcard in response to my application, asking whether I knew anyone they should know I knew, such as significant alumni or donors. If so, it would behoove me to update my submission accordingly. Bleck.

My stepfather, John, said, "I can dig up a connection with a donor or alumni at Duke Medical School, and we can see if that has any sway over the law school."

I appreciated his offer, but something about being accepted to law school through a forced connection would probably always make me doubt I belonged there in the first place.

Honey Blonde ushered me to the door about seven minutes into a half-hour interview, rescuing me from further discomfort at my going mute on the topic of college football.

It never dawned on *me* to ask *them* what was so hot about their law school that I should choose it over other alternatives. Never mind that I didn't have any alternatives. I was extremely grateful the law school let me in the door at all, and understandably, they let me know they were the ones doing me the favor.

The following week, I received two phone calls. One from the University of Michigan offering me a full scholarship. Holy cow wow. A top ten law school on the other edge of the country wanted *me*.

The other call was from the University of Chicago, notifying me of acceptance and a generous financial aid package. I stood in my kitchen gripping the handset on the landline.

"Are you sure there's not a mistake?" I asked.

Just a few days earlier, Honey Blonde seemed to suggest I get on a bus back to West Virginia. If this phone call were legit, and not a prank, then life was awfully strange.

The man on the phone extended a friendly invitation to visit Chicago that spring, meet the professors, and stay with a current student, who would show me around and take me out for a night on the town with other admitted students.

None of this who-do-you-know, how-many-generations-have-you-been-southern bullshit.

Upon reflection, Honey Blonde seemed sincere. She conducted her interview in a brilliant manner. She tested whether the University of South Carolina and I would be a good fit for one another, and quite quickly, she illuminated that we would not be.

A stubborn part of me wanted to stay in South Carolina. I felt stung by the university's lukewarm reception. That part of me cried, *"But I want to love you! Let me try to love the gamecock rooster thing!"*

It didn't help that business people and local lawyers warned me that Charleston law firms only hired from the University of South Carolina. I may never get a job if I left and went Off to law school, which sounded preposterous to me.

My vision of the railroad tracks appeared again. I heard in my head, "You can stay home, go to a school that doesn't give a shit about you, and your train will stall at the local station. Or you can keep your brain on fire, and the train will rocket forward at warp speed."

In April, I flew to Chicago to visit, walked into the university, and saw T-shirts for sale that read, "The Law School at the University of Chicago: Where Hell Does Freeze Over."

By the end of the weekend, I prepared myself for a move up to Hell. If Charleston didn't want me after attending one of the best law schools in the world, Charleston could fuck off.

⊷⊱⊰⊷

On the way home from the airport after the trip to Chicago, I spotted a brown puppy running alongside a busy road next to my car. My first thought was, "Lily. Aunt Lily sent that dog to me."

I hadn't thought of my deceased Aunt Lily in years. Our little dachshund always escaped to her house for a good time. For a fleeting instant, my thought about Aunt Lilly and the puppy made perfect sense.

Then the dog darted off the road and into woods filled with marshland. There was no way I'd find the dog again.

The universe flicked its wand, and by the time I arrived home, guess where the puppy was? Hiding under our porch.

The dog crept out at Mr. Dynamic's bidding, then peed all over him when he scooped her up.

I didn't question it, but I knew for a fact that Lily sent that dog to me. I hoped the dog would like Chicago. Mr. Dynamic was staying in Charleston, and I needed the company.

⊷⊱⊰⊷

For a small-town girl, living alone for three years on the south side of Chicago was a daunting prospect.

In September, I foraged for every ounce of courage and determination I could find and moved into a gorgeous walk-up in Hyde

Park, a block-and-a-half off Lake Michigan with my heaven-sent dog, Xzena.

My very first impression of the school, the one I'd gleaned from the library book on law schools, proved accurate. The students were friendly, but most of the time, they didn't speak plain English. My classmates were Ivy Leaguers and worked for consulting firms and on Wall Street for a few years before law school.

They knew how the world of Big Law, Big Finance, and all the Big Money things worked in a way that I didn't even know how to ask about. Their minds maneuvered through intellectual concepts, easily conversing with professors, while I was still looking up terminology in my Black's Law Dictionary. Attending prestigious schools was their birthright, and they stepped into their roles with grace.

We were only about two weeks into school when the international law firm of Sidley Austin hosted a happy hour in their posh skyscraper to welcome us first-year students. After Sidley, another firm hosted a happy hour, then another, and another. Recruiting from the big law firms literally started before we barely cracked open our law books.

The law school itself hosted a welcome dinner with professors seated at each table. Most students and teachers were bright-eyed, engaged, and lively, but I sat next to the one poor prof who clearly didn't want to be there.

He stretched out, crossed his arms, leaned his head against the back of the chair, and yawned. He didn't bother taking off his khaki trench coat, as if he didn't intend to commit to the entire dinner.

I tried to start a conversation and received monosyllabic answers in return. I listened to the easy chatter around me and became acutely aware, once again, of my less-than-riveting conversational skills. My insecurity only fueled my stupid brain whiteout routine.

Time slowed. I grew comfortable staying silent in the company of this likewise quiet person.

Finally, dinner arrived and he removed his trench coat. Maybe his blood sugar had been low and the appetizer helped, or maybe he decided to suck it up and make the most of the evening.

He slowly indulged me with a few questions. He was very serious. His face never broke into a smile, but he wasn't a cold person. He seemed to listen, and he seemed to think about my answers.

Suddenly, he looked directly at me, fork and knife in hand between bites. He summarized everything I had told him about my background, furrowed his brow, and said, "These big law firms will recruit you hard and heavy, you will receive more job offers than you know what to do with, then they'll shove you in a box. Into a pigeonhole."

He enunciated his words, as if he were trying to make sure I absorbed them. "That's how they work. And that system works for a lot of people." He subtly gestured around the table with his fork. "But you will suffocate in a box. Don't let them pigeonhole you."

His words zinged straight into my bones. Maybe he offered that advice to every law student, every year. No matter. It resonated with me, as an individual.

We didn't talk much the rest of the dinner. I noted that he conversed politely, but minimally, with the law student seated to his other side. I didn't hear the same advice to that student.

At the end, he stood and looked at me again, with the same intensity he probably carried throughout his day. He pulled on his trench coat and said, "It's easy to get caught up," he looked around the room as if to say, *in this.* "But don't forget."

I knew I was in one of those moments, in the presence of one of those people, that I would remember the rest of my life, without even trying. What I heard from him was, *Don't let anyone pigeonhole you. Ever.*

As we dispersed, another student approached and asked, "Hey, which professor were you seated next to?"

"Professor Obama. Barack Obama."

⋄⋄⋄

One of my classmates threw a Halloween party that fall. I called Mr. Dynamic before I headed out, and an anger demon answered the phone. "You're not up in Chicago to party. You are *not* going."

I was baffled that someone would try to tell me what to do. "Excuuuuuuuse me?" I responded, a nifty phrase I'd learned that might stall a conversation when I couldn't think of anything else to say.

For the first time in my life, I lived by myself and came and went as I pleased. I took stock of my circumstances and determined I was doing quite well on my own, in a major metropolis, to boot.

The conversation went round and round, Mr. Dynamic barbing me just enough to keep me engaged before one of us hung up.

I slumped onto the linoleum floor of my kitchen. An Oprah episode fell into my memory where women talked about their experiences with abuse, and Oprah offered the golden nugget: the identifying pattern.

The cycle where someone else's bad behavior is your fault, then you get the cold shoulder of abandonment, then an apology, then enough good behavior to keep you around. Repeat.

Suddenly, a pattern clicked into place with Mr. Dynamic. Angry outbursts where he attempted to control me, against which I rebelled. Then he'd storm off to bars and even strip clubs, according to the receipts he hid, before crawling back. Not that I would have minded the strip clubs, if I'd only been invited or had even known.

This time, I bet he would call me the following day, apologetic and loving. I checked my heart. Stonier than ever when it came to him. I cared about him, wanted the best for him as a human being, but as for him and me, it was over.

I felt so ashamed of myself. For a supposedly smart person, how had I been so dumb that I got caught up in the oldest relationship pattern in the book? My carefree classmates were out celebrating my favorite holiday while I had to pick myself up off the floor and deal with the latest heavy sack of sludge that I dragged into my life, something that pissed me off. I wondered if I enjoyed being mistreated and misunderstood.

I would have chastised myself further for settling for a relationship that didn't have the full-on, soul-level connection zing. But after Mason, I consciously gave up on that requirement as futile. Because, I believed, any such person wouldn't stay on Earth for long, or he'd live in too many experimental dimensions at once like Mr. Strange, or he'd succumb to alcoholism and not even be a straight dude.

I took off whatever I cobbled together for a Halloween costume. I had too much to reconcile with myself to go out.

A large bouquet of flowers arrived the following morning, right as I predicted.

Over the next months of the breakup process, I discovered that I still didn't miss him. He discovered therapy.

"OH MY GOD!" he said during one conversation. "Turns out, I have a subliminal communication pattern I learned from my mom, who beat the hell out of us kids growing up when she went on rages."

That his mother was physically abusive was not a new revelation. That he now linked it to his own behavior was. "And I'm *furious* with my dad for NOT PROTECTING US!" He was in a full-blown emotional awakening, fascinated with the science project of his own psychology.

I shared all this with my family.

Dad: "Never did like that sonofabitch."

Mom: "You're absolutely fine on your own."

And Grandma: "Honey, give it one more chance. No one will ever take care of you as well as he does."

So when Mr. Dynamic asked me to go to therapy with him, for Grandma's sake, I agreed.

Within minutes, I came down with my first migraine. Never in my life had I experienced such debilitating pain, not even dancing on a broken foot.

I recalled a time when Mom dated a man who wanted to marry her. She told someone at work, "I've decided to say yes." Then she fell straight to the ground, passed out cold. She called off the marriage plan.

With my mummified heart gathering dust somewhere, apparently my body was forced to take over. I never wanted a migraine like that again, so I listened and said goodbye to Mr. Dynamic.

FIFTEEN

B OOK BY BOOK, I learned how to think about complex, abstract notions in a logical manner, and law school flew by in a blur.

Living in Chicago for three years did not. The city and the lake were spectacular. Food, theater, and architecture were second to none. But there was something missing.

I missed whatever it was in the air that made the atmosphere glitter. I looked around for Dracula and couldn't find him. He must have stayed in Charleston.

I tried to ignore my growing resentment of all the time I was wasting by not living in a magical place. I loved Charleston but detested small-minded southern culture that I continually rammed into.

Maybe I needed to pack up the entire city of Charleston in the trunk in the attic with all of my other desires that led me down the dead-end road to heartbreak. Everyone had told me I wouldn't get hired in Charleston anyway if I went and did something stupid like expand my horizons.

Find a new magical city. Move forward.

In response to that pondering, I landed a summer job on Easy Street at Kirkland and Ellis in Washington, D.C. First-year law students are lucky to get any job whatsoever, but one as prestigious as K&E, in the D.C. office, seemed off the chain.

K&E was one of only a few national law firms that didn't pigeonhole its attorneys into finite practice areas or even teams. It was a sink-or-swim, individualistic structure that seemed tailor-made for anyone who got bored easily and had an entrepreneurial spirit.

Dad's older sister, Jill, lived near a metro stop just outside of D.C. in Vienna. She was an intellectual, humorous writer, and she invited me to dinner at the National Press Club and exposed me to all that D.C. had to offer a budding lawyer with big possibilities.

"Washington is the most exciting city in the world," she said. "Working as a lawyer in Washington is like being a producer in Hollywood."

Her look said, *"Leave small towns behind. Don't even talk to me about returning to some backwards tourist trap in South Carolina."*

While D.C. didn't feel like a new forever home, Jill was right. My brain raged on fire all summer.

Dad was so proud of my summer internship at K&E, particularly when I walked him through the white marbled lobby with expansive views of the city. He fumbled with his camera and couldn't snap enough pics when we reached the bank of windows that overlooked the White House.

I enjoyed being out of school and working on real cases. So much so that I foot-dragged on writing an essay to apply for *Law Review.*

"Just one little essay, and you're on," a partner at K&E encouraged. "It's a prestigious credit." He, like most of the lawyers at K&E, clerked for judges their first year out of school, and he had also clerked for the United States Supreme Court.

He even guided us summer associates through a private, behind-the-scenes tour of the Supreme Court.

"Justice Ginsburg's robe is *so tiny!*" I squealed. I wanted to touch it, but I worried the Justice might get creeped out if she learned someone pawed at her robe.

"Go for that *Law Review* position," the partner whispered.

My mind might have been on fire, but the idea of spending the next two years slogging through even more theoretical legal reading and writing sounded so boring, I couldn't bring myself to do it.

The law stimulated me, but I wasn't in love with it, a nice distinction from my previous all-consuming need to dance. After law school, I wanted to go to work and go home, with time and energy to walk the dog, plant flowers, and work out.

"You didn't apply for *Law Review* because you wanted to spend that time walking your dog?" the partner asked a month later, politely hiding his disbelief. I shrugged and nodded.

Still, the Something Missing feeling gnawed at me.

Which made absolutely no sense. I'd already made it to a firm I liked, with a view of the White House, in a great city, with endless glittering opportunities. What more could I possibly want?

I looked around and couldn't find my imaginary Dracula in D.C. either. But I did hear a coffin lid, maybe the one that housed my heart, faintly creak open.

⚜

I visited my grandparents in West Virginia at the end of the summer, trips that increasingly brought on inexplicable levels of anxiety from the land itself. I barely survived my childhood there and didn't want to taunt the reaper in those mountains more than necessary.

I had stopped visiting for the holidays, opting to travel or visit Mom and John in Williamsburg, Virginia instead. When I did foray into West Virginia, I drove. Fog and high winds frequently delayed flights out of the regional airport, but as long as I could see my car, I had a certain escape.

All of my aunts and uncles, and everyone I knew in high school, fled for opportunities elsewhere. Dad swore if I ever even thought of returning for good, he'd chase me back across the state line with a hot cattle prod.

Even Grandma and Pops repeatedly gave lip service to the notion that children were raised to spread their wings and explore the world, not stick around and take care of them. I wanted to cherish as much time with them as possible, but that meant traveling into West Virginia. The anxiety was crushing, and I couldn't fully explain it.

On this trip, for the first time in my life, I consented to a car ride with my cousin Shaun. He was proud of his new-to-him red convertible, and showed off how he'd refurbished the body and the leather seats, details that were lost on me.

As he explained the new stereo system, he said, "Ooooh!!! Listen to this new song! You've heard of Christina Aguilera, right?"

Prior to law school, I was a pop music junkie. But I had to admit, I couldn't remember the last time I'd listened to the radio.

"Uhhhh," I made a face at him, suddenly feeling very uncool and out of touch, but also trying to hide that my skin was crawling. I couldn't sit still, trapped in his car for long. It wasn't him. It was the geography. I wished I could hang out with Shaun, and with Grandma and Pops and relax, for Chrissakes.

Shaun was saying, "She's a singer and a *dancer!* You're gonna love her." He turned up the volume on Genie in a Bottle, then put the top down on the convertible.

"How long are you here?" Shaun asked.

"Till tomorrow. On campus interviewing starts for next summer jobs."

"It's August. You interview *now* for a job that starts *next summer?*"

"Yeah. By the time classes start in September, we'll all have jobs, so we have nothing to worry about during the school year."

"Well, hot damn. I never heard of anything like that."

"Me neither." I glanced at him sideways, chuckling with him at this strange new world I plopped into.

"I was hoping you'd be in town long enough so I could take you to the club. We could go out dancing." I didn't want to go dancing in Shaun's biker bar, and he must have sensed it. "Don't worry, I'd have your back. No one would mess with you."

"I live on the South Side of Chicago, you know," I retorted, again unable to wrap my arms around why I felt safer in my notoriously crime-ridden neighborhood in the city than anywhere in Southern West Virginia.

"You look kind of stressed out. Doing much for fun? How do you not know Christina Aguilera?" he jabbed.

I started to explain that the law school's second motto, right after "Where hell does freeze over," was "Where fun goes to die," but Shaun apologized. "I'm teasing. You're the different, creative one. Don't let anyone make you think that's a bad thing. You don't have to conform."

The don't-lose-your-weirdness plea from Shaun landed right when I felt certain that my past experiences didn't fit into a future at Kirkland & Ellis. For instance, from the moment I stepped foot in law school, and then a law firm, I had to quickly clarify that yes, while I had been a professional dancer, I was a ballerina, not a stripper.

Maybe to satisfy my inner rebel, I always added, "Not that there's anything wrong if I had been a stripper." To which most folks pulled back slightly, perhaps wondering if I might still be too rough around the edges for polite society.

I sat up straighter in the seat, feigned boredom over the dilapi-dated sites in town, and shoved Shaun's reminder of my "non-con-forming" side up in the trunk in my mental attic.

"Don't you miss Charleston?" he asked, not letting up.

Ouch. Thinking of Charleston physically hurt. "I do. But there are so many opportunities for me right now."

"I guess you have to take them. At least you're not wasting every weekend drinking till you puke in the toilet like the rest of us."

I didn't tell him that I had spent the entire summer overly-wined and martini'ed in the best establishments in Washington on the firm's dime. It seemed an embarrassing snobbery of riches, and Shaun might think I looked down on an evening with him in a local bar.

I suspected Grandma was still standing on the front porch peer-ing into the night, waiting for our return. "Grandma would worry herself into a heart attack if we went out drinking and dancing."

Shaun agreed and deposited me back to Grandma and Pops' safe and sound. Grandma was already heading down the driveway in her nightgown, her hair in a shower cap, pretending she came to tell Shaun goodnight, but more likely, to hurry me back in the house.

⟡

During on-campus recruiting week, every major law firm sends attorneys onto campus for a first round of interviews.

San Francisco was the hottest market heading into 2000. But San Fran didn't have the turnover of young lawyers as much as other ma-jor markets did. Available positions were few and far between.

I became convinced San Francisco was the answer to my Something's Missing issue. Oceans, cliffs, sunsets, maybe it was a more cosmopolitan version of Charleston. It was *California* for

Chrissakes, the state that manufactured magic and exported it around the world.

In the last week in August, I stood in a darkened hallway outside the cramped interview rooms. I had the last slot of the day for the only San Francisco position. I reminded myself that conventional wisdom said a girl needed to go first or last in any audition in order to be remembered.

Uproarious laughter bubbled out from the other side of the door. Crap. My classmate, Tom Bradshaw. Bradshaw was quick-witted and sincerely likable, with an infectious laugh.

My palms sweated all over my resume. The lucky Ann Taylor black suit I wore was not enough. Flush conventional wisdom down the drain on this one.

I needed to learn how to think fast on my feet and spit out all the right words, right then and there. I had mustered up enough conversational skills to get me through the summer in D.C. Overall, though, I still preferred to listen and absorb before talking, an unhelpful trait in that moment, heading into the cooler-than-you San Francisco vibe.

I glanced at my watch. Thirty seconds to go. Bradshaw's interview would be over, and I needed to verbally dazzle.

I decided I would do just that, from then on in life. I threw back my shoulders. Fake it till you make it.

I then held that posture for fifteen more excruciating minutes while the interview with Bradshaw went way over into my time slot. By the time he walked out, beaming, I knew I was done for.

"Kill it!" Bradshaw lightly swatted at my shoulder as I entered the small office. I swear I saw a white fluffy cloud under his feet, floating him down the hall.

I looked at the interviewer and pointed toward the door after Bradshaw, "Sounds like y'all had a great time! Everyone loves him!"

The words came out mealy, dripping with false brightness and insecurity. Bluhhhh.

"Y'all?" the interviewer responded, arching an eyebrow, without glancing at me or smiling, his eyes perusing my resume. "So you were a *dancer?*" His face took on the expression I get when I see a bug in the house.

"Yes." I chose to skip the not-stripper explanation.

He gave me the courtesy of a few more moments, during which I bombed. Thanks to the epiphany out in the hall, however, I pushed myself to engage in what little conversation I could resurrect, more so than I had my whole life.

A channel emerged between my mind and my vocal chords. It was a roughed-in version, but goddess almighty, finally there.

"I'm sorry, we can't give you an offer" was on my answering machine before I arrived back at my apartment.

I wasn't disappointed, even though San Francisco was now off the table. I only wish I'd had the courage to be more forthright, and tell the interviewer before I even sat down, "Let's both go home. You need to hire Bradshaw."

If I had done that, I might have had a shot at the position. Or at least a more interesting, human conversation.

For the rest of the interview season, I stopped acting like a starving dog overly appreciative of one stale morsel. Unlike every other dance experience, where rejection and failure were the norms, I now stood in a spot where employers wanted me and my classmates. I stopped trying to impress everyone, and instead, sought out honest conversations with each lawyer, in each firm, to see if the firm would be a fit.

I learned that there were a zillion ways to show up as a lawyer, and that Kirkland & Ellis in D.C. was by far my favorite place. All I had to do was graduate.

But the pesky problem of Something Missing remained. Each time I checked, I discovered that Dracula still lived in Charleston, because living in Charleston remained my deep desire.

❦

Fast forward.

2005. I was a fourth-year associate.

My assistant walked into my office with my itinerary containing flight information to New York the next day, plus train tickets leaving from Penn Station. The train traveled by the scenic Hudson River and would carry me to a preliminary hearing at a bankruptcy court in a small town outside of New York City.

The hearing was a mere formality, really, with a list of rote questions, which is why the firm sent a still-green lawyer to do the job. I grew nervous just the same at the thought of navigating the crowds in New York, then asking questions of a renowned businessman accused of stealing millions of dollars from our clients. I hoped I could keep it together and my voice wouldn't crack.

Thank God I didn't live in New York. Or Chicago. Or D.C. I discovered that after about two days in any city, I wanted to escape. Even on a vacation to San Francisco, I was happier in the surrounding vineyards and villages.

After law school graduation, I joyously fled back to Charleston, where contrary to all the admonishments, I received big law firm job offers.

Everyone in my life thought I made a horrible decision turning down K&E and D.C., and that maybe, like Dad, I was secretly afraid of Great Success. But as soon as I made the decision to return to Charleston, at least a portion of my heart moved back into my chest.

From there, it worked like a hot-air balloon that carried me all the way through my final year of law school.

I took a job at a firm, got married, bought a house downtown with a courtyard I could landscape, and a view of the rooftops over the peninsula. We would live happily ever after with our two dogs and two cats. Mr. and Mrs. Perfect in their Perfect Life.

❧❖❧

If I paid attention to my insides, I felt mildly out of sorts in my skin and still felt the stirrings of Something's Missing, as if I weren't *entirely* living my purpose. Something about my perfect life felt... pigeonholed. Hrmph.

I couldn't put my finger on what else, exactly, I wanted. "You need a creative outlet," Will Lewis offered. "Something completely unrelated to the law to satisfy other parts of your brain, that's all." Will was a high-energy partner on our team who wrote music, played guitar, and painted.

"Tell me what you see here," he said one day in his office. He pointed to an abstract painting he was working on.

Something about the messiness of the painting frightened me. Not about Will. About myself. "I see the deep guts of my mind."

He smiled. "Exactly. That's what my head looks like inside. I find that it's not so terrible when it's out on the canvas or on the page."

"I'm afraid that once I start to let out the gremlins, the whole house of cards will collapse." I wasn't sure why I said that.

"So what?" Will asked.

I rolled my eyes lightheartedly and got back to billing hours.

When I returned to my office, words swam on my screen. I couldn't concentrate on preparing for the hearing in New York.

A mildly familiar sensation crept up the back of my neck and across my scalp. The last time I felt this way had been at least fifteen years earlier, when I ran all night from my own mind, until memories of Jason caught up with me, wrestled me to the ground, and flooded my brain.

I searched my mental files. There wasn't anything else I'd forgotten in my life. Sure, I'd stored a bunch of emotional stuff up in the attic, but I knew what was there. I had my shit together.

The tingling over my scalp didn't stop. A memory *did* want to surface, but it wasn't about me.

A story from Dad . . . about his mom, going mad, talking to herself, "yelling at the spirits." Her behavior was horribly shameful to Dad as a kid, primarily because it was chalked-up to her drinking too much, publicly, and all hours of the day.

What if Dad's mom drank herself to death because she couldn't tell the difference between insanity and real spirit communication? What if that madness in our family outed itself in me right when I reached stability and success? Why was I so deeply petrified of Will's painting—or to try painting or creative writing for myself?

NOT the right time for these musings, girl. Get a grip! I barked to myself.

My Self didn't listen.

I suddenly recalled that Dad's grandmother and uncle held seances in their front parlor, according to Dad's breezy tales. "Uncle Charlie was said to be a medium, but he called it a curse. He worried people would think he was crazy because he would fall into trances. He couldn't fully control it," Dad shrugged it off. That was pretty much the extent I knew about the spiritual side of his family.

The idea of sensing and hearing my own dead people, like Jason and Aunt Lily, still seemed to be natural, albeit the actual experiences were rarer and rarer as I grew older.

I thought of Edgar Cayce and all the telepathy books I'd read when I was younger. They were quite substantive. The fantastical topics weren't approached in a fluffy manner.

There had to be spirit communication that was different from schizophrenia, or falling into trances like a loony toon, or visions and voices in your head popping out into 3-D Earth life.

But what if you couldn't tell the difference? It was the same concern that stalked me as a child, when ghosts leapt out of the shadows and into my room.

Maybe Will was almost right. I needed to start exploring some of these philosophies creatively. If I were headed down the path toward madness, the more I understood it, the better I'd be able to hide it.

I ignored the voice screaming at me to go back to work and opened Google instead. Some force made me search for "seance," then "mediums."

Image after image of psychics with crystal balls, heavy eyeliner, and 1-900 numbers came up. Sprinkled throughout were old ladies stuffed under fifty layers of scarves with placid smiles. My choices were aging hippies promising kittens and rainbows, or fearmongers, promising to lift curses or mail love potions.

I quickly shut down the search and peered out the door, hoping no one walked by and saw my screen.

Enough of that. No way was I taking Will's advice and inviting this lunacy out into the open. I had a plane to catch the next day, and I needed to show up as a put-together professional.

If I had been paying attention, I may have noticed the shadow of a long, thin finger sliding across my office wall, reaching across my desk and into my ribcage to tickle my heart. Dracula.

I hadn't thought of that made-up old fool since I decided to move back to Charleston, five years earlier.

ACT THREE

Union & Resonance:
The Whole is Greater than
the Sum of Her Parts

SIXTEEN

I SEARCHED FOR my train through the throngs of fast- moving crowds in Penn Station. I located it, hurried out of the chaos, and plopped down with relief in a window seat.

I reminded myself that this hearing was no-lose for me. My only task was to meet this businessman face-to-face, assess his demeanor, and get a few basic facts cemented on the record.

I also had a secret weapon in my pocket, thanks to Craig Burgess, a partner on our team. When I first started practicing law, one of my first assignments involved a series of innocuous witness interviews with Craig. At the end of one, Craig said to me in private, "She's lying."

I furrowed my brow. "How do you know?"

"I felt it right here." He touched his solar plexus. "Any time some- one lies to me, it's like a subtle catch. A tickle."

"Whooooaaa."

"Everyone lies to lawyers. Opposing counsel, witnesses," he nod- ded toward the door where the next witness waited in the hall. "Our own clients."

"Our own clients will lie to us?" My voice squeaked in disbelief.

He chuckled at my innocence. "They're the worst. Just pay attention. Your brain will tell you they're not lying because the story will make sense, but your body will feel it. See where it comes up. Throat, forehead, solar plexus."

From then on, I tried to hone my inner lie detector, and this hearing promised to provide additional practice.

I arrived at the hearing in the fall of 2005. The rundown federal building was very small considering about fifty people already waited. The businessman allegedly owed money to everyone present.

The human body can give off up to 50 different microexpressions that last only 1/25th of a second but can reveal when someone is lying.

The man was a professor and entrepreneur whose most recent scheme either lost or buried 40 to a hundred million dollars in offshore accounts from Lichtenstein to Cyprus. The investors were pissed.

I sat directly across from Mr. Offshore, who appeared at ease in the circus. I asked my questions. There were no surprises in his answers.

When I finished, something didn't make sense. The financial transactions involved were so complicated, however, I didn't know how to ask follow-up questions.

I learned through my previous disasters questioning witnesses that if something doesn't add up, I shouldn't be ashamed to play the dumb girl in the room and ask again. This time, I was, in fact, the dumb blonde and laid it on thick.

"Mr. Offshore, I'm not an expert in investments like everyone else here. What did your company actually do with the investors' stocks and bonds?"

He started to give the same wanh, wanh, wanh ... My face turned red. There was only so long I could keep everyone there listening to me fumble around. Then, something in the tenor of his voice tickled my ear because the words were out of resonance when he said "stock" and "pool."

Go ahead and be really idiotic, Girl.

"I can imagine an empty swimming pool with a bunch of people's cash thrown into it. But how do you 'pool' stock? I mean, where is the stock sitting?"

"Oh, I sold the stock."

"Ahhh." He wasn't lying. "Then you had the swimming pool of cash that you could spend elsewhere."

"Yes."

"So there's no stock, and no money left in the pool?"

For one second, if a pin dropped in the room, it would have sounded like a bombshell. Then the investors in the room erupted in shouting.

Mr. Offshore kept his gaze on me and said gently, "I'm very sorry. But there's no money left." His last sentence triggered the vibrations in my ear again as not resonant. There was money *somewhere*.

⌁⌁⌁

Resonance wasn't finished with me for the day, however.

On the plane ride back to Charleston, I opened a magazine someone left in the seat pocket in front of me. Inside were short interviews with 10 influential people on a variety of subjects.

Oprah Winfrey said the key to her success was the ability to connect with people authentically. The only way to authentically connect with another human being, she said, was to honestly communicate with herself, rip-off-the-band-aid sort of honesty, every day. Then each time she opened her mouth to talk with a guest, she spoke from that pit of honesty in her belly, for better or worse.

I suddenly wondered what that would feel like.

I read further. Oprah said a big part of her process had been confronting a childhood of abuse, acknowledging how that shaped her into adulthood and not holding secrets around it.

The tickle of resonance versus dissonance I felt when listening to Mr. Offshore mushroomed into a sonic boom.

I flipped the page. Supreme Court Justice Sandra Day O'Connor, in a separate interview, noted a statistic that girls didn't raise their hands as much as boys did in class, and that girls were less likely to speak, even when they had the right answer. She wished girls were encouraged to use their voice at an earlier age.

What if I held back in speaking — and held back from unleashing my deepest desires in life — because there was still a thing in me that kept me silent, something I was mortally ashamed about?

There was the truth nugget.

It had been there all along, buried under every other emotional layer and life experience I needed to mine and work through first.

I had never given a name to the abuse from my grade-school babysitter. I never forgot about it like I repressed memories of Jason. I only once tried telling someone, Mr. Dynamic, who before his own awakening, replied, "Move on. That has nothing to do with anything now."

From that moment with Mr. Dynamic, I divorced it from my emotional record and filed it away in the trunk. I followed his advice better than he did.

Even to myself, I never labeled it abuse. But Oprah called a spade a spade, and she didn't speak about it with shame. She spoke from power, like a person comfortable in her inherent rights as a being on this Earth.

A knowing took hold of me, and I acknowledged with dread that it wouldn't fade. It was too *resonant*.

I needed to confront, in myself, the impact from the sexual, emotional, and physical abuse the babysitter inflicted on me as a child. I needed to own the horror of my experiences. Because, from where I sat, as long as I remained afraid of my own mess, the experience prevented me from living as a free person.

On the heels of these revelations came the quaking in my boots, *oh fuck, shit, goddamn, this is what I have to do now?*

Well, not in that exact moment, as I sat stuffed in the middle seat in economy class. Instinctively, I knew I'd never be able to move forward in life, and reclaim my full heart, until I dragged this last, albeit ginormous piece of ick into the sunlight.

I sat stock still for the next hour of the plane ride, cradling this fragile piece of my younger self that dropped from my subconscious into my care.

In the row across the aisle sat a young girl, perhaps eight or nine, the same age I had been when the abuse started. It struck me how vulnerable she was, a happy little person. When I thought of myself as a nine-year-old, I felt much older. And oddly, more responsible, weighted down with someone else's secrets.

A nine-year-old IS A LITTLE GIRL! I shouted back in my head. I had also once been a happy little human, carefree and innocent.

Then came the memory of how every evening, after Mom came home, dismissed Cruella, and drove me to dance class, I showed up in such severe physical pain, heaviness, and shame that it took the full hour-and-a-half through tap, ballet, and jazz, moving my limbs, the compliments from my teachers about my grace, line, and technique, to feel worthy of my detestable body again.

I noted that it didn't help that dance is a verbally silent art. And that the only instrument in dance is the dancer's body.

Then came the memory of Cruella's brother, who Mom told me well after I'd left West Virginia, that in high school, he'd been accused of molesting a young boy. Something was up with those kids.

I caught myself. They were old enough to know better. They weren't kids.

My brain enacted a forced stop. I dozed off and on, trying to avoid flopping onto the shoulders of my seatmates.

I have no tools, I thought. Oprah didn't do it alone. She literally had a large television network with producers and assistants, through which she helped people navigate dark human experiences such as disgusting abuse.

I needed a team approach. I wondered if Dr. Z would see adults for an overdue childhood issue. There was one person I could count on to snap into gear and direct me on where to go therapy-wise.

Mom.

Mom and my stepdad, John, were visiting over Veterans Day weekend in November, a few weeks away. I had to tell her.

I had to tell my husband first. I knew if I could say the words out loud to myself, he would be okay hearing them. I just had to summon up the nerve to speak to them.

I felt robbed every time I thought of Will's painting. If other people are free to create and express, why can't I be?

Another piece of my heart crawled out of the trunk in the attic and lumbered toward my chest. When it arrived, I vowed to never be afraid or ashamed of my own ghosts in the shadows ever again.

With that, I fell hard asleep, straight up in the middle seat, for the rest of the flight.

Mr. Perfect was so upset for me and took it in with his custom-ary quiet sympathy. He preferred not sharing any details of our lives outside the sanctuary of our own four walls, so he suggested we not tell Mom and John, or anyone else, really, because then we'd have to take on their reactions.

He opted for the approach that, "It's out in the open enough, just between us. We can try to find a therapist, if you need, but it doesn't seem like this issue has held you back in life." On the outside looking in, his assessment was true.

My insides balked though. What he may have meant was, *Is this really a Big Deal? How disruptive will this turn out to be to our daily lives?* Neither of us had tread into this territory before, so neither of us knew.

Primarily, his approach felt too much like pandering to shame around the topic and never mentioning it again, where I wanted to be Oprah-level free. So I lurched forward.

Mom and John took the news like the healthcare professionals they were. I was prepared to tell Mom that if she did the whole "I'm such a bad Mom for letting this happen" routine, she needed to take it out on her own therapist.

Under no circumstances did I blame Mom or feel like she was responsible. But I couldn't get right with myself and take care of her too. Mom was one step ahead of me and assured me the last person I needed to worry about was her.

In late 2005, there were very few resources for adults seeking guidance through the treacherous waters of their own childhood abuse. Most resources were devoted to children.

Unfortunately, Dr. Z wasn't really an option given that online sessions weren't a thing, and telephone calls wouldn't have sufficed. I needed to start from scratch and unpack the trunk in front of a stranger. I wasn't sure I had the resilience to do that.

The alternative scenario presented a life diminished by fear, unspoken shame, and unresolved ick, costumed in the suits, stilettos, and gorgeous, high-end clothing of my lawyer persona.

My biggest fear had always been the idea of regretting roads not taken because I didn't have the courage to pursue something I wanted — or, more likely, that I buried what I wanted so deeply, Dracula couldn't even find it, which was accurate in that moment.

I had no idea what I would do if I didn't practice law. I only knew with certainty that standing between me and my future was this Issue. My future self, that old lady I saw in the vision on the coast of France, wasn't haunted by roads not taken, held back by any Issues, or tormented by nightmares with alligators.

I found a crime victim's clinic that didn't seem to fit my circumstances. I didn't see myself as a victim, like someone who survived a robbery or attempted murder.

But it was the only place around, so I called. Several times. Each time, my mouth went dry, I started shaking, and I hung up as soon as the receptionist answered. My physical reaction alone told me I was on the right path, dreadful as it was.

After my third try, she rang me back. "I know you want to talk to me. So let me start by saying, it's the doctor's job, not yours, to determine if we can help. Can I make you an appointment, sweetie?"

Weight flew off my chest. Contrary to so many other instances in my present life where I sought to show up as perfect and self-sufficient, hiding my mental mess and insecurities, the receptionist stated that it was enough to ask for help.

According to the website, in partnership with Yale University, the clinic had the most comprehensive, up-to-date research on the long-term effects of crime and abuse on victims. Doctors from all over the world interned there.

During the intake interview, the psychiatrist asked, "What's your greatest hesitation in talking to me?"

"I'm not sure I have a problem. I feel like something's holding me back. I'm not a crime victim. I hate the word victim." In spite of my words, my mouth felt stuffed with cotton and my voice quivered. Everything in me shook. I had no control over this new shaking business. I recognized my heart clunking back to life and Heart was now the driver of the train.

I continued, "My abuser wasn't even a real adult. Well, legally, maybe. I don't know. It was a long time ago."

I could tell she'd heard all this before. "Forget about what you think of yourself. Think of another nine-year-old."

I thought of the little girl on the plane.

"You're the lawyer here," she continued. "If what happened to you happened to another girl, would she be a crime victim?"

"FUUUUUCCCCKKKK YES!" If what happened to me occurred to any other child, I could tear the abuser apart limb by limb with my bare hands.

"See? We can help you. If you want it."

⸺⁂⸺

In early 2006, the National Crime Victims Center at the Medical University of South Carolina enrolled me in their cutting-edge outpatient program.

I was diagnosed with complex PTSD, which is similar to what war veterans suffer. Apparently, victims of long-term child abuse and veterans are similar in that both scenarios trap a person in a situation of repeated physical danger, over which they have zero control and cannot escape.

As a result, our brains form a Y, separating the acts and the memories from the emotions attached to them. Literally, a brain break. It's one of the oldest survival techniques we have.

In the case of complex PTSD, the Y remains. The emotions don't go anywhere. The chemicals get stuck in a cup until the cup explodes on innocent triggers, like falling into a full anxiety attack over fireworks, or in my case, my irrational fear of the entire state of West Virginia, my fear when speaking, or even my fear of allowing myself deep desires.

For me, the PTSD wasn't just from Cruella's abuse. That was only the start.

From there, I went to NCSA where many of the teachers used the guise of "training" to unleash their meanest capabilities on girls with big dreams and growing bodies, deepening my loathing of my body.

Then I went back to West Virginia, the scene of the original abusive crime, where I lost the person closest to me to suicide.

No wonder I was suicidal by the time I was fifteen. My experiences on Earth led me to believe I was safer outside my body than staying in it. That's pretty rational.

It's also oddly rational, from my Heart's standpoint, that it needed decades to heal, sequestered in the trunk in the attic. Out of necessity, Brain took over, until it, too, couldn't manage in its broken state. By then, Heart was ready to gallop to the rescue.

Meanwhile, Alligator was trying to tell me, through nightmares, to stop shoving away the pieces of myself that were dying.

I felt so relieved to be seen as the shattered Humpty Dumpty I was. My therapist warned that it would be painstaking to puzzle myself back together — heart and mind, emotions and memories, body and spirit, fears and desires — into an integrated whole, but she knew we could do it.

She sent me home with a two-page pamphlet for family members to help them know what to expect and how best to provide support.

What I could not do, she said, was place myself in a situation where I had no control. I had to be extremely picky about who I shared with while I went through my Repairing Humpty Dumpty phase.

That was difficult when it came to Dad. Dad was remarried and more emotionally stable than when he was single, but I couldn't count on him not to say something snarky or call Mom behind my back after he'd been into the wine and cuss her out in his own helplessness. So I left him out of it.

The sheer amount of packed-away shame and sorrow and angst could only be nibbled in crusty bits over months. Even though each crusty bit liberated me.

It soon became obvious that I couldn't keep up with work. While my therapist assured me extreme brain fog was normal, I had to tell my team leader, who I innately trusted. He needed to understand if I dropped the ball on a project that it wouldn't last forever.

To my surprise, he said, "Let's get you on a reduced goal for temporary medical purposes." Meaning, the firm would cut me slack on the hefty, billable-hour goal.

"Does anyone have to know why?" I worried about having a black mark in my personnel file: *CAN'T CUT IT DUE TO CRAZY*. "I'm not crazy," I promised. "It's actually the opposite."

"You'd be shocked how many partners throughout this firm have come to me with similar issues. However, they're in their fifties or sixties before they deal with it, and by then, there's addiction, DUIs, suicide attempts, and nervous breakdowns. Yes, they are crazy. I'm proud of you for facing this head-on, now."

Fat tears spilled from my eyes. Other high-functioning people in the high-performing firm were a mess inside too.

⁘

Grandma and Pops presented the last big hurdle of bringing the skeleton out of the shame closet. My only motivation for telling them, at their advanced age, was to alleviate my guilt for not spending enough time with them. I needed to apologize for why I rarely came home and why I felt I needed to flee from the entire state as soon as I'd arrived.

Back around the dining room table, for Sunday supper, we gathered. Mr. Perfect, me, Mom, John, Grandma, and Pops. After supper, I took a deep breath and let out the words. They never really got any easier.

Mr. Perfect cried silently. He was more awkward than me when it came to saying the right words, but his tears were a steady hand on my back.

Grandma set her jaw, and Pops looked down at his hands. He tried to speak, but a sob cut him off. Hearing Pops cry unleashed more waterworks for everyone at the table.

"I never wanted you to think I was running away from you," I said. "I'm sorry for not being here more often."

"Oh, honey," Grandma reached over to my hand. "We never thought you didn't want to see us." She pulled herself up a little straighter and forcibly brightened her face. "The past is the past. We can all let it go now."

Mom and John lashed out at the same time. "Let it go?!" Mom gasped.

"Kitty!" John snapped. "You don't just let things go. You work through them, slowly, over time, and one morning, you wake up and realize, it's done. But you can't force things under the carpet or they'll never get resolved."

"Well," Grandma stammered. "That's what I meant." Grandma had tried her usual, and this time, she was outnumbered.

Pops finally found his voice, but he couldn't raise his head. "Andrea, I'm glad you're telling us now. Because," he choked back another sob, "if I had known anything back then, I would have killed someone."

He meant it.

I couldn't stand to see Pops pull his handkerchief from his pocket and wipe his tears, but I also never felt so accepted and protected in my life by everyone around me, family and work family.

I also began to feel free, free from fear, and free to speak, free to make mistakes, and free to fly, or splat.

From that point, I reclaimed everything I'd stored in the trunk in the mental attic. I went through each wretched and poignant experience lovingly, handling with care all the previous pieces of myself. I also started to reclaim the mountains and time spent with Grandma and Pops.

There was an inside joke in my marriage that Mr. Perfect loved stability and routine so much that I couldn't rearrange the sock drawer without stressing him out.

When I tried to share with him the techniques and exercises the clinic gave me as homework, which were miserably difficult yet psychologically fascinating, he responded with silent suspicion. I sensed that my efforts to rearrange my brain struck him as threatening.

So we fell into a pattern of him asking, "How did it go?" To which I replied "Fine."

It meant enough to me that he asked. Once the clinic released me from the program, I think he looked forward to returning to our regularly scheduled programming, which didn't require facing and processing jagged emotions and twisted-up memories.

Instead, I felt free enough to add creative outlets, finally heeding my colleague Will's advice. I started taking hip hop dance classes and yoga at the gym and bought a personal laptop so I could write snippets of fiction. I craved a place to experiment with tales of ghosts, gothic creatures, and all things that go bump in the night, including the things that go bump inside our heads.

One teeny thing kept rattling around in my head. Mr. Perfect never read the two-page pamphlet the clinic sent me home with on the first day. I nagged him enough that he finally took it into work, where he placed it face-down on his desk.

SEVENTEEN

❦

I N 2007, AUNT JILL, Dad's sister, published her book *Family Spirit*, a comedy inspired by Uncle Charlie, Grandma Sabina, and their seances in the 1920s.

"It's based on all those kooky spiritualists in the family," she laughed when I called to congratulate her. "I'm convinced Grandma used her cane to rap under the table, signaling Uncle Charlie to fall over in a trance and cry out, 'It's the Great Beyond!'"

From our conversation and the pages of her book, Jill clearly thought the family seances were the greatest hoax going, that Uncle Charlie was just old and couldn't stay awake, and that folks who believed in the seances were too gullible.

Next time Dad visited, he brought with him The Family Box, a caved-in cardboard box of genealogy charts, newspaper clippings, U.S. Congress memorabilia from Great-Granddad Alf, even letters describing Uncle Charlie and Great-Grandma Sabina's seances.

As we rummaged through The Box on my couch, I asked what he thought. "I've had too many people tell me about Grandma's seances and the strange things that happened in her house," he said, his voice thoughtful. "Remember, I told you that man *heard* music pouring out of Uncle Charlie's chest that one afternoon in the field. There's more in heaven and Earth than dreamt of in Jill's philosophy," he mused, loosely quoting Hamlet.

I've always been more interested in people's experiences, perceptions, and beliefs, rather than what's objectively true, as I don't believe that humans have the capacity to perceive all there is. I agreed with Dad.

"You do believe in Something Greater than ourselves, don't you, Kid?"

"Of course."

"You hear the spirits? Feel 'em?"

"Usually in the middle of the night or when I least expect it. Just a bunch of weird stuff, and it's random. I used to worry I was crazy, but I don't feel that way anymore." I still hadn't told him about the PTSD or the abuse that contributed to it.

"No, you're not crazy." He gnawed on his cigar. "Sometimes I hear them, and I wonder what the hell they want. Then I don't hear them, and I wonder where the hell they went." He chuckled and looked at me through his bottle-thick glasses. "Hit or miss thing, for sure."

Dad slipped into stories of his mother, Hattie, and how the family basically abandoned her after her older sister was murdered. As always, he spoke with great sensitivity and forgiveness about Hattie and himself as a young child. He never dwelt long on the memories, preferring to muse over them briefly as he chewed on a cigar, then glide into the next story.

Hattie died before I was born, and I never felt the same generosity toward her that he did. Hattie was apparently a natural medium like her mother and Uncle Charlie, but from the stories, she was clearly undisciplined in all aspects of her life.

For the first time, however, I wondered if she also experienced a form of PTSD after her sister died. Society wouldn't have been equipped to help her with her mental health, and her family didn't hone any of her abilities, much less her intuitive ones.

Hattie was only fifteen years old when her only sister, Della, was killed, allegedly by her husband. Certain townspeople took revenge into their own hands, kidnapped Della's husband, and lynched him. Afterward, rumors swirled that Hattie's father had ordered the killing of the young man, but no one was ever accused or charged in his murder.

Grandma Sabina and her brother Charlie held a seance shortly after the murders. A blue light appeared in the parlor and landed on Della's photograph. Della's voice rang out for all to hear and she said, "My killer is not on this plane."

No one knew what that meant, but folks did start to wonder whether Della's husband wasn't the murderer after all.

Della never communicated again.

Grief encapsulated the family. Hattie, on the eve of blossoming into society, became lost in the shuffle. After losing her only big sister, she craved attention and mentoring.

Her dad was a big-time politician in the United States House of Representatives and a newspaperman. He traveled the country. He educated her brothers to become journalists and groomed them to take over the newspaper. Her family offered her a secretarial position at the newspaper, but she eventually proved herself unable to hold down a job.

Perhaps more than anyone else in the family, and perhaps directly resulting from Della's death, Hattie easily sensed and openly communicated with the spirit world. But she had no patience for meditating around the parlor table in a seance.

She preferred drinking and flirting, resorting to extremes merely to be noticed, so much so that the sheriff frequently escorted her home for disorderly conduct. Unsurprisingly, by the time Dad came along, no other parent would allow their kids to visit his house to play with him.

Dad was a little boy when his father divorced Hattie. Aunt Jill escaped the house and the entire state when she was eighteen, so Dad, at eleven, was left to look after his emotionally-explosive mom.

In tenth grade, Dad became a page in D.C. to the Speaker of the House. For the next two-and-a-half years, Hattie repeatedly called him while he was on duty on the floor of the U.S. Congress, claiming to be on her deathbed, begging him to come home.

She drunk-dialed him one too many times, and Dad gave in over Christmas break of his senior year with one semester remaining. Dad was convinced his mother would die any moment and he'd never forgive himself if he weren't there.

Hattie lived another five years, "yelling at the spirits" who haunted her living room until the very end.

I realized the spirit world didn't drive my grandmother mad. This world did. Hattie had trunkloads of grief and pain and quite possibly, a broken brain.

I still couldn't forgive her for all the harm she caused Dad, which then rippled throughout all of his relationships, but I could understand the situation a little better.

⸻

In 2008, I mingled in a large conference room in the Washington, D.C. office of the Baker Botts law firm, listening to a small group of lawyers discuss which colleges they planned to visit with their teenage children.

One lawyer turned to me and asked, "You remember those days, don't you? When your daddy took you around to visit colleges?"

I guffawed. For an instant, I knew he had to be kidding.

I thought of the time Dad rescued me that Thanksgiving weekend, after running away to the edge of life, when I had no plans to finish high school, much less attend college, when I was tussling with what would become twenty years of complex PTSD. Yeah, I remembered those days.

Then it dawned on me that my law colleague — and the other kind, expectant faces looking back at me in the conference room — were serious. To them, I must have presented as *normal,* enough so that I fooled them into thinking I grew up with the kind of lifestyle and experiences that placed a Spring Break College Tour on my teenage calendar.

I regained my composure and nodded. "Pivotal time. For sure."

I turned to the windows and looked out over the city, blinking in disbelief. There I stood, a practicing lawyer, working on a case with some of the country's elite, white collar criminal defense attorneys, and they thought I was like them. Normal.

I pulled off a heist.

⚜

The Big Case that took me to that Baker Botts conference room exposed me to lawyers who were passionate about the law and criminal justice, like Dad. There was no separation between their work and their life purpose. I got high off their energy, which spotlighted in myself that I had no heartfelt drive for my work, and I definitely wasn't yet living my purpose.

I sat in Dulles International Airport in D.C., waiting for my flight back to Charleston, reluctant to leave the vibe of our group. I felt more easily connected with and inspired by this team of lawyers, basically a bunch of strangers, than I had felt in *years*.

This connection shimmered, even through a profession I respected but no longer wanted to dedicate my life to —

Oh, crap.

I looked around at the gates boarding to New York, Santa Fe, Vancouver, and realized, for the first time, I didn't want to go home.

It wasn't just my job I didn't want to go back to. It was Mr. Perfect.

I sat with that agonizing truth for the next few hours on the flight back to Charleston. Airports and airplanes were turning out to be portals to myself.

Mr. Perfect loved our lifestyle and bragged that his wife was not only a lawyer but also a partner in a Big Law Firm. It seemed, however, as if my PTSD embarrassed him, not that many people knew about it.

Maybe it was simply that raw emotions and messy truths were uncontrollable and therefore, too unruly for him to bear. Maybe he worried I'd come out the other end a different person, and he was correct.

I reminded myself that he supported me through the therapy, through wanting to write, and wanting to dance again in hip hop class. He never tried to shut me down or shut me up.

But the two-page pamphlet written by the clinic for family members remained unread, face-down on his desk, by that point buried under a stack of books.

When I got home after the D.C. trip, Mr. Perfect notified me - for the first of a zillion times to follow - that I had changed, in the same firm tone a parent uses when seeking to correct a child's poor choices.

I responded, "I hope so! I hope to change and grow for the rest of my life. You will too! Let's goooooooooooo together!"

"I don't understand what you're talking about," he said. "I'm good with where I am. Fine with how things were. I don't have energy for *this*."

"You're not even *trying*," I howled. My Heart felt ginormous, and I wanted our relationship to take up more space in it. Big Emotions only served to make him stand up a little straighter, and a little farther away.

It should have been clear from that first go-round that our life trajectories had fallen askew.

Mr. Perfect never signed up for a life of radical growth or a wife who plummeted head first into personal exploration. The Mrs. Perfect he married thought she had her act together, and that woman turned out to be bat-shit-wrong.

I didn't understand, at the time, that I couldn't force anyone to skip down my dark alley of transformation with me, on my timeline, no matter how much I assured them it was safe, magical even. So when Mr. Perfect refused to skip with me, I grew resentful.

I felt pigeonholed and blamed him for it.

He felt betrayed and left behind.

⟡

It took at least a year, but we finally grew so frustrated with each other, and so bored of the same argument, that we separated.

There were times I worried that I was the living embodiment of Kali or Shiva, the Hindu goddess and god of destruction. I was well aware that I was throwing a hand grenade into my life. Perfect house, perfect job, perfect husband, check. All of it just happened to be perfect for someone else.

I cried for months on end. I cried over him. I cried over the idea of selling our perfect-for-us house. I cried over the rooftop view I'd never see again.

Mainly, I cried over the person I wanted him to be and he wasn't.

We had been separated for a good while when I went on a girls' trip to California. While out there, Mr. Perfect called. He said he was ready to grow, ready to move forward with our relationship. I felt so relieved, I said yes.

Within the hour, I threw up.

I didn't listen to my body. We reconciled, then after a few months, separated all over again, this time with less drama.

⁂

I was almost out the door for work one morning when my uncle called. I barely even said hello, when he stated, "Shaun killed himself last night."

Everything in me deflated.

It didn't make sense. My cousin Shaun was doing great, wasn't he? He had a job he enjoyed, he had just remodeled his house, he was only 45... he had also just come through hip replacement surgery and repeatedly complained about the pain. Apparently, his doctors removed him from the painkiller Oxy too suddenly and too soon, which not only caused horrific pain, but also severe depression and screwed-up brain chemistry.

My uncle explained that the responding law enforcement officer sat up with Shaun's mother, Nan, the entire night. "He wasn't in his right mind because of the Oxy withdrawal," the officer assured her.

She'd told the officer, "Shaun started drinking heavily from the pain, then for the first time in decades, he said he wondered about his daughter. He said he never should have given her up for adoption. That was the last thing he said."

That broke my heart into a million pieces.

I hot-tailed it to West Virginia to be with my family as fast as the car would drive. By this point, I had no lingering, misplaced anxiety over visiting the state.

I hadn't talked with Shaun recently. I felt terrible for him, terrible for his loneliness, terrible that I hadn't connected with him in his worst time.

Mom talked with Shaun a lot in the months and weeks leading up to his death. He told her he didn't feel right and that he was worried he was depressed. Shaun was psychologically intelligent, vigilant about his own mental health. Mom was convinced that, as the officer said, his brain chemistry wasn't right, and it was due to the mismanagement of Oxy. It seemed to me Shaun had descended into one black hole of a moment that he couldn't get to the other side of.

Shaun's funeral was a standing-room-only, raucous affair. His friends had a band, and the pianist pounded the church piano so hard, even the roof wanted to bounce.

"Shaun loved music," the singer told us. "For a skinny white dude, he sure could dance." Shaun could DANCE?!

Maybe if I'd gone out with him when he invited me, I'd have known that, I berated myself.

When we filed out of the church, it was ninety-one-year-old Pops, straight-backed and strong, who Shaun's mother clung to for dear life.

In years past, Pops lamented that he and Grandma outlived everyone they knew. He didn't want to make any new friends, he said, because they'd just go and die on him, and he was sick of funerals.

This one was particularly hard. The older generation shouldn't have to bury the younger one. But thank God Pops was there for Nan.

He all but carried her down the steps, then held her on the sidewalk, the crowd pausing behind them, bearing witness to a mother's grief.

⁘

A year before Shaun died, I learned that a lawyer in Charleston died by suicide, and within days of that, an unrelated teenager did so as well. I didn't know either of these men, but my brain fell into a looping, gripping obsession with both of them.

I discovered that the lawyer was forty-five, had a wife and a young child. And twenty-five years earlier, he'd attended a local, private high school during a time when a ghastly, years-long, sexual abuse crime spree was perpetrated against the boys at the school.

I lamented that if only he'd known about the crime victim's center or some place similar, or believed that he could come out the other side after abuse has thrown buckets of shame on you, he might still be alive.

Then, I heard that another teenager died in a single-vehicle, drunk driving incident, and the community showed up by the hundreds, memorials on the beach, hand-made signs outside his house and everything. But the teenage suicide victim? No community outpouring for his family and friends whatsoever. Nothing but whispers.

I was so disgusted by the societal shame surrounding both suicides that my bones wanted to wretch.

I then realized I was spinning out over these two men as I did each time I learned that someone died by suicide. The point of the PTSD therapy protocol was not to run back to talk therapy every time life triggered me. The point was to trust my own tools first.

I dug around in my psychological tool box. My personal laptop emerged.

Over the next months, I wrote an unflinching essay on every single thing I thought, felt, and knew about suicide, and I wrote about still living on the other side of it. I allowed myself to write words polite society wouldn't have the stomach to swallow.

I had no one to protect, as no one would ever see what I wrote. It was incredibly satisfying.

And it worked. From then on, even when Shaun died, I didn't spin out over suicide. I didn't fall into the abyss of obsessive thought patterns — at least on that topic.

That doesn't mean I didn't grieve. Out of all my losses, Shaun's is the one that filled me, unendingly, with the most regret. I rarely expect anyone to stay alive, but he's someone I took for granted who would.

⁂

A few weeks later, a friend of mine held a summer solstice workshop on a Saturday afternoon. "We're going to make intention bowls, purge ourselves in the fire of the sun, then dance in the surf of the ocean," she said. "You should come."

It sounded like a day wasted on fluff and flake to me. Between billing hours, writing snippets of short story ideas, working out, then crashing from the work week, I didn't allow myself much wasted time.

Stefaney was the most no-nonsense, not-flake person I knew outside the legal community though. What I heard her say was, "Girl. Lighten up. You need this."

So I went.

Stefaney instructed us to write what we wanted on a small piece of paper. We would place the wish in the bottom of the container that we then filled with salt and topped with crystals and flower petals.

I didn't know what to wish for. Without a vision, the intention bowl and its stupid crystals seemed useless. I had promised myself to stay at the firm until the Big Case went to trial, rationalizing that after that, my Next Thing would miraculously appear on its own volition.

So I wrote, "Something unexpected this way comes…"

Boy, did it, within the hour.

A woman in the gathering told us about Mami Wata, the mermaid goddess. Captured, enslaved Africans would pray to Mami Wata for safe voyage as they made the perilous journey across the Atlantic Ocean.

"But," she warned, "they had to stop praying to Mami Wata as soon as their feet touched land, lest Mami Wata try to lure them back into the ocean."

The obsessive switch in my brain flipped to "ON." I later Googled everything I could think of and found nothing indicating any historical event where enslaved people followed Mami Wata back into the ocean.

Through a series of phone calls, I found an old man who lived on St. Simons Island in Georgia.

"I forgot about that legend," he said, his voice husky. "But I can tell you a ghost story about a boat landing." Where there are ghosts, there were once people.

I was so excited, I leapt out of my chair, closed my office door, and asked him to please tell me more.

"There's a boat landing where I live, called Ibo Point. My grandmother told us that there were ghosts around the boat landing. She said they rattled their chains. And they sang. She heard their voices fly up into the night."

Something in my chest snagged on the word *sang*, as if my heart throbbed. It was the opposite sense as when someone lied. Resonance.

The old man knew nothing more. Unfortunately, neither did Google or the maps when I searched for Ibo Point, uprisings, St. Simon's ghost stories, nothing.

I tried working that afternoon, but a voice took over my head. I felt a woman showing me a scene, through her own eyes. In my mind, I saw a man's back, a man she loved. I saw her hand reach for his shoulders, but then I felt as if she were jerked from behind, removing her from the man, while he stood in the water facing the sea.

I felt all of this as if it were happening to me.

I left work, went home, grabbed my personal laptop, drove to my favorite coffee shop, and wrote.

More details came. Splashing, shouting, then the woman standing on the shore, her shame at not being in the water with her man. I felt her mouth closed, forced silence.

I thought back to those nights when Mason and I channeled characters for his short stories and remembered Mason saying, "Some characters won't let me go. They're *real.*"

When I finished, I sent the story to Stefaney, clarifying, "I made it up, it's fiction, but this woman wouldn't leave me alone."

Several years later, Stefaney called. "Honey, you're not going to believe this. Your story about the Mermaid Goddess at Ibo Point has been proven true. The woman talking to you in your head was real."

EIGHTEEN

ONE PART OF me couldn't believe what Stefaney was saying. Another part of me acknowledged that when I leaned into what might seem inexplicable from the outside, my internal compass nudged me toward what did make sense.

On one passage from Africa to Georgia in 1803, the captured humans on board vowed to never step foot on American soil as enslaved people. When the ship pulled into the landing, chained though they were, they jumped in the water and sang, "Mami Wata brought us here. Mami Wata will take us home."

The ghost story was true. There *were* ghosts at Ibo Point who rattled their chains and sang. Maybe ghosts and their stories weren't mere sillies after all.

And Stefaney's intention bowl exercise wasn't useless, even though I didn't know what to wish for.

I plodded along one painstaking billable hour at a time, waiting on the Big Case to go to trial, yet increasingly needing to quit my job. The argumentative chatter in my head only grew louder.

*Where are you going to work next? How will you pay the mortgage? Fine, Smarty Pants, sell the house, but you still have to pay rent somewhere, and this town is dang expensive. You have a great team of colleagues and the most interesting cases around. You're just going to walk away from a good gig? What the hell do you **want**, anyway?*

And my personal favorite: *It's not going to get any better than what you already have. The grass won't be greener, chick-a-dee.*

My anxiety skyrocketed over nothing and everything. On days I didn't go into the office, I couldn't even drive down the street where it was located.

I knew enough about anxiety and how my brain operated to know that I was nearing a breaking point. I knew I had to leave the firm. I knew I wanted to love my work and feel like I was growing toward something purposeful. That's all I knew.

That's when I heard the dog pad down the hallway outside my office at the law firm and misshapen dark objects, like a piano hurtling through the ceiling, fell into my peripheral vision.

With the visions, I reacted as any sane person would. I involuntarily jerked away, which was fine when I was by myself, but not in a conference room with colleagues. Sheesh.

Other than the visions, I had no physical symptoms. After many tests, in 2008, I was diagnosed with atypical migraines, caused by a hyperactive optical nerve, likely triggered by stress.

No shock there. And no immediate end to the work stress in sight.

Two very long years later, the Big Case went to trial in the winter and spring of 2010.

Mr. Perfect and I listed the house for sale, and I awarded myself four weeks off from work. I rented an apartment in Buenos Aires for the month of May and looked forward to exploring the city by myself and writing.

I needed to stay at the firm until the house sold, but it was suddenly no big deal now that I felt the future arriving. I willed myself into believing that I would soon be finally, fully free.

Right before I left for Buenos Aires, I planned to meet a male pal at the movies on the evening of Easter Sunday. It was definitely, most assuredly not a date. He was also going through a divorce, and Mr. Perfect and I had been mutual friends with him for nearly 15 years.

When I woke up that morning, apparently still half asleep, my foot slipped on the top step of my long flight of hardwood stairs and down I went, tumbling like a sack of potatoes until I hit the bottom. I didn't break anything, but barely managed to crawl back to bed where I stayed until it was time for the movie.

As I drove up to the theater, my pal was already waiting outside. Good Lord, have mercy, he was *gorgeous.* It's like he was glowing. How did I not notice that before?

We had easily talked into the night on multiple, previous occasions about everything under the sun. I knew he was adventurous, open-minded, and I'd known him forever, long enough that I trusted him with every fiber in my being. Until that moment, he'd been a Pal.

Suddenly, I saw a fire horse.

I wondered if I'd hit my head on the fall earlier that morning and either knocked myself senseless or finally woke up.

I hobbled out of the car and pretended like my eyes weren't bulging out of my head. For the entire movie, my hands shook and all the hair on my arms stood on end.

After the movie, Fire Horse said, "When my divorce is finalized, I'd like to ask you on a proper date. If that's ok?"

I tried not to let my handbag slide out of my sweaty palms. "Yeah, I'd like that."

If I had called Mom that evening, I would have sounded exactly like she did when she called me after she first met my stepfather, John. I didn't call her though, because we both wouldn't have our divorces settled until that summer, and I had four weeks in Argentina in front of me.

At the beginning of May, Fire Horse took me to the airport, refusing to take my Buenos Aires phone number. "You need to go without still thinking about people from home."

During that month, the migraines and their intrusive visions stopped. The nagging voice in my head moved out. My anxiety transmuted itself into creative energy.

Fire Horse was the first person I saw when I returned to the United States. We eloped that December.

⁘

The Fire Horse is a sign in the Chinese Zodiac. They are independent thinkers, uncommonly intelligent, charismatic and quick-witted, enthusiastic about life, and energetic.

My particular Fire Horse is also an expert space holder. He doesn't care what mistakes and flaws you show up to the table harboring. He cares deeply that you are entirely, authentically you, weaknesses, strengths, dreams, and failures. He isn't afraid of pushing buttons, with the intention that you see yourself as you are and, hopefully, get a big laugh out of it.

When people asked why we got married, I said, "Because I have more freedom to be myself with him than without him. If I come home and say I want to dye my hair blue, he'll drive me to the beauty store. If I want to run off to the circus, he'll say, sure, let's talk about it."

Unsurprisingly, he understood that working at the law firm was driving me toward a nervous breakdown. I needed to do something else. Life is short, let's go!

The day the house sold, I gave my notice at the firm, and Fire Horse bought me the blue hair dye. I was finally connected enough with myself to be in a full Heart, Brain, Body, and Soul relationship like this one.

⚜

Shortly thereafter, Dad's sister, my aunt Jill, died unexpectedly.

Losing Jill was a blow for everyone. For Dad, she was the only person who shared his childhood experiences.

After a very traditional funeral, everyone gathered at Jill's house. Dad burst into the living room. "Seance!" his voice boomed.

"Yep, time for the seance," agreed my cousin Martha, Jill's daughter.

Jill's other daughter, Barbara, voiced what we were all thinking. "Mom would not approve. Not a good idea, folks."

Dad said, "Too bad. Set up a card table and gather 'round."

I looked at Fire Horse, trying to discern if he had already identified the closest exit. But he rubbed his hands together and said, "Finally, the fun part!"

No one in the modern generation knew how to cobble together a seance.

"For crying out loud, has no one watched a ghost movie?" Dad asked. "Sit in a circle and hold hands. Chant. Call in the Great Beyond. It can't be that difficult."

"You lead it then, Dad," I suggested.

"I disrupt the spirit channels or something." He flitted his hand around his head. "I'm going outside." That was the first I heard of

Dad having any experience that led him to believe he disrupted "spirit channels," whatever that meant. A good half of the funeral party high-tailed it out to the driveway with Dad and the cooler of beer and wine.

Another cousin took charge and picked Martha and a few other relatives to sit at the table. The remainder of us plopped onto the surrounding sofa and seats.

"We need a grounding force," she said. She looked around the room. Her eyes landed on Fire Horse. "You, come here."

Sitting in curiosity to observe something-off-the-wall is one thing, but getting yanked right in the middle of it, in a brand new family, can stretch a person. I hoped my poor husband didn't want an annulment before we got back home.

To my relief, he was game and joined the table.

A hush fell over the room, for all of thirty seconds. Impatient as ever, Dad burst in. "Anything happen?"

Martha said, "We just got started. Jesus, Uncle Jack. Quiet down."

"Y'all are a no-good bunch of amateurs," he said. Dad could say things with a straight face and grumbly voice, yet his words sounded light and funny.

He raised his right arm, palm open toward the ceiling, closed his eyes, and portrayed his best version of a TV evangelist. "I HEREBY CALL IN THE SPIRITS OF THE GREAT BEYOND! I COMMAND THEE TO ENTER AND MAKE YOUR PRESENCE KNOOOOOWWWNNN." His voice dropped on the last word.

Dad opened his eyes. I tried not to giggle. Bossing around spirits who had ascended to a higher existence didn't seem the best way to go.

Five seconds later, Dad had enough. "I'm going back outside. Like I said, I disrupt the channels."

The ten or so of us who remained around the living room once again fell into a meditation. Minutes passed, enough to fall into a much-needed relaxation.

Then Martha snored. She was so exhausted, she fell asleep sitting straight up at the seance table.

We all jolted back to the present. "Well, that's enough of that," one cousin said.

Martha cried out, "Mom!" I followed her gaze out the closest window, where a beautiful butterfly danced. "That's Mom," Martha repeated. "She sent us that butterfly."

We disbanded the seance and grabbed food and drinks. The whole family, even those who ventured back inside from the driveway, took turns admiring the butterfly that hovered outside the window for the remainder of the afternoon.

When Martha returned home, she saw a similar butterfly in her backyard for days.

"A butterfly," Dad said when we were back at the hotel. "No flickering lights. No thunder booms, no lightning bolts. Just a butterfly. Hmph."

Dad called a few weeks later. "I've felt Jill around in the evening, checking on me. You think I'm just making that up because I want her around?"

"No, Daddy. Not at all."

"I wonder if she did send that butterfly. That would be more like her than rattling the house to the ground."

⌘

I can't say where the first two years went after I stopped practicing law at the firm. I started writing a novel, fictionalizing Dad's side of the family, framed by the murders of Della and her husband. But mainly, I think I slept, fatigued from the previous decade.

In 2015, I had the option to practice law again on a very interesting, large, white-collar fraud case, on a contract basis, which is similar to consulting. I worked with a team out of Florida and New York, who I'd known from the Big Case.

This time, however, I got paid by the hour. No billable hour expectations. I could work from home, ten hours a week or a hundred. Up to me.

That structure made all the difference in the world to my mindset and gave me plenty of time to write, live a full life, and of course, walk the dogs, while working as part of a familiar team again.

I listened in on a conference call with our accounting expert one afternoon, when Grandma walked through my living room wall.

Grandma had been on her last breath for a few years. That hadn't kept her from flirting with Fire Horse.

The last time we visited, Grandma was fast asleep in her recliner next to Pops in their apartment at an assisted living facility. Fire Horse walked in, Grandma bolted upright, tilted her head sideways, and smiled. "Well, hellllllooooooo, handsome!" I hadn't heard that sing-song voice out of Grandma in years.

On the afternoon when her essence walked into my living room, it came as no surprise that Grandma had passed. I couldn't see her body, but what I sensed was precisely like what might be depicted in a movie: a clear, gel-like form walking through the wall.

It was as if her discarnate soul still had the substance and density of a human body, because she tripped over my dog sleeping at my feet. The dog grunted like someone kicked her. I heard Grandma's voice, inside my head, say, "Oh, what a pretty dog."

Grandma circled behind me, and I caught a whiff of scents swirling around her. I smelled her kitchen from when I was little and the carpet on the floor that had been replaced when I still crawled on it, memories long forgotten.

She ascended up, to my right, and I heard joyous cries of women, both hers and her sisters, as if Grandma walked into a surprise party. In my mind's eye, I saw a portal of light open in my ceiling. Grandma flew toward it, ecstatic, her density expanding like glitter blown in the wind.

I couldn't help but feel thrilled, an irrepressible grin plastered to my face. She was 97 years old when she died. Time to party with her sisters.

I checked the clock. I wanted to match it with her actual time of death.

Sure enough, within the minute, my uncle George called in on the other line. The accounting call was wrapping up, so I took the call.

"Mother's passed. Just now." His voice sounded so heavy, I had to gag myself from spurting, *She's so happy! It's a party now! It's SO FREAKING AWESOME!*

⸺⸺⸺

Pops wanted Fire Horse to drive him to the funeral. Those two related to each other from the get-go, and Pops showed it by simply saying, "He's a good driver," or "He's good to me."

During the ride, Pops said, "She left me." He was mad Grandma died first, as that was never the plan. He figured he still had a good way to go before life ran out of him, and he was mad about that too.

People loved Grandma, and there were a lot of folks in the community who attended her funeral. It's not like anyone wanted her back in her aged state, but her passing was the end of an era. No one was ready to hear about Grandma's after-party.

At the funeral, Pops motioned toward me. "Hey, hey," he said to get my attention. Pops was hard of hearing, and the worse his hearing became, the quieter his voice dropped.

I leaned into him so I could hear, and he pointed around the room. "All these people are here for her, not me. You won't see these people at my funeral."

"No, Pops," I argued. "They're here for you."

He shook his head.

My joviality over Grandma's After-party outed itself on the dark side. I said, "You're right. A lot of these folks are in worse shape than you. All of us are going to die before you do. No one's going to be left to attend your funeral. Sorry."

He pursed his lips and shook his head again.

⁂

For almost the next two years, Pops received more attention than he had his entire life. Grandma had always been the cheery face, the extroverted one, a natural magnet, while Pops was nonverbal, methodical. He internalized stress and expressed emotions through grouchiness. For the first time, nurses, physical therapists, the family, everyone fawned over Pops.

He loved it.

He was still mad at Grandma for dying first. I tried telling him that maybe she was getting things ready for him.

He answered, "Don't lie to me."

On one visit, he told me, "She really left me this time. She's no longer upstairs." He pointed to the ceiling. "I'm not crazy. I know there's no actual upstairs in this building. I mean the other upstairs. She hasn't visited me in a long time. She's gone."

I decided to tell him about what I experienced when she first passed. He took it in and nodded.

"Pops, if Grandma's with her sisters, do you really want all of these women right here in the room with you?"

I asked this for two reasons.

One, he seemed comforted by the idea that Grandma was with her sisters instead of Nowhere To Be Found or Gone From Him Forever.

"She would be with her sisters," he said.

Two, my cousin and I had recently visited Pops at the same time, and while we ended up ignoring him, our conversation devolved into lots of high pitched, feminine laughter.

Pops had shaken his finger at us. "HEY, HEY. STOP HOOTING." Like scolded teenagers, we tried to giggle into our hands.

I asked him, "Can you imagine all the hooting if Grandma brought the party with her sisters down here?"

He made a face.

A while later, he said, "Hey, hey." I leaned into his recliner. "What if I don't know where to go?"

I took a moment. I knew he was asking about the afterlife.

Pops had memorized maps, streets, routes, and the layout of the land before he went on any trip, so he'd feel confident on the journey. He wanted a plan.

I didn't have an answer, but it didn't feel right to offer platitudes like, "Trust! You'll know what to do!"

I tried anyway. "Grandma will be there to meet you."

"What if she's not?"

I suddenly remembered that Pops loved to swim. Rivers, oceans, lakes, didn't matter.

"Jump in the river, Pops. If you don't know where to go, jump in the river."

He nodded. He had a plan, one that made sense to him.

⁊⁊⁖⁖⁖⁖⁊⁊

In the summer of 2017, I heard Pops' voice in my head, "What if it's time?"

I assumed I was simply thinking of our last conversation, replaying it in my mind. But suddenly, I remembered a dream from the night before. Grandma had visited and said, "It's time."

I paused watering the plants in the courtyard of our home and jerked upright. In case what I heard was actually Pops talking telepathically, I answered in my head, "Pops, jump in the river. Grandma's here."

I ran inside and told Fire Horse, "I just remembered Grandma came to me in a dream last night. We have to get in the car. Right now. Pops is going swimming."

Like Grandma, Pops had been fading in and out for a long time. This time felt different.

Uncle George, who took on the mantle of Bearer of Bad News, called when we were still several hours away from West Virginia. "Pops fell again, and this time —"

"We're already on the way," I said. I hoped we'd make it.

After paying the toll at the turnpike booth about 30 minutes out from where Pops had been taken to the hospital, the driver's side window would not roll back up. Rain started pouring into the car sideways. "I think the window fell off track," Fire Horse observed calmly.

We were down to one cat and one dog, both of whom went with us wherever we did. So when we arrived at the hospital, I ran inside to find Pops while Fire Horse kept the pets from leaping out the window to follow me.

It made no sense to him to wait helplessly in the car all night with the animals and a litterbox, so he unscrewed the driver's side door in the rain, lifted the window back into place with one hand, jammed the screwdriver under it to hold it in place with the other, then ran inside to join me.

Pops had always wanted Fire Horse to be the one to help him in and out of his chair or the car. Pops trusted Fire Horse wouldn't let him fall. If Pops was going to die just then, both of us needed to be there.

We took turns sleeping between a chair and a cot in Pops' room, relieving my uncle George who'd been with Pops for months previously.

The following morning, Mom called and said she was taking the earliest flight she could get, and other family members hit the road toward West Virginia.

Within a few moments of talking to Mom, the air felt still. Fire Horse and I met eyes, and we nodded to each other. We surrounded Pops on either side of the bed, and held Pops' hands and arms.

I saw, in my mind's eye, the same portal of light open up in the ceiling that I'd seen when Grandma passed. I felt Pops' relatives and Grandma peeking in. I felt the same profound comfort as I had when Grandma's time came.

I said, "Pops, everyone is here for you. If you're ready, you can go now."

I became of two minds at once. Did I say that because I wanted him to know that all the family was heading to the hospital for him, so he felt cared for and safe? Or did I really refer to all those who'd passed before him and were ready to escort him out of Earth?

In that instant, he stopped breathing. I guess I meant both.

After a few moments, Fire Horse looked at me and mouthed with his signature piercing humor, "You just killed your grandfather."

I mouthed back, "He only felt safe to go because you were here."

⁕

Pops was wrong about his funeral. Just as many people came to say goodbye to him as had attended Grandma's service.

At the end, everyone filed out, abandoning Pops in a casket, in a strange place, in the hands of strangers. How long would he be left alone?

My thoughts were irrational. Clearly, the entire cemetery staff was nearby to execute the next steps of the burial. But I could not make myself leave, even after the rain started again. Pops was my first best friend. I reached for him when I was nine months old and never stopped.

My uncle Jerry held me as I sobbed. "I can't leave him here all by himself."

He said, "Honey, you don't have to. We can stay as long as you want." I remembered Pops doing the same for Nan, Shaun's mother, at his funeral.

Fire Horse and I stayed until the bitter end. We watched the undertakers lower his casket into the ground and muddied our hands and clothes throwing dirt on the grave.

With Pops settled safely next to Grandma, I could leave. It was now truly the end of an era.

⁕

On the ride back to South Carolina, I fell asleep in the passenger's seat, pondering who actually killed Grandma Hattie's sister, Della.

Around midnight, I jolted awake. "Hey!" I startled Fire Horse from his highway hypnosis. "I'm going to tell ghost stories for a living. I love ghost stories. I've collected a ton of strange, true stories about Charleston. Why don't I write them down and entertain a crowd with them?"

For years, Charleston was the top tourist destination in the country, and in some years, the world. Making money through any facet of tourism was a no-brainer. Fire Horse agreed.

Within moments, an entire business model was clear to me, as if it had already been written, and all I needed to do was arrive at that page in the book. "I'm going to start at the jail and the graveyards. I have to get back inside the jail."

⚬⚬⚬

A few months earlier, Fire Horse surprised me with a night, just the two of us, inside the Old City Jail downtown. The idea wasn't to get a good night's sleep. Hopefully, paranormal activity would keep us up all night.

The gothic, fortress-style building was designed to scare the hell out of anyone passing by. It had long been closed as a jail and became a haunted attraction for ghost tours and paranormal investigations.

I refused to take a tour of the Jail or hear anything about the history of the building before we spent the night inside. I was annoyed by my erratic blips with the spirit world. The blips worked when they worked, such as when Grandma and Pops each passed and the Ibo Point story. But outside of those limited scenarios, the blips made me look and feel like a kook, forcing me to chalk up my experiences to "atypical migraines" or "just a dream."

I determined that I would go into the Jail cold and either come out with an undeniable encounter, preferably one I could verify in the history books, or the spirit world was going to have to leave me alone once and for all. I would resort to using their voices for fiction and supernatural storytelling, and I wouldn't have to worry about whether I was making up the encounter or whether it was "real."

The cells had been removed for scrap metal in World War II, so what was left of the crumbling building were the concrete, architectural bones, three floors of large, open rooms that felt like ballrooms, with fireplaces in every corner. Little lighting and no furniture or creature comforts, to be sure.

After exploring the building in the dark, and both of us seeing the same shadows move across rooms where no one but us inhabited, we retreated to a room that felt more airy than the others, welcoming even. We lit candles, and I felt guided to leave water in the hall.

I'm more of a glamper than a camper, so Fire Horse brought an air mattress to lounge on and a pump with two fully charged batteries. Both batteries lost their charge immediately.

The building was a damp icebox in the winter, so even though we didn't intend to sleep, we huddled in our sleeping bags on the concrete floor for warmth.

When we inevitably dozed off, the spirit world started yammering.

Frank stood behind my head and chattered incessantly. I could see his round face, see that he was a prison guard, and I could see his mouth moving.

When I tried too hard to hear precisely what he said, I jerked awake. Ugh!

Which meant I woke up Fire Horse. "What is it?! Did you see something?"

I shrugged, not wanting to wake myself up further. Apparently, I needed to be in a half-sleep state. After several rounds, I asked Fire Horse, "Can you hear it? All the banging?"

He didn't.

For the rest of the night, I heard Frank and various banging and raucous sounds when I fell into a mild dream state, which simultaneously seemed like I was falling backward in time, hearing noises from a jail a century earlier.

I repeatedly jolted awake, harshly rammed back into the present. Silence surrounded us. It felt as if Fire Horse was there to anchor me, ground me in the present, so I could drift into other sensory perceptions.

By the time the sky lightened, I said, "It's Frank."

"Who's Frank?"

"Maybe I was dreaming."

"Lie back down and ask him who he is."

"He's a guard, and he wants to tell his side of the story."

Through articles, a book, and a photograph, I identified Frank as a guard in the Jail who was fired by his boss in 1935. Afterward, Frank insisted on telling everyone who would listen, including the newspaper, that his boss wrongfully terminated him. He wanted his side of the story told.

The Jail experience was phenomenal. I set my intent, went in, communicated with a spirit, and verified as fact what I'd sensed. I needed to get back there.

⊛

After Pops' funeral, when we returned to Charleston, I walked into Bulldog Tours and asked for a job. Bulldog had the rights to give tours in multiple historic properties, a graveyard and the Jail.

A few weeks later, I had my own private key into a graveyard and the passcode to the security system at the Jail. I rediscovered my fourth-grade love for telling ghost stories, particularly to kids visiting Charleston on school trips. I felt more at home prowling around Charleston after dark in gothic attire than I'd ever felt in a law firm in my fancy suit and heels.

In the middle of one such tour on a narrow street next to the graveyard, with a row of wide-eyed children looking at me, Mr. Perfect hurried past.

I sensed he was mortified seeing his former law partner of a wife now peddling ghost tales to grade-schoolers. I wished he could see something more heartfelt and significant in the moment, but I had to let that wish go. More pressing, I needed to finish the story and send those kids to bed with their imaginations blown open to the moon.

Overall, I became obsessed with the streets at night, the shadows flickering in the gas lanterns, and primarily the Jail. I felt called to the Jail like a woman possessed.

I meditated in there every day, morning, noon, or night. I had no direction to my meditation other than to sit in silence, open my awareness, and allow the spirit world to communicate with me, if they chose, and if not, I just sat still.

The Jail taught me how to read space, and how to use my body to receive sensations for the mere purpose of the experience itself, without judgment or the need to be "right." I stopped worrying about whether I could verify the communicator in the history books and allowed my imagination free reign.

I had already trained the logical, practical side of my brain through law school and a decade of law practice. So why not set my mind totally free?

I worked through many fears sitting in that dusty, ruinous fortress. I grew comfortable in the dark, with the building, with the nudges and inexplicable stirrings around me in there, and mainly, I grew comfortable with myself.

During one meditation, I saw a clearing in a forest. For days, that's all I saw, though I felt someone approaching in the woods, growing closer to my awareness in each session. I intuited that I needed to keep sitting in this clearing versus allowing my brain to go nuclear and demanding that whomever approached needed to move faster.

I was shocked to find that the person approaching was Jason.

Suddenly, he was right there, as close to me in that moment as he had been in physical life. My heart burst open. Energy pulsed through my chest, as if a long-buried casket had broken apart. Golden light poured in.

I heard his voice in my head. "Open your heart. More. Love enough to risk loss all over again, even a tragic loss. That's how much you have to allow love in. Don't hold back from love."

I thought I already had an open heart. But in that moment, my capacity to allow love exploded exponentially. If I thought I loved Fire Horse before, I really loved him now. Same with the cat, the dog, the flowers in the garden, humanity itself.

The message burrowed even deeper. I also needed to allow myself to love the activities and things I loved, to want what I wanted, dream wherever the dream led, no matter how bizarre or outside the lines the desire bled.

Holding back wasn't going to stop future losses and failures, or lessen the pain arising from them. Might as well love large and dream big along the way.

⚜

The next time I logged into my laptop, a Facebook ad scrolled across my screen. I clicked through and met my first psychic teacher. She was grounded, deeply intelligent, and authentic.

Then my mediumship teacher appeared. Then the next mediumship mentor arrived, and the next.

Each one, right on time.

Lo and behold, after years of searching and Googling, yearning and healing, the teachers appeared.

ENCORE

T HE PLAN I had of telling ghost stories and leading paranormal investigations began to include the idea that perhaps every now and again, someone would surreptitiously enter my backyard through a garden gate, and I'd give them a psychic or mediumship reading. Ha.

My first mediumship mentor gave me an exercise where I had to do one reading a day for thirty days, preferably on strangers.

This exercise was deceptively difficult and exhausting. Practicing on strangers meant I had to open my mouth and say out loud, "I'm a psychic and a medium," without turning fifty shades of red and stuttering. I braced for the world to roll its eyes.

Instead, Mom sent me all of her friends. Dad sent lawyer buddies. Friends of friends sent me their friends. I was blown away by the outpouring of YES that bombarded me from every direction.

Within the course of the year, way sooner than I ever imagined, I gave up the ghost tours and paranormal investigations. The first thirty sessions turned into twenty or thirty a month, then groups, then larger groups, and the Travel Channel booked me as their paranormal expert for an entire season on the show, *True Terror with Robert Englund.*

Along the way, a friend who's a psychologist mused that while some healers work slowly over time to lead people to transformation, our psychic mediumship session delivered catharsis in forty-five minutes.

"I've been called cathartic before," I laughed, although this time, it wasn't something I felt burdened by or ashamed of.

Dracula wasn't done with me yet.

Several years earlier, Fire Horse and I traveled to Transylvania, Romania with Dacre Stoker, a descendant of Bram Stoker, the man who created the perfect villain a/k/a my personal guide, Dracula.

Dacre has spent decades uncovering truths behind the novel and his famous ancestor.

Until this point, I focused on the story of *Dracula*, not its creator. So right when life can't get any stranger, it does.

In 2021, Dacre had the idea of including me in a joint presentation of his research, with a Halloween twist. He proposed that I present the portion of his research that revealed Bram Stoker's attraction to the supernatural and what was termed as "fringe" sciences in the late 1800s, such as telepathy, mediumship, and mesmerism. Thanks to my great-grandparents and Uncle Charlie, I understood Bram's pull toward psychic and mediumship phenomena and the spiritualism of the time.

I also learned that Bram was a lawyer. He loved the theater, and happily quit law to manage the popular Lyceum Theater in London. In the off-time he barely had, he wrote a novel creating an irresistible dark force, weaving in the enduring mysteries that exist at the edges of our consciousness. *Dracula*.

The more I learned about Bram Stoker, the more I admired and resonated with him.

The Charleston Library Society hosted our event. The institution is one of the oldest libraries in the country, housed in an appropriately grand Beaux Arts-style building, with two-storey flying ceilings, marble floors, and a grand piano just next to the stage. Its members are made up of professors, businesspeople, and many of my former law colleagues.

I couldn't believe I had the opportunity to stand on a stage with Dacre Stoker and discuss my favorite topics. A problem remained, however.

When I first approached the Library Society about the event, I had hyped up Dacre, my degree in literature, and the fact that I was a former lawyer.

I left out my current job. I worried the director would throw me out the front door if I brought the words "psychic" and "medium" into those hallowed halls.

As dress rehearsal approached, I asked Fire Horse, "What if they say that I can't introduce myself as a psychic medium?"

He replied, "Everyone is fine with you. You're the only one making it weird."

"I'll be standing in front of my former professors and a bunch of lawyers! They're going to think I've lost my marbles."

I gulped down bowling balls of fear and hoped for the best. I felt mildly more at ease when I saw the library had placed a skeleton sitting upright on the piano bench, boney hands on the keys.

On Halloween weekend of 2021, for two evenings, I appeared next to Dacre in front of nearly 100 people each night, including folks I'd known in earlier careers.

I was introduced as a psychic medium, a lawyer, a professional performer, and a Dracula expert, someone with interests akin to Bram Stoker himself.

I was not escorted from the building. Instead, we were greeted with a big fat YES in the form of a thrilled audience.

At the end of the second performance, as we were leaving the stage, the skeleton fell over onto the keyboard of the piano. A loud, dissonant BUUUUUUNNNNGGG echoed through the great hall, startling us all out of our skins for a second.

It was perfect.

◦ ◦ ◦

Every time I talked about a group session or a reading, Dad asked, "Did any spirits show up?"

"Yes. No one would come see me if they didn't."

"How do you get them to show up?"

"Dad, they never fail us. We have to learn how to see and hear them and take what we get."

"Jill and old Judge Abbott have been around me lately." Judge Abbott was Dad's long-deceased legal mentor. "What do you think they want? Can you ask them?"

"You're the one feeling them. You ask."

"Hmph." He chewed on a cigar stub. "I sure do miss them."

"Maybe they're letting you know they're around for you."

Not much longer after that, Dad fell and broke his hip. Calm as ever under fire, he called while he waited on the ambulance, like it was no big deal.

He asked if it would be too much trouble to pick him up from the hospital. I was more than happy to be there for him.

When he came out of surgery, he said, "Kid, the funniest thing happened when I was under. You're never going to believe who I saw. YOUR grandmother."

"Hattie? Your mom?"

"NO! Grandma Kitty! Your mama's mama. I saw her clear as day sitting at the end of my bed. Out of all the people, I couldn't believe she was the one checking on me."

Dad and I had the same dark humor, so I said, "You must have thought you ended up in the wrong place for a minute." He laughed.

Dad never came home again. He soon fell into respiratory failure and remained good and dead for minutes before he was revived and ventilated.

He was moved to the closest ICU that had a bed available, which was two hours away from any family. I slept in his room, then moved into a hotel, and wore the same clothes for days on end.

After four days of ups and downs, he popped back. When he saw me, his eyes grew wide. "Good Lord, Kid, you look like shit. What the hell happened to you?"

I laughed and filled him in. Dad knew he had died and wanted to tell me all about it.

"It was amazing! I saw a door, and it's so easy, you just shoot right through it and you're on the other side!" He sounded tremendously excited. "I saw all of my life laps," he said and drew horizontal lines in the air with his finger. "Wait, we call them timelines here. I could see I'm at the end of this one," he said with no concern or sadness. "It's a miracle."

He looked at me, suddenly solemn. "Wait, are you dead too? I'm so sorry you had to die too."

"No, Daddy, we're both alive."

"Well, shit. I know I'm alive."

"I mean on Earth. We're both here on Earth."

He shook his head and looked around his room. "Ahhh. I'm in an acclimation area. We're here until I get used to being dead. You can visit me here because of what you do. The medium thing."

Against my better judgment, I argued with him. "No! Daddy, you're alive in your body. We're going to get you out of here! You're healthy!"

He wrinkled his brow and looked around again. "Nope. I'm dead. They'll come to get me shortly. I've been gone for a while. Did they already have my funeral?"

I gave up arguing and decided to meet him wherever he thought he was. Besides, his words were riveting, and he showed no signs of distress. In fact, he was more at peace, more innocently enthusiastic than I'd ever seen him.

"No funeral yet."

"I miss my friends, my community, my compadres. But I don't want them to die in order to visit me here."

Dad started to fall asleep and suggested I leave for the night. "Go to sleep, Kid. Take care of yourself. I'm okay. I'll just wait here until they come get me." He waved his fingers at me and smiled. "Too-da-loo."

Dad fell asleep and didn't wake back up.

He gave the best of parting gifts. He told me what he experienced on the other side. He was eager, filled with verve, and ready for his next adventure. When I thought of Dad, my heart burst with joy and love and hope. When I thought of myself and our family, I sunk into heavy sorrow and self-pity.

I remained at his side for a long while. There would never be an easy time to leave.

Then fire alarms went off in the entire hospital.

My skeptical mind weighed the coincidence. But the bigger part of me thought, *Dad*. Never short on drama, demanding physical signs and clear instructions from the Great Beyond.

Don't you know what to do in a fire drill, Kid? Get out of the building.

Dad was no longer in that body, and it was time for me to quit crying over him in that room. He was out in the larger universe, and I needed to join him.

He and I both knew we'd keep communicating.

WELCOME TO THE
GREEN ROOM
✸

I BELIEVE THAT up to 95% of all long-term psychic, mediumship, creative, and artistic development is continued *self work and personal development*. That means perhaps only 5% is learning and perfecting specific skills.

In the physical performing world, that 5% is called "tits, splits, and tricks." You can certainly get by on tits and splits alone, but not forever, and not if you want to be evocative and authentic.

So I constructed a Green Room where we can make mischief with the thorny, sticky, majestic 95% part of ourselves.

✸

The Green Room is a backstage area where performers prepare before a show or crash and party afterwards.

It's dedicated in-between space, the haven between backstage chaos and onstage lights and action, and the crash pad after show time before re-entering the outside world.

In this book, the Green Room chapters offer liminal space, a sanctuary between my experiences in the memoir and your experiences playing with these pages. Here, transformation can simmer, your imagination can streak through the universe, and your Heart and Soul can boogie on down — because truly, no one's watching.

Just as every theater has its ghost light — that single, bare bulb left illuminated on an empty stage to prevent accidents and keep resident Spirits company — the Green Room provides Ghost Lights, Program Notes, and exercises to address the issues and themes raised in the corresponding story chapters.

Through each chapter, you'll discover vignettes, practical implementation strategies, reflections, deep-dive questions, research from diverse fields, and sacred practices designed to help you:

✷ deepen your connection with yourself and therefore with others, both incarnate and discarnate;

✷ strengthen your courage to find and follow your desires, wherever they may lead, and

✷ along the way, hone your own intuitive abilities as you follow the roadmap to awaken to the unseen world around us and become more comfortable walking with the unknown.

Ghost Lights to
Illuminate the Green Room

1. No one has access to the ultimate truth. Within the Green Room, there will be no dogma and no finite conclusions, even as your brain craves and demands certainty.

2. Try to accept that there are ideas, concepts, and realities that are unknown and unknowable. That's where Magic and Miracles live.

3. Take what resonates, leave the rest. This is true of any exploration of self and the Great Beyond.

4. Recognize when you belittle your imagination. It happens. More than we care to admit. Imagination is the bridge between our everyday reality and the land of Magic and Miracles.

5. Allow yourself grace. There is no right or wrong way to do you, boo.

Terms of Art in the Green Room Chapters

1. **Clairs = Clear**

Our "clairs" are what we bundle together and think of as our Sixth Sense. Derogatively, they are lumped into the age-old insult, "It's just your imagination." We have a lot more spidey senses available up there in our Imagination than we might expect.

* Clairvoyance = clear sight
* Clairaudience = clear hearing
* Clairsentience = clear physical feeling
* Clairempathy = clear emotional feeling
* Clairsalience = clear smelling
* Claircognizance = clear knowing
* Clairgustance = clear tasting
* Clairtangency = clear touching

Experiencing our clairs in an "objective" manner refers to times when we see, hear, etc. something happening in the 3-D world, outside of our minds, yet most of the world cannot see and hear it. Such as seeing a ghost, or hearing a voice when no one's physically there.

Experiencing our clairs in a "subjective" manner refers to when we have experiences that remain safely tucked in our minds.

2. **Psychic:**
    a. Most people use the word to indicate future-telling or fortune-telling. Or it indicates someone is reading body language, facial expressions, or current thoughts.
    b. For our purposes, however, "psychic" means receiving information, without words, from someone's Soul, while they are still incarnated. When I give readings, I'm reading the client's Higher Self, on a Soul level, not their body language, facial expressions, or current thoughts. Some folks call this type of reading a Soul Reading.

3. **Mediumship:** communicating with the souls of discarnate beings, including deceased people and animals, and spirit guides.

4. **The Divine:** God, Source, Spirit, Higher Self, the Universe.

5. **Catwalk:** the interlocking scaffolding in the rafters of a theater, over the stage, the orchestra pit, and portions of the audience, where lighting, sound, and sets are hung. The Catwalk provides the broadest perspective of *everything* happening in the theater. For us, the Catwalk will serve as our Imagination Bridge, for those times we need to climb upward and play with seeing ourselves and circumstances from a different perspective.

6. **Witch Tips:** Guidance that's mystical and mischievous, practical and true. In this context, "witch" does not refer to the use of witchcraft or paganism.

7. **Dose of Magic:** Your cue to do an exercise. I highly suggest *doing* the exercises, rather than merely passively absorbing them.

Let's go!

CHAPTER ONE
PROGRAM NOTES
Imaginary Friends &
Memories of Past Lives

❧

C HILDREN HAVE WACKY perceptions because they aren't yet indoctrinated into Society's Accepted Notions of Life on Earth. Very young children haven't yet been shamed into keeping their mouths shut. Accordingly, this chapter in the story forces us to dive into Children's Woo right out of the gate.

❧

Ghost Light 1: Folks can start to experience supernatural sights, sounds, and phenomena at any age in life.

While mine started as a child, and I didn't outgrow them, please know that it's NEVER too late to join this carnival!

A friend of mine lived a normal and very busy life, without much deep reflection on the Great Beyond. At age forty, he decided to try one session of Reiki energy healing to see for himself what all the hype was about.

He expected to relax during the session, and instead saw lights, heard sounds, felt physical waves of energy cascading over him, and then sensed the undeniable presence of specific loved ones in his life who had previously passed away. All as he lay there on the massage table, trying to work in a nap! It was a life-changing experience for him.

There are no rules regarding time or life phases as to when these "awakenings" in our perception occur. I hope we have realizations and awakenings throughout our entire lives, little bubbles of truth, expanding and deepening our wisdom.

Sometimes, they come in with trumpets and fanfare. Sometimes, they arrive on a whisper.

Most of the time, they are inconvenient. We can grow into these truths, or periods of awakening, and they become our new normal.

However, truths can disrupt how we perceive our jobs, relationships, friends, even entire communities and lifestyles. Sheesh. Other people might not react to the New You with bouquets of butterflies and rainbows.

But who can say no to this carnival when it comes to town? I can't.

Ghost Light 2: Our fun night time experiences as children may have been dismissed by our parents as "just imagination" and therefore, they're harder to remember.

Interestingly, most people don't remember their fun, nighttime experiences as children without parents reminding them. And most parents have forgotten too. Probably because most parents dismiss such experiences in themselves and their children as "just imagination," even when it's clear the child is seeing or interacting with something that's "not there."

Sometimes, clients ask me to read their home when strange phenomena occur around a child, or where the child is happily interacting with nothing.

More times than not, through a mediumship reading, we discover that Grandma, Granddad, a great-grandparent, or relative is the one looking in on the child, like my Aunt Lily checked in on me. The child is interacting with the relative, and the relative is playing with the child.

Even more frequently, that deceased person knew the child before they passed away, although that is not always the case.

Sometimes, then, fog emerges from the back of the parents' memory indicating that they, too, felt naturally and innocently connected with an ancestor or a being like Man-Toy when they were a child. They then ask me, "Am I making this up? Is it possible that . . . ?" Or, "I always felt close to that relative, but I don't remember ever meeting them."

Sound familiar? If so, I get it. I've pooh poohed many of my own observations, discarding them as fanciful, imaginary.

Dose of Magic:
Reflection/Journal Prompt

Let's go back to your early childhood. If you can't or don't want to remember it, feel free to make up an alternative.

To help anchor you into this time period, play for a second. Did you sleep with the light on? Why or why not?

I insisted the light be off. Any monsters lurking in the UnderBed could find me more easily in the light. Duh. In the dark, I could safely hide or crawl out of bed and sneak around the house in the shadows.

Besides, Man-Toy and I could see each other in the dark just fine.

As an adult, when I heard about children having imaginary friends, I would have said I didn't have one. Man-Toy didn't seem like an imaginary friend. He was Man-Toy, a Being in his own right.

Do you recall seeing, feeling, or simply being aware of any imaginative creatures, beings, or even deceased ancestors as a child?

If the question alone immediately caused your mind to blurt out, "Maybe, but," then stop. No "buts." "Buts" indicate rationalization.

Go back to the first tickle. Revisit the question.

Allow the answer to arise without judgment. Let it be hazy. It may take a few days, a few months, maybe even years.

Let's travel further into the past.

Memories and Imaginings of a Previous or Alternate Existence

There's an idea that we incarnate multiple times, each time to learn a lesson or experience a previously undeveloped aspect of ourselves. Even if you never had a past life experience, join me up on the Imagination Catwalk to play.

Of course, past lives can't be "proven" in a manner that would stand up in a court of law or in the Court of Most Common Opinions. That pesky skepticism won't stop us from having fun pondering the notion.

Ghost Light 3: Children may remember past lives or an alternate existence more easily than adults.

Perhaps because children are closer to their previous existence—be it a past life or the life between lives—and don't yet have conditioning to frame the current life, they may be more likely to remember conversations, scenes, and full lives that seem not to exist. They may also be more susceptible to inexplicable night terrors.

You may have heard of the famous and well-documented case of James Leininger who began having night terrors when he was two years old that suggested he was a pilot in World War II. Statements made by young James eventually identified the pilot, the aircraft, the location of a plane crash, and so forth.

The University of Virginia's Division of Perceptual Studies subjected James's case to a rigorous review. The Division focuses on various aspects of consciousness, with some scientists researching reincarnation and children who recall past lives.

The doctors studying young James authored a fascinating abstract, narrowing the evidence to rule out fraud and fantasy and concluding that:

> "The documentation in James's case provides evidence that he had a connection with a life from the past... An understanding of the link between the apparent memories and the emotional and behavioral issues these children experi-

ence may be helpful to families, particularly in situations in which the parents are inclined to dismiss the possibility of a past-life connection.

"Awareness of cases such as James's, ones with documentation of a close agreement between events from a life in the past and memories a current child expresses, may lead the parents to be less likely to discount their children's reports and more able to help them through the experience."[1]

Certainly not all childhood behavioral issues can be chalked up to past life traumas, particularly when a child's current home life is abusive or tumultuous. But employing a broader perspective, as UVA suggested, may be a helpful tool in the box.

Usually by age seven, all past life memories fade back into the subconscious mind for young children.

Ghost Light 4: We don't go backwards in consciousness.

Whoop!

What if...you've never been wiser than you are right now? You've never been braver, you've never been smarter, you've never been witchier than you are Right Now.

Gonna say it again.

You've never had more awareness intuitively, psychologically, emotionally, or mentally than you have Right Now.

I hear a lot of folks claim to be high priestesses, warlocks, oracles, ancient Egyptian rulers, and so forth in past lives. Which may be true, who knows? Not all rulers and magical folk are wise leaders or well-rounded humans living full, productive lives.

---

1   Jim B. Tucker, M.D., (2016). The Case of James Leininger: an American Case of the Reincarnation Type. *Explore, 12* (3), 200–207.

I also hear folks lamenting the loss of being "in tune" with nature or the unseen. Again, that might be true, as most of us no longer live in mere survival mode. We don't need the reptilian portion of our brain to remain hyperactive and overdeveloped, particularly at the expense of rising consciousness and awareness.

In other words, there's no need to yearn for a former glorified version of yourself who's not as badass as you are today.

Here's the good news. If consciousness doesn't go backward, you didn't irrevocably lose your mojo or leave it in a cave in Atlantis. You weren't more magical in any version of the past than you are right now. Hmmmm.

Ghost Light 5: Past life scenarios should not be used as an excuse to spiritually bypass or escape current life problems.

What's the dang point if we can't use past life scenarios as a crutch to excuse our current bad behavior?

The same could be said for unresolved current life issues, traumas, and hurts, right?

Any story about yourself that surfaces in your awareness as a past life memory or as an imaginative alternate life could be used to understand, confront, heal, then change circumstances in your current existence. For example, it's not helpful to tell yourself, "I was a witch in a past life and tortured for it. Therefore, I'm going to hold back from living my full truth now."

The first sentence may be true, but the second sentence shouldn't necessarily follow. There might be very palpable reasons you're holding yourself back that could be healed, such as fears of being seen and heard, a lack of acceptance in your family or relationships, or imposter syndrome. Does it matter whether those fears originated further back than before you were born in this life?

Maybe. Let's play.

When I give readings, I set my intention that a past life scenario will come up only if a pattern of behavior no longer serves the client's best interests and, therefore, needs to move from the shadowy subconscious into the blistering sunlight. Otherwise, a past life scenario is a mere curiosity and will have no transformational impact or connection to the client's current life.

For some of us, it's easier to grasp a pattern in a story that's removed from our current lives. We can view the circumstances from a distance, treating it like fiction. We can see how actions trigger reactions.

We can make parallels between the story and our current lives without getting caught up in overwrought emotions or over-rationalization. Usually, it's also easier for us to feel compassion toward removed, maybe even fictional characters, than it is toward ourselves and loved ones, particularly when we're caught up in a destructive pattern with them.

Think of this as sitting up on the Catwalk, watching the story and choreography unfold down on the stage, while simultaneously witnessing the audience's reaction. So yes, the distance and a story can help reveal a tired old pattern that needs to take a hike.

Ghost Light 6: There are also times when a past life story illuminates a deep desire for something missing in our current lives.

A friend of mine led a client through a past life regression when the woman presented feeling inexplicably blah. During the session, the woman saw herself living in a different city, surrounded by luxurious Victorian and Edwardian furniture and decor. She felt deeply happy in that environment.

Turns out, the woman was highly dissatisfied with her contemporary home, current decor, and possibly even the city where she lived. She hadn't given herself permission, however, to create a different atmosphere for herself, which, in turn, proved to be the tip of the iceberg. There were a lot of accessible, affordable experiences she desired that she wasn't giving herself permission to indulge in.

What if the life this woman envisioned during her session was not a past or alternative life, and instead was the product of a nifty brain trick designed to bring a repressed desire into her conscious awareness?

Does it matter whether she could find her former street address, her former name, and look herself up in the library to prove her previous existence?

I think not. I think it matters that she used the session to live much more fully Right Now. With her pattern identified, if necessary, she could follow up with a therapist to understand and heal why she continued to engage in self-denial.

⁕

I have no idea why I had night terrors of fire and rats. Am I currently scared of fire and possess an aversion to rats? Yes, but I think healthily so.

Neither prevent me from enjoying my fireplace or a campfire. And I employ two cats to keep mice and rats out of the garage.

Dose of Magic:

If your desire for Something More seems inexplicable, explore it. Allow that desire to surface.

For those of you with unexplained alternate-life scenarios rising into your mind, acknowledge the experience rather than trying to seek a conclusive answer about WHY the experience happened. The more you allow yourself to sit with uncertainty, the sooner a pattern of behavior or desire may surface that could be celebrated or healed.

What are your experiences? Do you feel like you've had past life memories intrude into your current life? Negative? Positive?

For those of you with no alternate-life experiences, opt for curiosity. Place your rational mind on the bedside table for a few moments, and let your imagination go. You don't have to explain yourself to anyone, and none of it needs to make sense.

Color outside the lines. Play with your so-called Imaginary Friends. I'm sure they miss you.

Witch Tip
**At the end of the day,
the more deeply we understand ourselves,
the more fully we can live Right Now.**

For Further Inspiration

※ The classic resource on how a past life can affect the current one is *Many Lives, Many Masters* by Dr. Brian Weiss, for those of you looking for an easy-to-read case study.

※ For more recent and ongoing research involving children's memories of reincarnation, you may be interested in the books by Dr. Jim Tucker of the University of Virginia.

CHAPTER TWO
PROGRAM NOTES
Instinct Versus Intuition

❧

THIS CHAPTER IN the story flicks on lights in different parts of our brain, depending on the stimulus.

For instance, how many times have you shared a sensation or a sixth-sense impression, and someone rolled their eyes and said, **"It's just your imagination"**?

Then you started to doubt yourself.

If your impressions were not "just" your imagination, what else could they be? These "imaginative hits" could be coming from your **instinct or intuition.**

Ghost Light 1: Most people conflate instinct with intuition, which are each the result of significantly different brain functions.

If you've ever been bullied or abused, I guarantee you operated out of the instinctive part of your mind in those frightening and miserable moments.

You may have also employed a hefty amount of imagination to facilitate an escape plan—or to plot all the ways you could get back at the perpetrators, such as reducing them to three-inch squeaky toys and tossing them to the meanest Chihuahua in town.

On the other hand, when you're in the flow in an activity like I was when dancing or reading as a child, or when I'm writing or giving readings now, Instinct can take a nap.

Intuition comes online and drops in nuggets of wisdom and understanding. Or makes a ballerina leap off the page of a magazine.

When we don't tease apart instinct from intuition, we tend to jump to conclusions based on instinct. If we welcome in the whispers of intuition, however, we can live better in harmony with our true selves.

Ghost Light 2: Instinct exists in our most primitive, reptilian part of our brain.

Instinct:
* keeps us alive;
* operates on duality: fear or safety. Black or white. No in-betweens.
* is INSTANT and REACTIVE.

You don't need much information to act on instinct. Instinct is what makes you slam on the brakes in an intersection before you even consciously realized that another car had run the red light.

Instinct doesn't give you time to think. By the time you realize you're in danger, your body has already made the decision toward safety, to stay, go, move, change course, run.

Even if you're in an emotionally or verbally toxic situation, with no imminent threat to your physical body, I'm pretty sure your inner

Reptile is screaming at you to either run or fight for your safety. You should listen.

Dose of Magic:
Cross Examine Your Instinct

Outside of these "am I safe" situations, give yourself time to think before making a decision based on instinct alone.

Let's say you really want to start a new business, apply for a new job, take a leap on a new client, or a new relationship, and your inner alligator gets agitated... hmm.

So many clients have told me that they really wanted to do XYZ but that their "instinct" said not to. That is true, Instinct probably did say no.

For example, does it feel desperately unsafe to speak publicly? That's a big fear for most people, so yes, it feels unsafe. But is it unsafe? Probably not.

Working more deeply through fears, clients have understood they can thank Lil Alligator Instinct for doing her job and proceed toward creating a new future anyway.

Psychologically, our instinct can easily fall prey to manipulation. Social media, news channels, lawyers, and politicians all use fear-based messaging to keep us in reactive, instinctual mode—making us easier to control.

Witch Tip:
**Instinct kicks in when we
REACT to a stimulus.**

Ghost Light 3: Intuition is activated in the newest part of our brain. Intuition is PROACTIVE.

My favorite definition of Intuition is: "the ability to understand something immediately, without the need for conscious reasoning."[2] The key phrase is "to understand." Not react to a fear stimulus.

Ghost Light 4: Communication through our intuition is maddeningly subtle.

Intuition is not going to scream at you and cause your body to jerk away from a bus that you nearly stepped in front of. Intuition is so subtle that we all tend to ignore it.

Intuition comes when we allow ourselves access to our own higher consciousness. I believe we receive intuitive hits all the time. But there's only so much we can access at any given moment.

Intuition is more than one part of our brain. Intuition is connection: mind, body, and soul; the emotional body, the mental body, the physical body, the spirit.

Witch Tip:
**Intuition is always available —
when we open ourselves to receiving guidance
WITHOUT grasping for a specific answer.**

Ghost Light 5: Premonitions—Instinct or Intuition? Both.

Let's take the tragic shooting incident that Dad endured. I believe his intuition gave him the premonition to buy a gun, something he'd never done before. His instinct propelled him to open his desk drawer in the necessary moment and use it.

---

2   *Google Oxford Languages Online,* s.v. "Intuition," accessed July 10, 2025.

A few years ago, I scheduled a rafting trip down one of the most rigorous rivers in the country. Class Fives all day. I love water, and I'd wanted to run that river for decades.

Then a woman died on the river the first day the season opened. Our trip was three days later. I woke up in the middle of the night feeling her presence, and I grew anxious about our own safety on the trip.

I went anyway. I KNOW BETTER, and I still didn't listen to the premonitory intuitive hits I received.

Then when we were assigned to boats, I felt like we were in the wrong boat, even though the other strangers in our group seemed great.

Lil Alligator Instinct started bellowing, Intuition was jumping up and down, and I ignored them both. Interestingly, two other people who were assigned to our boat looked at the river before we got in and walked away from the trip.

Early on, all of my worst river nightmares came true. Our boat flipped. We were caught in a whirlpool, I came up under the boat, I gulped and breathed in buckets of water, stuck in the washing machine of the whirlpool that finally spit me out, and I swam-if that's what you can call it — the remainder of a Class Five rapid with a 40-foot drop for over 200 yards.

Fortunately, my body took over in the water. My body knew when to relax and let the water carry me, and knew when to swim like hell.

I think Intuition told me not to go in the first place, sensing something might be off. Instinct told me not to go once we reached the riverside because my physical safety was at risk. Instinct saved me in the water and instructed my body what to do before I could think about it.

Clearly, my best intuitive moments are saved for my clients and not myself. If you've ignored the intuitive nudges, then all the flashing red lights, know that you are not alone.

Going forward, let's all stop doing that.

Where does imagination fit in?

Ghost Light 6: Imagination is the vehicle that carries us into our instinct and our intuition.

Our imaginations catapult us into fears, some justified, some not.

We should question our imaginative conclusions when our lives and safety aren't truly threatened, and unleash our imagination when we're embarking into the world of intuition.

For so many of us, Lil Alligator Instinct has a wildly active imagination, while the shuttle bus between Imagination and Intuition is broken down on the side of the road.

Let's get that bus cranked back up with the next notion.

Ghost Light 7: Everyone can read a photograph of their own people! It just takes trusting your imagination.

For some folks, photographs of people who are still alive will appear to be "alive" on the page. They'll have a zing, or a glimmer, or a twinkle in their eye. It will be subtle and fleeting, but it will be there.

For other folks, pictures of living people will appear flat. Just a pic.

On the other hand, for some of you, people who have passed away will appear to move in their photo. For me, if someone is deceased, their eyes in the photo will seem to be "living."

Think about superstitions in some cultures against taking a picture because it would capture a person's soul. Likely, those folks caught a movement, in their intuitive mind's eye, when looking at photos. Some people would see the flicker when looking at a photo of a currently living person. Others would see it when the person died.

It was perfectly natural for me, as someone born with mediumistic tendencies, to see the deceased ballerina twinkle to life and jump off the page. Pictures of living people, to me, appear flat.

Dose of Magic:
The Ballerina Jumping Out
of the Photo Intuitive Exercise

Don't try to get this one "right." Just test yourself to see which way your natural spidey senses want to carry you.

Pull out two pictures of people you know. One of someone currently alive, and one of someone deceased. Yes, pets work too if you're more drawn to animals.

If you try this exercise on strangers whose vital status you are unaware of, your brain will go nuclear and drown out your intuition. So let's not start there.

Don't overthink this.

GLANCE at the two pictures. One subject is alive, one is dead. Look into their eyes. Do you sense a difference between the two photographs?

Which one dances for you? Which one appears to be flat, simply a photo?

I promise you, somewhere in your body and in your mind, you reacted on the first glance. It might take a little practice, with different photographs, to discern how intuition feels to you. But it's there, I swear.

When we make decisions or jump to conclusions based on instinct alone, we may be far from our own personal truth. Many of us made instinct our best friend in order to survive childhood.

But as adults, if we allow ourselves to feel our way into intuition, an entire world opens up, one that requires subtlety, quicker observation of a tickle, more emotional intelligence, more empathy — and more honesty with ourselves.

CHAPTER THREE
PROGRAM NOTES
Limitless Imagination &
Big Heart Energy

⸎

THIS CHAPTER INVITES expansive, limitless imaginings! But how often were you told as a child, *That's just television. It's made up. It's not real life.*

Or a pesky curmudgeon tried to put a lid on your imaginings or your desires? Such as, you aren't good enough, smart enough, rich enough, not Enough enough.

How deeply is it embedded in you, to this day, that something you desire or a type of life you crave somehow isn't for you? That you're "not allowed" to have what you want?

It's very common.

It's also common to forget what we want because we convinced ourselves that we couldn't have it. Then, we don't even allow ourselves to wish on stars and dream, for the mere sake of wishing and dreaming.

A friend of mine spent years feeling listless, trying different modalities and hobbies, such as psychic and mediumship classes, yoga, energy healing, varying forms of mystical arts, all of which she was very good at, but none of which felt like Her Thing.

Through this self exploration, she finally uncovered the forgotten desire she harbored since she was a child. She wanted to play bass guitar in a band. Not impossible, at all. As soon as that desire resurfaced, she bought a guitar and found a teacher.

Another friend rebounded after a terrible health issue, and on her hospital bed, she turned to her husband and said, "I've always wanted to play piano! I can't die without learning how to play the piano. Why have I never said that out loud before? What's so complicated about signing up for piano lessons?"

It sounds simple. But working through all of the resistance, negative self-talk, or a tremendous health scare, just in order to remember these desires, was not simple.

We're going to work on these themes for the next several chapters. Let's start with unchaining our Imaginations from the doghouse we sent it to.

Ghost Light 1: Our brain is wired to resist novelty, preferring to cart us down familiar roads rather than create new neural pathways.

Mel Robbins has a five-second rule which states that if you feel urged "to act on a goal, you must physically move within 5 seconds or your brain will kill it."[3]

My editor of this book states it another way: "In five seconds, the part of your brain that puts words and meaning to things will start telling you all the reasons you SHOULD NOT go after what you desire."

3   Mel Robbins. *The 5 Second Rule: Transform Your Life, Work, and Confidence with Everyday Courage.* Savannah, (GA: Confidence Project Press, 2017).

The negative talkies erupt as soon as we think, "Ooooooh, I'd like to try that!"

If we know about this pattern up front, then we know to outrun the negative talkies as we sprint toward our desire. At minimum, we can smart-mouth back, "I hear you, Negative Nilly, but you're not always right."

Ghost Light 2: Our hearts cannot lie.

I want to be an astronaut! I want to run off into the sunset with the hottie love of my life!

It is impossible to have a desire that is completely out of reach. The problem is that your Resistant Brain will try hard to shut down your heart.

I can't be an astronaut because I'm too old and wouldn't have gotten into Astronaut Academy anyway. The Love of My Life is probably already married, and besides, wouldn't even like me.

When Brain wins, you forget what Heart wanted in the first place.

I probably wouldn't even like being an astronaut — too much math and hard work. I don't want the headache of bothering with Love. What a joke Heart is.

In order to shush the brain talkies that drown out our Heart cries, we have to learn how to play with our imaginations again — without judgment and without attaching to a specific outcome.

Creative Visualization

Creative visualization is a tried and true technique, using all of our clairs — our extra senses — for performers and athletes to embody how to feel during a game or a show, imagining precise techniques, and plays, and what it feels like to perfectly execute them.

This technique can be used for any purpose, however, to bring a feeling you desire into your body, to test whether you want the Thing you think you want, or to give your imagination permission to soar just for the fun of it.

Many of you have already been using all of your clairs without even knowing it. I'm going to prove it to you right now.

Some may come more naturally to you than others. And over time, some may wax or wane.

Dose of Magic: Creative Visualization Made Easy

All you have to do is read the list of following questions and allow your imagination to respond. No overthinking.

Imagine a mermaid.

I bet none of you have seen a true mermaid in real life nor have you been one in recent memory, so you must use your imagination here.

* Is this creature a mermaid or a mer-man?
* What color are the scales?
* What color is the skin?
* Where do the scales stop and skin start?
* Look at the hands — are the fingers webbed?
* If you were to touch the mermaid, what does the skin feel like to your human touch?
* What do the scales feel like?
* Are you a little creeped out by touching a mermaid?
* Put yourself in the body of a mermaid: What's it feel like having one flipper instead of two legs?
   * Try to place your reaction out of the way, only sense the sensation itself, as it would feel to the mermaid

* What does it feel like to be a mermaid swimming through water?
* Do you use your arms to swim? Or can you swim like a dolphin, bulleting through the water?
* What color is the water you're in?
* Look around, what are you seeing with your own eyes?
* What's it like to swim with your eyes open and see underwater?
* What do you eat?
* Does everything taste salty? Or are you in clear water?
* How does it feel to breathe underwater?
* What does it sound like underwater? Can you hear better than humans or is it muffled? Or do you FEEL and perceive sound in a different way altogether?
  ☾ Maybe you feel sound waves coming at you?
* What does it smell like?
* Can you breathe outside of water?
* Do you enjoy sunbathing on rocks and luring sailors to their death?
* Or do you rescue sailors?
* Can you sing?
* Which is your most fun hobby?

Come back to land...

So many people say they don't know how to creatively visualize, but you just did it. And you used all of your clairs.

❦

The real **dose of magic** in this exercise is to start allowing your heart, under the guise of silly ol' imagination, to awaken and whisper to you, **"I want this madly fantastical thing that's impossible, but I want it anyway..."**

It might take practice to allow yourself the freedom to unchain your imagination enough to listen to your heart.

I want to be an astronaut because I love space, and stars, and black holes, and universes, and I can self-educate on those topics and pretend I'm flying through space in a rocket — or just in my space suit. Or I could actually apply to Astronaut Academy — or a course offered by NASA to the public.

I want to run off into the sunset with my Hottie Love because I want to feel loved, and accepted, and excited, and inspired, and sexy, all of which I can pretend is in my life right now through my Imagination.

If you have no idea where to start visualizing, you can try a number of prompts.

You can imagine a body without pain, without weaknesses. Dr. Joe Dispenza was told he would never walk again after a cycling accident. Over the next six months, while he had nothing else to do — confined to a wheelchair anyway — he visualized his spine healing. Guess what? It did.

You can imagine a beautiful scenario for your children or your partner, or you can imagine your dog running free on the beach or in a field. Sometimes, it's easier to identify and imagine what others want than it is to tap into our own heart's desires.

And feel free to channel your thirteen-year-old smart aleck. *I know I won't be a famous painter by tomorrow because I don't even own any paint, but back off, Mr. Resistor! I'm just pretending, geeeeez.*

Witch Tip:
Exercising the muscle of imagination
creates new neural pathways in our brain.

You don't have to commit to a meditation. You can play with your fantasy world when a song comes on that wants to transport you, or while you're washing dishes, taking a shower, or pulling weeds.

In those moments, I double dog dare you to ask yourself, **if you absolutely knew you couldn't fail, what would you do?**

More importantly, how do you want to feel doing it?

Let your imagination run hog-wild.

Big Heart Energy

Ghost Light 3: Electromagnetic waves emanating from our heart can be detected up to three feet away. That's Big Heart Energy!

Your auric field is the electromagnetic energy surrounding your body — many consider this part of the soul's energy.

This field around you is a source of power. Performers play with this field by expanding their energy in large theaters to reach the audience members in the back row. They also shrink their energy when executing a sleight of hand in front of an audience. Public speakers expand their energy when they want to grab and hold the attention of the audience, or a jury.

Psychics, mediums, and healers sit with this energy in an exercise called "Sitting in the Power."

Sitting in it, acknowledging what it feels like swirling around your body, and taking a few breaths can recharge you when you are down. Sitting in your heart energy is also a way to feel what your heart is communicating, without language.

You don't need to sit for long. A few minutes or the length of a song is good.

Dose of Magic:
Sitting in Your Power

My favorite version of this meditation is a short, guided one on YouTube by Tony Stockwell.

Other times, when I feel out of touch with myself—perhaps when I'm overloaded and I've shoved down emotions for later processing — I'll play "Nuvole Bianche" by Ludovico Einuadi, a pianist. That song never fails to drop me right in my heart, then release any emotion trapped there.

No words, no storytelling to myself. Just raw emotion. Tears are welcome.

Witch Tip:
**Sitting with the power emanating from your being
is tremendously healing and illuminating.**

These two practices — creative visualization and sitting in your power — work together to reunite your heart's desires with your body's energy.

When you give your imagination permission to play, you remember what you truly want. When you sit in your heart's electromagnetic field, you feel the power to claim it rather than passively allowing your resistant brain and negative talkies to dictate your life.

For Further Inspiration:

✳ Scientist Gregg Braden has extensively researched and written about Heart Intelligence and Trauma, and Brain and Heart Cohesion. He teaches techniques on how to heal the heart, even after the brain has healed, and how to make decisions based on all aspects of our being, in cohesion, in bite-sized videos. He's found all over the interwebs and in multiple books and platforms.

✳ If you really want to geek out on the brain and theories of cohesion, see *Becoming Supernatural* by Dr. Joe Dispenza.

CHAPTER FOUR
PROGRAM NOTES
The Resistance:
Desire is Dangerous

✎❧

YIKES, Y'ALL. This chapter in the story slams us with crushed spirits.

It also introduces the cognitive dissonance or sense of betrayal that arises when we follow our heart's desire, maybe even succeed, yet we feel like a failure and a disappointment to those around us.

There's the old notion that the team will only win if the coach is brutally mean, beats them down, and yells, "You're the best players in the world! Why are you so worthless? I expect MORE out of you." Like my ballet teachers at NCSA.

These Not Enough seeds are planted when we're young and first start to dream big.

Let's break down how those seeds then blossom into False Truths.

1. Desire propels us to push forward, to play, to experiment with The Thing, to express our wants and to love freely.

2. Then someone tells us, "Silly little goose. Desire led you into the dark woods and abandoned you. You can't handle it in there. You're not enough. This Thing is not for you. Run for your life!"

    We may resist and fight back for what we want, if our desire is strong enough. But over time, the mantra gets stuck in our head. *Not Enough. Not Enough.*

    Who gets blamed? Desire. We conclude that it was wrong for us to want in the first place.

3. We then marry Desire to rejection and failure. As if one can't come without the other.

4. Therefore, desire is dangerous.
    Poof!
    When Desire = Danger, we have the perfect formula to birth the fear of desire itself.

5. When fear kicks in, what part of our brain activates and takes charge? Instinct.

This pattern is precisely why we stay in "safe" jobs and relationships way past their expiration date, even as these situations crush our spirits. Or why we bury our desire to find new work, play an instrument, start painting, writing, or embark on a spiritual journey or a trip to a new locale. Or engage with ourselves and others in a deeper, more fulfilling manner, without holding back.

This is why too many people lay on their death beds in a state of quiet despair, safe from the danger of all the Things they wanted in life.

I always wanted to jump into the hole. But I was scared to bother the doormouse.

It is not wrong or dangerous to want a different life for yourself. It is not dangerous to want a different partner. It is not dangerous to want at all.

Even when the False Truth demons jump up and down and scream that we'll fail, we'll be rejected, thrown out in the cold, and betrayed because we're Not Enough.

Living in close relationship with ourselves — a/k/a our imagination, intuition, desires, and so forth — is no different than a relationship with anyone else. It must be developed, and trust must be earned over time. It takes time to evict the False Truth demons.

Ghost Light 1: Societal norms instruct us to FEAR the unknown and FEAR the dark and, therefore, to fear what we want.

If our Resistant Brain avoids novelty, then society pulls out the bullhorn to echo it. The known is safe. The unknown is dangerous!

The unknown is also usually painted as dark. And "dark" is dangerous!

If you feel this way, you're normal. It doesn't mean we have to continue accepting this norm as our own personal truth forever and always with EVERYTHING though.

Many years ago, if you were highly intuitive in certain cultures, you were called a witch. In some cultures, the term "Witch" equaled respect. But most cultures touched by organized religion deemed it to be a bad thing.

Therefore, if a woman lived as she desired, she was deemed a "witch" and could be duly punished for it.

⁕

Take the case of Bridget Bishop from Salem, Massachusetts, the first person executed during the Salem Witch Trials on June 10, 1692.

Bridget was known for her independent spirit and unconventional behavior. She owned and operated taverns, dressed in bright red clothing, which was provocative at the time, and was described as assertive and outspoken.

According to witness testimony, she was married three times, argued publicly with her husbands, went about strange places at odd hours, and refused to be agreeable when disputes over property and business dealings arose.

All in all, she refused to conform to Puritan expectations of female behavior, placing a target on her forehead. Even so, she trusted her own judgment.

Her "desires" — to dress as she pleased, run her businesses independently, and speak boldly — were labeled as evidence of witchcraft by a community that expected women to be submissive and modest.[4]

---

4   Paul Boyer and Stephen Nissenbaum. *Salem Possessed: The Social Origins of Witchcraft.*

It worked. Bridget was feared. In turn, women feared behaving like Bridget.

I guarantee Bridget knew this *Witch Tip:*

**When you develop trust in yourself,
and stand firmly in your Wants and Needs,
you have a direct link to your higher consciousness,
which means you have a direct link to the Divine.
When you're secure in your inviolable link to the Divine,
you can't be controlled easily.**

Woop.

We've been taught to fear our own divinity, to fear our own selves, and our own power. We've been taught that something dark might be lurking just beyond the veil of our conscious mind, or deep in our hearts.

We've been taught to doubt ourselves, to fear our truths, and to fear what we want in life.

Ghost Light 2: "When you look him straight in the eye, the Devil is a letdown."

So said a character in the Netflix series, *Narcos*. In other words, facing fears can bring light.

We can't live and sleep comfortably in our homes if we're afraid to peek under the bed. We're going to work on looking fear in the eye, from the safety of this Green Room, and disentangle it from Desire.

Cambridge, (MA: Harvard University Press, 1974); Bernard Rosenthal. *Salem Story: Reading the Witch Trials of 1692*, (Cambridge: Cambridge University Press, 1993).

Dose of Magic:
Turn the Mr. Resistor Fear Demon
into a Squeaky Toy

For this exercise, I want you to put judgment to the side. Toss away labels of "good" and "bad" and observe from the standpoint of having an experience. I recommend journaling for highest impact. Pull out a pen and paper and puke up what's begging to be purged.

1. What felt like a block or resistance when you started the creative visualization exercise in the last chapter?

2. What felt like resistance with the idea that your heart energy is so powerful? Do you have resistance to sitting with YOUR own power?

    I did when I first started.

    I don't feel anything. This is too woo. This is stupid. I can't sit still for seven minutes. Maybe other people have "power," but I don't.

    Over time, Sitting in the Power or Sitting in My Heart has become a sanctuary. And yes, you have the same measurable electromagnetic field around you that I have around me.

3. What self-talk suddenly erupts in your head when you think, I want...

    For me, it's always, *I don't know what I want, so why bother?* Which is a Big Lie. We always know what we want, and we're probably afraid to ask for it. At bare minimum, we know how we want to feel every day.

Now for the fun part!

Write the word FEAR on the top of your page.

So many of us get blocked by the very notion of fear that we immediately shut down and don't even explore the word, much less what's underlying our fear. What we're doing in this exercise is learning not to be afraid of fear itself. Like, not becoming even more anxious over the fact that we're anxious.

If it's easier, imagine that you're sitting up on the Catwalk watching Fear and another version of you playing as actors down on the stage.

Set your intent that you're not going to be afraid of fear itself. Hold space for anything that arises for 60 seconds at most, all the while knowing that you're safe doing this exercise, and Fear cannot reach you up on the Catwalk. You can laugh at it, play with it, taunt it, and still acknowledge how it affects you.

* Write or doodle every single thing that the word "fear" makes you think of. Everything, no judgment.

* How does the word make you feel?

* Does it make you get all prickly?

* Do you scoff at it?

* Do you withdraw from it and want to run away?

* Do you want to punch Fear?

✳ Does fear also make you think of words such as betrayal, disappointment, abandonment, shame?

✳ Where does it sit in your body?

✳ Does it show up at all the wrong times, especially when your life is NOT in danger and you're perfectly safe physically, emotionally, and mentally?

On another page, write DARKNESS.
Start brainstorming.

✳ What is darkness to you?

✳ Are you afraid of it? Or allured by it?

✳ What are you afraid of when it comes to your own Imagination? Or the idea of your Intuition? Has someone told you those notions are "dark" and they meant that as an insult?

✳ What is it that you are afraid of in your own perceived darkness?

✳ What if all of your imaginings, dreams, wishes, desires were your private source of divine light?

When we stifle our perceived darkness, we are also stifling our connection to creative force energies, which means our connections to ourselves, to the Divine.

What would be possible in your personal life if you didn't view darkness as dark? Your professional life?

Ghost Light 3: Desire is not married to fear.

Just because you feel fear doesn't mean that you have to shut down what you want or how magical and authentic you crave your life to be.

Witch Tip:
The goal isn't to eliminate fear.
It's to stop letting fear make decisions about your desires.

When you can observe fear without being controlled by it, you reclaim the right to want what you want.

Mr. Resistor Fear Demon may be a frequent actor on our stage whenever Desire and Imagination and other versions of our True Self appear, but over time, when you play with him and look him in the eye, he can shrink to the size of a Chihuahua's squeaky toy.

For Further Inspiration:

 My friend, David Strickel, is a channel who created a spiritual framework called Trust Your Abundance. He has books, videos, and a course if you find yourself stuck by the concepts raised in this chapter. Learn more: **www.thestreamofdavid.com**

 If you love your dark side, like I do, then the master of calling a spade a spade when it comes to Fear is Shawn Coss, ER nurse and creator of *It's All in Your Head,* a beautifully communicative, illustrated book of fear monsters regarding mental states, phobias, mental illness, and all the ways we mentally torture ourselves. You can find him at: **anymeansnecessary.com**

✳ If you're feeling High Level Brave and want waaayyy more depth in uncovering secret desires and fears than what I've offered here, then by all means, jump head first into shadow work. Tread carefully. It's not for everyone.

✳ Dr. Caroyln Elliott Lovewell turns this topic upside down and humorously in her work and in her book, *Existential Kink*. Others approach this work differently, so if she's not your jam, then boogie on.

Credits:

In this chapter in the story, Rabbit pulled his statistic about the ideal skinny ballerina from Alessandra Ortiz, "Changing the Perception of the Ballet Body," WorldWideBallet, October 17, 2015, https://world wideballet.net/ blogs/news/54300420-changing-the-perception-of-the-ballet-body

CHAPTER FIVE
PROGRAM NOTES
Spiritual Bypassing &
Ethical Boundaries

e⅋⅌

THIS CHAPTER BEGS us to explore spiritual escapism and spiritual bypassing, which I engaged in during this time period.

Ghost Light 1: Spiritual escapism or bypassing means turning to notions of the soul, the spirit world, energy, quantum, or other dimensions and realities for the sole purpose of AVOIDING the emotional, mental, or physical pain and suffering in this reality.

As an extreme example, think of the "spiritual" person who is actually quite shallow. Someone who repeatedly and consciously avoids acknowledging yours — and their own — suffering during grave situations. Someone who meets your pain with a smile, "It will all be okay! The world is beeeeeee-you-teee-fulll! Just breathe and be grateful to the Divine!"

We'll talk much more about this harmful, false-positive foolishness in later Program Notes.

Spiritual escapism, when applied to ourselves, is not entirely use-less, for sure. For children, or for any person in an abusive situation where physical escape is not available, dissociating from our bodies or our physical reality can be the only survival option in our toolbox.

For many people, escapism is the preferred tool to avoid tough situations or confrontations. Folks escape into work, church, certain demanding and time-consuming hobbies that no longer serve them just to avoid dealing with emotional or mental pain and suffering. Obviously, some folks escape into addiction.

For me, during this time period, I felt like I had to stay and suc-ceed at NCSA because I was finally surrounded by other artistic weirdos, even though the adults made us miserable. I couldn't have explained it at the time, but for instinctive, survivalist reasons, my anxiety spiked to the moon every time I thought of returning to West Virginia.

And the training at NCSA was deemed "normal" for the dance world at the time, if not exemplary and critical to our future success. The whole "you're lucky that we care enough to beat you" mentality.

Melissa Hayden's tropes didn't help either:

✳ "If it feels good, you're not doing it right."

✳ "It doesn't matter if it *feels* good. It only matters that it *looks* good."

But my classmate Katrina didn't look good up close. Her skin tone turned yellow and gray, and her eye sockets grew sunken and dark. Her state of being was normalized and praised because she was so thin.

Sheesh.

Ghost Light 2: Melissa Hayden's notions are society's notions.

Women wore corsets, women's desires are dangerous, boys don't cry, suck it up, baby, on and on. Doesn't all of this malarkey require a person to dissociate from painful, earthly truths, particularly when we're children and teenagers?

Ghost Light 3: If you or someone you know experiences "body dissatisfaction," you're in the overwhelming majority.

According to www.nationaleatingdisorders.org, "69–84% of women experience body dissatisfaction, desiring to be a lower weight than they currently are, and 10% to 30% of men exhibit body dissatisfaction with the primary concern being a desire to become more muscular."[5]

The Mayo Clinic says, "Body dysmorphic disorder is a mental health condition in which you can't stop thinking about one or more perceived defects or flaws in your appearance—a flaw that appears minor or can't be seen by others. But you may feel so embarrassed, ashamed and anxious that you may avoid many social situations."[6]

This makes me so very sad for all of us who've been made to feel ashamed of our bodies. If this resonates with you, here's a whole casserole of Grace.

Ghost Light 4: Bullying and abuse is the number one cause of body dysmorphia.

Sigh.

---

5   Reviewed by Paula Edwards-Gayfield, M.A., "Body Image and Eating Disorders," NationalEatingDisorders.org, accessed July 10, 2025, https://www.nationaleatingdisorders.org/body-image-and-eating-disorders/

6   Mayo Clinic, "Body Dismorphic Disorder," MayoClinic.org, accessed July 10, 2025, https://www.mayoclinic.org/diseases-conditions/body-dysmorphic-disorder/symptoms-causes/syc-20353938

I escaped into non-addictive, mind-expanding drugs and spirituality, hoping there was something higher and better Out There that would rescue me from the Life on Earth Here that made absolutely no sense.

Dose of Magic: Journal Prompt

⁂   Have you retreated to spiritual concepts to avoid a painful reality?

⁂   Perhaps as a child? Perhaps now?

P.S. Eat heaping spoonfuls of Grace in honor of you and your younger self as you ponder these questions.

> HOLD UP!
> *I thought you encouraged us to spend time in our heads through Imagination?*

It's coming, Rabbit. Hang on...

Ghost Light 5: The upside of escapism is that it can buy us much-needed time.

Sometimes, we can't begin emotional processing or healing until we're out of the physical situation that's causing us harm. So, in the meanwhile, we can learn new spiritual concepts that interest us or throw ourselves into a project that needs completing.

On one hand, my spiritual escapism opened me up to tools to see Katrina's skin tone and know that underneath the teachers' praise of her, something was wrong.

On the other hand, what could I do? Not a thing.

I felt helpless and increasingly dissociated from myself and surroundings as all us little girls, who were blossoming into curvy teenagers, were fat shamed and deemed Not Good Enough.

The thing is, we shouldn't live in Escapism forever. Ideally, we'll take the time in Escapism to build tools that are handy for us back on Earth, when we're ready to fully return to this reality.

Witch Tip:

**Spiritual bypassing or escapism
can be a reaction to avoid painful truths.
Think: Instinct.
Conscious use of imaginative, spiritual exercises
invites all the hard realities to the party, in due course.
It's proactive.
Think: Intuitive.**

Claircognizance & Objective Clairvoyance

I knew something was wrong with Katrina, even though I had no facts to support my "knowing," which is an example of claircognizance, "clear knowing."

My "seeing" Katrina's skin color as yellow and gray is an example of objective clairvoyance. Others couldn't see her color as off, while I saw specific shades on her actual skin, not in my mind's eye.

I came to learn that for me, gray = lack of vital force energy, maybe a physical depression, and yellow = mental illness or depression. I would learn the following year what caused her eye sockets to appear black and sunken.

I met a woman once who would see, in her mind's eye, figurative snakes wrapped around someone's head when they were depressed. That's an example of subjective clairvoyance, meaning, "seeing" snakes was her symbology for depression.

Dose of Magic: Observe When You Experience Claircognizance and Objective Clairvoyance

If you start paying attention, your own symbology will likely appear. For instance, can you look at your partner or child and notice when they're coming down with a cold or fever *before* they exhibit physical symptoms?

I'm certain you've experienced a knowing when you felt something was off with a loved one, especially when you couldn't put your finger on what was bothering you. Try to observe these moments without judgment or questioning.

I have a journal dedicated solely to these moments so I can note when a pattern appears. You may want a symbology — or mystical moment — journal too.

Quick Detour on Ethics:
Boundaries #1

Ghost Light 6: Outside of a close loved one, never — and I mean never — give unsolicited messages or observations.

The above exercise is meant only to assist you in developing tools to communicate with yourself.

Without significant training and time spent in developing healing, psychic, or mediumistic skills, you may do more harm than good while communicating an unasked-for observation, even if your intent is to help.

I have years of training in these skills, and I would never communicate a message or observation to someone unless they ask first. Truly, even then, they have to make an appointment and hire me. Hold yourself to that same standard and disciplined boundary.

… Unless it's your kid or grandkid, who will probably give you an eyeroll in return, or yell at you to back off.

Ghost Light 7: Best practice if you feel like you have an overwhelming sense about another person is to do the old-fashioned thing: pick up the phone and call them.

Your sense is probably accurate. Reach out.

"Hey, you've been on my mind! How are things?"

If their situation matches your observation, make a mental note of the symbology you received or how you felt. You can say, "That's interesting. I had a feeling something was up."

For the love of all things holy, however, do not tell them you saw snakes on their head — or whatever literal image came to you.

Even if someone surmises that you're a crackpot, 99% of people will also start to think something is wrong with them and they're about to die. They won't be able to shake that fear for years, if ever.

And maybe they're actually awaiting results of a brain scan. You don't know.

You can see how relaying such a message, without training, could cause more harm than good.

Likewise, don't tell a stranger in the coffee shop that you sense that their dead father is always around them blanketing them in his love. Dad may have been a serial killer and a child molester.

Not. Helpful.

You get the drift.

Quick Detour on Ethics: Boundaries #2

By discussing my previous use of LSD, I am NOT promoting or recommending drugs or chemical cocktails for any purpose whatsoever.

Folks have told me that I should try ayahuasca, that I'm not "fully" healed until I've done so, or that all my previous mind-expanding ventures are nothing compared to a medicine journey to Peru where I must puke up my toenails for three days in order to have a "legitimate" experience.

Some folks have also looked down on my choice of red wine over smoking weed.

Good for everyone who has experienced life-changing healing and integration with the use of any modality, chemical, natural or otherwise. There are studies on the benefits of marijuana and psychedelics, and there are reputable people who facilitate medicine ceremonies—who will not bully you into partaking in their services — if you feel pulled to explore these routes.

Witch Tip:
**Don't let anyone convince you that you are Less Than,
not one of the cool kids, or not "fully" anything,
unless you have XYZ experience.**

Middle fingers up to anyone who tries to belittle you into doing something you don't want to do or that you feel is not right for you.

CHAPTER SIX
PROGRAM NOTES
Reframing without Rewriting: Skip the Forced Forgiveness & Insincere Gratitudes

❧

I
T's NEVER TOO late to heal a wound. Even one you didn't know was still there.

Sometimes, when we get triggered unexpectedly, we realize there's a tenacious old monster squatting in our basement, and he's been lurking down there for decades. It's annoying to find him there, but we then have the opportunity to evict that sucker once and for all.

More Information Can Lead to Clarity & Less Isolation

As I wrote these NCSA chapters, the shame of failure continued to rise in me for that one sliver of my life that seemed unreconciled, and still felt humiliating.

I didn't feel comfortable saying I went to an elite ballet school when I disappointed everyone at said school. Imposter syndrome shrouded my dancing years from the 1980s all the way into the twenty-first century.

Yet, each of the vignettes in the story appeared in my memory with startling clarity, right down to what we were wearing and the smells of the sweaty ballet studio.

I procrastinated one afternoon and Googled my old teachers' names. Intuition took the wheel on that one.

I found a lawsuit with sixty-five plaintiffs, including many of my former classmates, accusing some of the teachers at NCSA of abuse. Before I saw the allegations in black and white, I never thought of the training as abusive because it was normalized in the industry.

To my great dismay, according to the allegations, many of my classmates, who I viewed as successful, suffered the same reaction that I did over the following years. Failure, shame, skewed body images, depression, anxiety, suicide attempts, and abandoning their love of dance.

I felt at once validated and heartbroken.

The lawsuit dragged my shame monster out of the basement and into the open.

But the driver of the lawsuit was the allegations of sexual abuse at the hands of certain "esteemed" teachers, who held the power to determine whether the students graduated or earned their connections and referrals for jobs.

When I read that some of my mates were sexually abused on the trip to Europe, my bones sobbed from a place I didn't know still hurt. Of course, they wouldn't have wanted to engage in a bubbly conversation with a younger kid on their return.

I can attest to many of the specific allegations, the nicknames, and the coarse, sexually charged atmosphere that the older students were subjected to — though, like I said, it was normalized in the industry at the time.

I can hear Melissa Hayden's voice, *"Honey, wake up. This is the business. If you can't take it, go home."*

To be clear, demanding training and high expectations are the norm in any athletic or artistic profession. There happen to be thousands of coaches, teachers, trainers, and institutions across the world who are exacting but do not cross the line into abuse.

⋅⊱ ⋅⊰⋅

Then a lightning bolt struck: I might have been saved from further abuse for leaving NCSA when I did. Holy cow.

Suddenly, I felt grateful for not being "good enough" to cut it there. Woo hoo, Failure!

Within moments of reading the lawsuit, my shame monster about my NCSA years dissipated into the afternoon sun, calling out, *"My work of taunting you is done here! Ta ta!"*

The experience reiterated this *Witch Tip:*
**Reframing does not require rewriting history
or engaging in premature acceptance.
Instead, reframing means seeing the full picture.
Sometimes, we don't have the full picture for decades.**

Ghost Lights for Reframing Issues in a Heart-Healthy, Authentic Manner

1. Reframing an issue does NOT mean rewriting history. If someone hurt you or abused you, by all means, please continue to call it out on the pages of your personal history book.

2. When we thoroughly heal a trauma, sometimes, we see the circumstances from a broader perspective.

3. Reframing an experience is not an excuse to ignore the icky monsters hiding in our basement.

4. Reframing an experience does not mean swallowing this hogwash: "I shouldn't feel so bad about my own pain and suffering because others had it worse." Your pain is valid regardless of others' experiences.

5. Reframing does not mean you must "forgive" your transgressor or analyze their situation so much that you understand yourself right out of your own pain and, hence, write yourself out of your own story. Please refer to #1.

I hear many people give lip service to the notion that they should forgive someone who hurt them when they haven't yet worked through all of the complicated emotions of the harm in the first place.

Forced forgiveness does NOT aid in healing, nor is it authentic. In fact, in many cases, forced forgiveness can repress anger that might otherwise propel us to seek justice, right social wrongs, or seek treatment for ourselves.

In due course, I believe, true forgiveness allows us to choose to stop giving our power away to the person who harmed us. It releases grudges and anger that no longer serves us.

Witch Tip:
Forgiveness comes as the result of healing.
It cannot be rushed.

Dose of Magic: Reflection

What if…

✴ It's not your duty to forgive another person, and

✴ You don't even have the capability to do so?

✴ **What if the only person you can ever forgive is yourself?**

Your only job is to forgive yourself, which is a BIG DEAL for victims of hurt and abuse, and for anyone who feels like a disappointing failure concerning certain life events.

So many abuse victims blame themselves for being "weak," for being in the wrong place at the wrong time, or primarily, **for not standing up for themselves or others, for failing to act.**

Children and young adults cannot grasp the implications of abuse and rarely possess the wherewithal to speak up or ask for help. When they do, their pleas may be dismissed.

The same is true for adults. There are times when it's not safe to speak out or stand up, or you simply cannot process what is happening in real time.

If the shame monster taunts you over any failure, remember our earlier discussions on Not Enough.

PSSST...
You're Enough.
Here, have
some Grace.

GRACE

Ghost Light 6: Skip the fake gratitudes.

Don't be grateful for things **other people** think you should be grateful for. Don't be grateful for the house you no longer want to pay for, the partner you no longer like, or the job you've grown out of. Don't be grateful for trappings of success that hold no meaning to you.

Don't use the act of gratitude to skip over dark, truthful emotions and force forgiveness.

Because...

Ghost Light 7: A situation can be horrible and a blessing at the same time.

Reading the allegations in the NCSA lawsuit brought full integration within myself on this issue: The situation I experienced felt abusive, my sense of failure was significant, AND I felt grateful that my so-called failure rescued me from further abuse. All points exist simultaneously.

Reframing requires full knowledge — hard work on You, Yourself, and You — then realizing one day that you've managed to pop out the other side and you think of a situation differently.

⁂

Parker Posey, in the story, provided a simple, positive example of reframing. She was encouraged to drop dance and pursue acting. As immature baby bals, with a single indicator of success, we saw her rejection by the dance world as a failure.

A few years later, long before she became a well-known actress, I could discern that she was the success for pivoting so easily, tossing her pointe shoes in the bin and heading to drama class.

Dose of Magic: Reframing Situations Without Forced Forgiveness & Insincere Gratitudes

Reflection/Journal Prompt:

✻ Are there periods in your life where your younger self is begging you for forgiveness?

Remember, you're the only one who can grant this wish. You might need to climb up onto our Catwalk and look at your younger self as you would someone else at that age. I bet you'd be way more understanding and compassionate toward that imaginary person than you are toward yourself.

✻ Maybe you feel that you should have left a situation, or should have fought, should have stopped fighting, should have stayed quiet, should have yelled, should have This, should have That?

If so, acknowledge it and tell your younger self, "I'm sorry if I let Me down. And I forgive Me for doing so. There's a lot I understand now that I didn't understand when I was younger."

✻ What if there were circumstances happening at the time that, even to this day, you know nothing about?

✳ What if you felt alone and isolated, yet other people were experiencing the same turmoil? Would that help reframe the picture for you?

✳ What else would help reframe the situation for you?

Further Reflection or Journal Prompt:

Is there a time when your setbacks later proved to be a synchronicity? Or your perceived failure saved your behind?

If there's anything you can reframe, without rewriting history and ignoring emotional truths, I invite you to do so.

CHAPTER SEVEN
PROGRAM NOTES
Flipping the Script on Stigmas

❧

S TIGMA = A MARK of disgrace.

Society can attach a stigma to many innocent or natural circumstances. Such as, back in the day, a woman who wore pants, or the main character accused of adultery and branded with "A" in Nathaniel Hawthorne's *The Scarlet Letter*.

Even when we are solid non-conformists to society's rules, we can still unconsciously fall prey to stigmas. Which is why we're shining a high-voltage spotlight on it.

Ghost Light 1: We can subconsciously attach a stigma to a situation or interest, separate from societal and family norms.

We can hold ourselves back from accepting a condition, such as clinical depression, or an interest, such as spirituality, because we don't identify as someone with that condition or interest AND because we believe that condition carries with it a shameful stain or blemish.

"I'm not depressed because I'm the type of person who gets things done, pulls herself up, puts a smile on when I walk out the door, and never lets anyone see me sweat. I'm not the type of person who has depression."

"I refuse to be branded with a Big D that I will see every time I look in the mirror."

"I'm not 'spiritual,' because those people are impractical flakes. I am not a flake."

I had a client who came from a line of female mystics, each of whom secretly passed down knowledge in the kitchen over whispers and tea. My client's husband thought the grandmas and aunties were ignorant and old-fashioned. It took my client years to accept her own interest in spirituality because she also believed she was too smart and modern to fall for the old auntie and granny stuff.

When she did tiptoe into That Stuff, she had to toss her personal stigma to the wind, while still acknowledging societal and familial disdain. She switched the covers on her spirituality books so it looked like she read romance novels.

To me, that was a win. She saw no benefit in fighting with her family over what she read just then, but she also didn't let her own stigma hold her back any longer.

Because mental and emotional health issues still carry layers of stigmas, let's walk through talking points on Depression as an example to bust apart ANY stigma-related myths that might be holding you back.

In this chapter in the story, my friend Vivi eviscerated any embarrassment between the two of us by openly sharing her experiences with depression, then held a mirror to my face.

On one hand, I thought, "Great. If she's correct that I'm depressed, then that's one more strange and bad thing about myself that will separate me from all the normal people in the world. I'm disgraceful enough as it is." Clearly, this self-talk dripped with the shame I attached to my own mentally sensitive nature!

On the other hand, I went into denial that there was anything fixably wrong inside my head, blaming my specific circumstances instead.

It is true that temporary depression can result from circumstances, and we can bounce back out of it once the situation changes. But a lot of the time, we slide into the brain chemistry of clinical depression, and when circumstances change, our brains don't.

Ghost Light 2: Depression can come on so slowly, we don't notice it in ourselves or our family members.

The spectrum of my world so slowly collapsed to the middle, I forgot that life wasn't always dull. I chalked up my earlier ecstasy with dance as the whimsy of a child, which I would have outgrown anyway.

I was no longer subjected to the extreme highs of hope and dreams that came with the opportunities NCSA offered, but I was no longer subjected to the stinging pain of failure and rejection either. My world went from wide-ranging emotions to apathy, from technicolor to gray.

In reality, I'm sure I began to sink into depression two years earlier — when I first attended NCSA for the school year—and our spirits were crushed in short order. My emotional state matched that of many others, so even if a teacher had been paying attention, I wouldn't have stood out.

By the end of the following year, Mom and Fanchon Cordell

noticed I was gloomier than the rest of the bunch, but even Mom thought I would adjust to high school back home and eventually return to my normal self.

Living with NCSA "norms" for over two years on a daily basis is not a temporary set of circumstances, on top of years of Cruella's abuse and grade-school bullying. There's no way my brain chemistry could rebound on its own.

Ghost Light 3: Depression has a wardrobe full of costumes, and they're not one size fits all.

Cloaking my clinical depression were stereotypes — that I bought into — of typical teenage angst. Aren't all teenagers self-absorbed, moody, mouthy, sullen, know-it-all misfits who hate their lives?

No. They're not. A stereotype I disproved myself throughout the remaining years of teenagedom when I threw out the it's-only-teen-age-angst costume.

It didn't help that I was a highly active, high-performing person, albeit with a grumpy face. Depressed people are supposed to lie around in bed all day, aren't they? Um, nope.

Ghost Light 4: Depression is a liar and creates faulty thought patterns.

I didn't believe Vivi when she suggested to me that if depression were the issue, then the issue could be fixed.

Most depressed people don't believe there is a solution. To close the circle on this faulty thought pattern, the lie goes: If there's no solution to my issue, then depression isn't the cause. It's just how I am.

Once again, nope.

Ghost Light 5: Acknowledging that we may be suffering from depression or other mental and emotional conditions influenced by external factors requires us to also face up to the fact that something is severely wrong in our lives.

Which means ... we must make a change.

We can't entirely rely on, "I'm the problem. It's me. Leave me alone."

Sometimes, we're depressed or anxious even after we've done self-work and gone to therapy because our external situation needs to change. The marriage still isn't working. We still need to quit the job. We need to pursue the Thing. Life needs a solid shake-up.

Usually, by that point, depression and anxiety are sucking all our energy, and we don't have any gas left in the tank to make changes. It's not helpful that those possible changes come with their own stigmas. Divorce, career identity, and so forth.

Argh.

Witch Tip:
**Some of us don't fit the mold or fit within the guardrails
of what we think of as traditional symptoms of depression
or other mental and emotional issues.**

That, coupled with personal and societal stigmas, and boydoggie, we can really be misunderstood and stay in a miserable place way past our eviction date.

Dose of Magic: Busting Through Stigmas that Keep you in Chains

In my personal set of values, a stigma should attach to actions such as abusing children, human trafficking, discrimination based on sexuality, race, and gender, to name only a few. These stigmas do not blossom from soulful, heart-driven intent. They probably don't prevent people from engaging in these behaviors either.

When you have a soulful, heart-led desire, stigmas should not hold you back either.

For example, there should not be societal and personal stigmas attached to the below, which is a very short list of common examples:

✳ Mental and emotional conditions
  ☾ Stigma: "There's something wrong with you, and you should be outcast from society."

✳ Empathy, compassion, kindness
  ☾ Stigma says, "You're weak, vulnerable. Too sensitive. Toughen up."

✳ Free thinking
  ☾ Stigma: "You're a wild card. You can't be counted on. You're dangerous. You're untrustworthy."

✳ Pursuing a career in the arts, or pursuing excellence and expertise in _____ (fill in the blank).
  ☾ Stigma: "You'll fail. Waste money. Your pursuit is worthless and childish. Grow up."

✳ Imagination and Intuition
  ☾ Stigma: "You're making things up. You're full of crap. You might be trying to scam me."

✳ Being poor or having a physical illness
  ☾ Stigma: "It's your fault."

You get it. Let's flip the script on stigmas.

Dose of Magic: Reflection/Journal Prompt

When you feel resistance to something you are pulled to explore or experience, including seeking help, ask yourself…What if a subconscious stigma is holding me back?

1. Have I adopted a resisting belief against doing this Thing my whole life? Or has it come on so slowly, I didn't know it was there?

2. Does it appear in costumes, such as a well-meaning granny or friend sweetly admonishing you not to do the Thing? Or, is a stigma hiding behind stereotypes that don't fit your situation?

I have a few lawyer friends who kindly ask when I plan to return to a law career, intimating that what I'm doing *now* isn't legitimate, that I'm wasting my education and experience, and so on. Their questions reveal their own belief in a stigma. Such as, do *they* feel disgraced or embarrassed by associating with a spiritual wild card like me? Hmm.

Does well-meaning granny feel uncomfortable because she's worried what the church ladies will say when they learn of your actions?

Witch Tip:
**Other people's discomfort with you may be real,
but you don't have to don their beliefs in stigmas.**

3. Are you engaged in faulty thought patterns regarding what you want because you're worried that the result will be A Mark of Disgrace on Your House and Your Entire Lineage?

Such as, *There's no solution out there for me. I don't need to try the Thing to know that I will fail anyway. I don't want the Stigma of Failure looking at me in the mirror every day. Or the Stigma of Flake, Loser, Outcast, Weirdo, Dummy for trying... My parents and children will bear the burden.*

If it helps, remember this stigma has you in chains. Is that making anyone proud?

4. Is it time to make a change? What are all the societal, familial, and personal stigmas that may arise when you take action toward your Heart-Driven desire?

Ghost Light 6: You can call out the Stigma for what it is, then flip the script.

Why is it a Bad Thing to _____ [Everything Stigma says] instead of a Heart and Soul Affirming Good Thing to _____ [Your heart's desire or soul-driven need].

Example: Why is it a Bad Thing to not practice law instead of a Heart and Soul Affirming Good Thing to integrate all aspects of myself and, in turn, help a lot of people along the way heal from grief, find their souls, and live a fuller life?

If fear of a Stigma is holding you back, remember, it's chaining you to the doghouse in the backyard.

Is that really where you want to live and die? We can do better.

Stigmas are tough to bust, and you may not recognize them immediately. If you don't, simply pay attention. The word itself will drop in your head when it needs to.

Or pop up onto the Catwalk and take a look at other actors in your life. I'm sure you will see someone else held back by the fear of a stigma that can be released.

Please don't be afraid to ask for help. Someone else might have a bolt cutter in hand who can assist freeing you from the leash.

If you've ever broken free from a stigma, acknowledge all the COURAGE it took!!! Wow. Congratulations!

For Further Inspiration: Call on Sinead O'Connor and Lil Nas X

* In 1992, Sinead O'Connor ripped up the photo of the Pope on Saturday Night Live. She was seen as cray cray because of social stigmas at that time. Also remember, at the time, the Catholic Church actively covered up instances of sexual abuse. Sinead's mother was a victim of sexual abuse by a priest, from which she never recovered. Not only that, her mother then severely neglected and physically abused Sinead O'Connor as a child. Having experienced devastating generational effects of abuse, Sinead stood up, spoke out, and ultimately was credited as justified and vindicated. Bust through the stigma.

* And Lil Nas X? He came out as gay in the American South — when southern black men couldn't be gay, AND in hip-hop, AND be a rapper, AND be a country singer. If he could flip the script on so many social stigmas, we can too.

CHAPTER EIGHT
PROGRAM NOTES
Me: I Don't Know How to Keep Living
The Mystical: I'll Show You

꩜

AVE YOU HAD any desperation-fueled experiences that even though no one else may understand it, you realize that, in a way, it was privately majestic?

Let's cut to the chase on the Big Issue in this chapter. I didn't want to die. I actually wanted to live more fully.

I just didn't know how to keep living under my current circumstances — and as a minor, I had no control over most of them. The only thing that made sense to my depressed brain at the time was to skip out of this dimension.

Ghost Light 1: If asking for "help" feels icky to you and brings up resistance, then consider it a share.

Consider sharing how you feel and sharing your thoughts. Your feelings and thoughts matter a lot.

Here's my dark share:

We're all going to die. So let's agree to this. We can procrastinate and die tomorrow. Or tomorrow's tomorrow. Things might be messy, but we'll get through.

If this speaks to you, please consider living to die another day. CALL OR TEXT 988

All you have to say is, "I don't know how to keep living." If you go here, you won't feel so alone: www.iasp.info/suicidalthoughts/

Witch Tip:
For me, having
mystical experiences
here on Earth kept me going.
Realizing the mystical
— and therefore, death —
is so close
made me curious enough
to stay alive
and conquer Depression.

Let's talk about how to drag the magic out of ourselves.

Ghost Light 2: We can't force specific supernatural or enlightening experiences, but we can learn to recognize them on a more regular basis.

Signs from the universe, or a specific message from a specific deceased loved one, or even memories of our own past or alternate life experiences cannot be ordered on demand. We can't roam into the forest and insist Bigfoot and fairies appear.

Well, we can, but no one needs to obey our commands. Our higher self and subconscious minds don't even obey our commands. It's exasperating.

When we do have a Bizzaro and Enlightening Experience, within the first five seconds, our brain will try to override the experience.

It was just a trick of the light.

Mere coincidence.

That wasn't really a message from my dear grandma. Wishful thinking.

Witch Tip:
**Bizarro Enlightening Experiences happen all the time,
and our Brain tells us to ignore it.**

What we can do is train ourselves to notice the Bizarros and the Bigfoots, and the Divine signs and impressions from our own consciousness. We can become better at telepathy, psychic hits of Knowing, and, of course, we can train awareness of the spirit world and communicate on their behalf if we're called to do so.

Intentions, Boundaries, and Surrender

This chapter in the story delved into a sudden, past life awareness, telepathy between Jason and me, a journey toward the Great Beyond — and a lot of mutual, open-ended intent.

Without realizing it, I was already using my current process. Before every reading with a client, I set an intention, create boundaries, then surrender to whatever comes.

Now I'll teach you how to use that process.

Ghost Light 3: Set Your Intention.

Intention setting in the context of spiritual experiences comes as a surprise to many people, even though it's the number one rule in the book for entrepreneurs, athletes, and creatives. You create a goal or an intent before you rush out onto the field or into a business venture.

In the spiritual arena, folks tend to assume they can demand a reaction from the Great Beyond, our Higher Self, or even other people! Making a demand is an intent, but our demands are usually too exacting, involve the free will of too many other people, and we aren't trained to recognize the responses.

A few good broad intentions are:

* I'd like to be more aware of the signs around me so I know when I'm intuitively on the right track, and I'm going to learn to pay attention to how it feels when I receive a sign;

* I'd like clarity on how to handle _____
    (my elderly pet's physical condition;
    (my child's situation at school;
    (The fight I had with my spouse;

* I'd like to land five new clients in my business this month;

* I'd like to see a sign from my deceased grandmother;

✳ I'd like to have a dream or even a waking memory about a past life;

✳ I'd like something silly to make me giggle today.

These examples are open-ended, which is why they work more easily than, "I demand a heads-up dime to appear on the southwest corner of Fourth and Main tomorrow morning at 11:11 AM, and at the same time, I want to catch a whiff of Grandma's freshly-baked bread, and to see a shooting star in broad daylight."

That demand is not impossible, although you might be setting yourself up for frustration.

The primary issue with that demand is that there's no room for Something More. If you're so focused on the sidewalk looking for your dime, you might miss the Granny's Bakery delivery truck with a logo of a shooting star on the side that drives through the intersection at 11:11 AM.

Witch Tip:
If you're up for it,
the Grand Slam of Intents is:
"Please send me what's in my highest and best good.
Thank you, thank you, thank you."

That one makes us all pucker up, no differently from when an adult tells a child that doing homework is "for your own good."

Sometimes, what's in our highest and best good in the overall scheme of things is NOT what we want in the moment.

The good news is, when we make an intent, we can caveat it.

⊷⊶⊷⊷

Wait! Who the heck are we talking to when we set an intent?

Talk to whomever you feel the most comfortable. We won't always know who we're talking to in Divine communication.

You can pretend you're talking to yourself, the Universe as a whole, an angel, an archetype, an imaginary friend, a tree, a bunny. **You can always talk directly to your own loved ones in spirit. They will hear you, even if you don't hear them respond.**

You can talk in your head, or you can talk out loud. You can write, or type, or draw. You can send thought images. I have several clients who send texts on their phones to a loved one who's passed away. There are no rules on this one.

Witch Tip:
**The more you practice setting intentions,
the louder they ripple through the universe.**

Dose of Magic: Reflection

Set an intention, right now. It could be for your day, your week, your year. What is it?

Ghost Light 4: Set boundaries.

The "highest and best good" intention naturally eliminates what's not in our best interest. However, when I set that intention, that also means I've consciously given permission to my subconscious, my Higher Self, or even the spirit world to send me signs I might not like or want to face.

For example, I have a recurring nightmare with a particular animal. It took me a long time to realize that the only time I have that nightmare is when something is bothering me, yet I'm refusing to deal with it. I'm okay with my subconscious sending me that message through a nightmare, even though I don't like it.

Over time, I have become not okay with the television or lamps coming on in the middle of the night, which they used to do frequently. It scares the bejeezus out of us to hear someone suddenly start talking downstairs or a light on when it shouldn't be.

While I enjoy the idea of maybe-it-was-magic, I couple the intention of "Send me magic" with the clear boundary of "BUT DON'T SCARE ME."

Dose of Magic: Setting Energetic Boundaries

When most people start playing with intentions and asking for signs, the fear of the unknown may arise. A fabulous boundary is to visualize yourself and home surrounded by rings of light, fire, a bubble, or guarded by whatever majestic beings look like to you.

You're constructing a magical, energetic, high-voltage fence around you and your home as you set an intent with clear boundaries.

Take a few seconds to imagine a beautiful, energetic boundary around your home and your family.

That's it! It's simple. If you want, you can make it more elaborate, pull out the cauldron, and throw in the eyes of newt, but it's not necessary. Your visualization is enough.

⌘

Examples of intent + effective boundaries include:

* Please send me five new clients, **who I can best serve** through my business this month. Thank you.

See how this combination is better than simply "five new clients" who may end up being mediocre, even though the revenue result remains the same?

✳ Please send me a sign or whatever is in my highest and best good today, but for the love of Dog, please deliver it gently. I don't need to be hit over the head with it. Thank you.

Ghost Light 5: A ginormous, necessary boundary is Permission.

You can give the Universe, the Divine, or deceased loved ones permission to send you signs and mystical experiences. You can also revoke these permissions at any time.

No one gets to root around inside your mind or your soul's history without your express permission.

The reason the psychic games worked between Jason and me is that we set mutual intents, we both gave each other permission to psychically play with each other, and permission to see into each other's past lives. And we practiced a lot.

Ethical questions can arise regarding permission when it involves the relationship between a parent and a child. You can set your intent to passively receive intuitive hits about your child or any other close loved one, and you're likely already doing so without even thinking about it.

Practicing telepathy with others, even family, is more intrusive than passively receiving intuitive hits, so always ask their permission first.

If you grant permission to others, you can likewise revoke it. You can give the Universe permission to send you signs and revoke that permission anytime.

Ghost Light 6: Surrender the Outcome.

This is the hardest and most important one, and we'll revisit it in upcoming chapters. Surrendering means releasing control over a desired result. Surrender requires trust, and trust takes time to develop.

Surrender allows the five clients best suited for us to show up at the door instead of fixating on Client A and insisting that you won't be satisfied until Client A hires you.

Likewise, the Beings in the Great Beyond have free will, may have a much broader perspective than what we have access to here on Earth, and may know better than you what's in your highest and best good and the best way to communicate it.

Surrender means, "Please send me a sign from my grandmother. I trust she knows best which sign to send me, and I trust that I'll develop the awareness to receive it."

Surrender also means, "The skeptical voice in my head tells me this new goldfinch at my bird feeder is only a coincidence. That may be true. It may also be true that it's a sign from Granny because that was her favorite bird and yellow was her favorite color. Thank you."

The best way, in my experience, to practice surrender is the Sitting in Your Power exercise we discussed in the Chapter 3 Program Notes.

Witch Tip:
**Conscious intention-setting coupled with surrender
leads to deeper, more meaningful connections
with ourselves and the world around us,
which in turn leads to more satisfying work and relationships.**

Doses of Magic:

1. **The Radio Exercise**—When you get in the car, set your inten-
    tion that the Universe will send you a message in the first song
    you hear.

    The radio works better than using a preset playlist. If you feel
    pulled to change the station, do so. This exercise trains you to be
    more consistently aware of everyday synchronicities.

    For instance, while writing this chapter, I hopped in the car on
    a break, and the first lyric to blare out of the speakers said, "I'm
    wide awake!"

2. **Clairvoyance exercise** — Hold an image in your head and set
    your intention to see it out in the world, wherever it may be.

    Social media responds frighteningly well to images in our head.
    But really, so does the Universe and our awareness.

    Using the example above, if you want to see a shooting star, be
    open to seeing it wherever it may appear.

3. **Times on the clock** — Set your intention that your awareness
    leads you to look at the clock at certain times. Fun ones are re-
    peating numbers, such as 3:33, 4:44, or 5:55. But pick any time
    you want.

    You can do the same with waking up. Tell yourself that while your
    alarm is set for 7:00 AM, you want to fully wake up at 6:55 AM.

4. **Try telepathically communicating with animals or pets.** Ask permission from the animal first, then observe the animal's response. Some pets are highly telepathic and enjoy the energy, and you'll hear a clear response in your head. Other pets will glare at you or walk away when you try to talk with them telepathically.

Keep practicing. Both you and the animals might need training to learn how to communicate.

Witch Tip:
All of these exercises are doable.
They take only practice and playfulness.

For Further Inspiration:

* The Telepathy Tapes at
  www.thetelepathytapes.com
  or wherever you listen to podcasts

* www.iasp.info/suicidalthoughts/

* *Entering the Circle* by Dr. Olga Kharitidi, one of my favorite memoirs of all time. Dr. Kharitidi relates her journey from skeptical psychiatrist to slowly being open to the mystical world and bringing shamanism into her practice to heal mental disturbances.

* Please know that if depression or mental illness runs in your family, as it does in mine on both sides, that does not mean you are carrying around an inevitable diagnosis of the same. For an excellent memoir on this, see *Crazy Enough* by Storm Large.

✻ *Illusions* by Richard Bach, a classic on the fluidity of our realities, messages from the Divine, and holding images in your mind, then watching them appear in 3-D reality.

CHAPTER NINE
PROGRAM NOTES
Nighttime Romper Room: Precognitive Dreams, Uniting with Loved Ones in Spirit, and the Remains of the Day

❧

ARE YOU A vivid dreamer like I am? Have you heard a voice plain as day just as you're falling asleep or waking up? Have you awakened and can see a dream-like event playing out in your room?

I scared the hell out of my husband once when I woke up and yelled, "Call 911!"

He sat up and asked, "Why?"

I pointed to my closet and screamed, "There's a man collapsing, and he needs help!"

He said, "Okaaaaayyy. Can you describe him?"

I saw my clothes move on the hangers as if someone had fallen into them, described the man and what he was wearing, then slowly came to the realization that my husband couldn't see him.

My husband responded, "Would you like me to turn on the light?"

❦

Here are a few additional questions I hear most:

✳ I had a very real dream with my Departed One. Did he actually visit me?

✳ Why is the ONE Deceased Person I want to dream about NOT visiting me in my dreams?! Have they forgotten me? Or abandoned me?

✳ I had a horrible dream. Is it going to come true?

✳ Why don't I dream at all?

What in the world is happening with our wackadoodle, and sometimes frightening, nighttime experiences?

To our waking minds, our dreams can seem layered, not linear, and experienced from multiple points of view simultaneously. It's hard to tease apart what portion might be premonitory versus a fear projected from our subconscious into our conscious dream state. Or whether it's merely the janitor coming to sweep out the dust bunnies from the previous day.

Witch Tip:
We rarely know with certainty
what type of dream we had.
It's likely that all types of dreaming
are happening at once.

Here are a few tenets that help me tease apart this discombobulating astral plane.

Understanding Our Dreams

Ghost Light 1: Our unconscious minds don't operate linearly or logically.

Sigmund Freud and Carl Jung are credited as offering the most significant thoughts about dreams during their lifetimes. They believed that our unconscious communicates to our conscious through dreams, offering insights into what we deeply want, need, or fear, which is inherently personal. Jung believed our unconscious used personalized symbols and metaphors, along with universal archetypes.

Therefore, we need to learn the language of our unconscious minds.

Ghost Light 2: Set an intention regarding your dream state.

An intention can be as simple as, "Hey, Wackadoodle Dream Self, I'd like to learn more about what my mind is trying to communicate to me." Or, "I'd like to awaken with insight on this topic. Make it clear, please."

Sometimes, we don't need to remember our dreams in order to awaken with clarity. A friend recently embarked on a business venture and sensed something wasn't quite clear in her business plan, as if she was peering through a foggy window.

By making that observation, she simultaneously set her intention to un-fog the window. She woke up at 2:00 AM with the path forward plainly laid out.

Also, we may remember one portion of one layer of a dream, and we might not even be remembering that accurately, which is why dreams can be disjointed. Pay attention to any fragments you remember. You can set your intention to be, "I'd like to more fully remember my dreams when I wake up tomorrow morning."

Ghost Light 3: Observe your own symbology.

The more you observe your dream state, the more you'll remember your dreams, and patterns will emerge.

For example, water is a direct symbol of consciousness to me. If I'm fully in alignment with myself, I'll dream about crystal clear, aquamarine water. If I'm bothered by something, the water will be murky, and I'll feel afraid of what's lurking underneath.

Dose of Magic: Start a Dream Journal

So many people have startlingly rapid breakthroughs of understanding and patterns when they keep a dream journal.

What is a recurring bad dream or good dream for you? Recurring animals?

Pay attention to even minor symbols. The devil is in the details.

Ghost Light 4: As we transition between states of awareness, our brains travel through mediumistic states.

In a mediumistic state, we hear, see, and participate in conversations on a different dimensional level. When I'm falling asleep, this state can feel like I'm eavesdropping on my Higher Self and that of others. I rarely retain any specific memory of this state, other than it feels familiar, and usually it feels as if I have a clearer understanding of truths about life.

This is also the state where we hear another person's voice loud and clear, as if they're in the room with us.

I believe this is the state my brain is passing through when my body "wakes" up and I see scenes playing out in my room. My brain hasn't fully transitioned back to 3-D reality, so I'm still aware of dreamlike activity.

One explanation is that our dreams and experiences in this state are a side effect of the brain attempting to make sense of random neural activity.[7]

This seems like a partial explanation. While it may be true, it doesn't account for all of our experiences in the in-between states.

Precognitive Dreams

Did you know that our bodies can detect future events seconds before they occur, with measurable physiological responses preceding emotional stimuli???

7   See Allan Hobson and Robert McCarley. "The brain as a dream-state generator: An activation-synthesis hypothesis of the dream process." *Am J Psychiatry.* 1977; 134(12):1335-1348. doi:10.1176/ajp.134.12.1335; https://psychiatryonline.org/doi/10.1176/ajp.134.12. 1335

If our bodies can detect future events, what about our minds while in a dream state? From my experience, I believe our sleeping minds are way more powerful than we can grasp. However, that doesn't mean that every bad dream is a premonition.

Ghost Light 5: The vast majority of bad dreams are not pre-cognitive.

Create a checklist for yourself when you have a bad dream.

⚹ First of all, is the dream bad because of the action or words that took place, or because you felt anxious, scared, or a sense of inevitable doom DURING the dream?

⚹ If dreams are a projection of our buried fears, what is the dream indicating you're worried about? A common fear dream is where we're driving and the brakes fail. The vehicle flies out of control. Usually, that's when we're worried life is going too fast, and we feel out of control of our lives.

⚹ When you have a bad dream about another person, what does that other person represent to you?

⚹ Is the dream illuminating that you're concerned about that other person? Or shining light on a relationship issue you're ignoring?

During my relationship with Mr. Dynamic, which appears in Chapter 14, I started having nightmares that he turned into an alligator, then puppies would turn into alligators. There's so much symbology there, but in short, I didn't need to worry about him. I needed to focus on myself and what the relationship was doing to me. As soon as I did, the alligator dreams went away.

Now let's tackle the big question: Are some dreams actually glimpses of the future?

Ghost Light 6: Precognitive dreams may not *feel* like anything at all. They are more observational.

In the truly precognitive dreams I've had, I felt nothing in the dream itself. I made an observation from an emotional distance, then woke up and said to myself, "I'm not dealing with this right now. I had no fear and no sense of impending doom."

It's not until a few moments later or, sometimes, not until the following morning when I'm fully awake that anxiety and concern creeps in.

It's hard to tease an observation away from our emotional reaction, however, particularly when they're only moments apart.

Ghost Light 7: All souls have free will. Your precognition is not set in stone.

You may have a very real sense of Something's Going to Happen, and it might not come true. That doesn't mean you didn't have the sensation in the first place.

We might be picking up on a heightened *possibility* that a certain event will happen. Whether it does or not depends on a lot of free will by a lot of actors.

Think back to my example of the extreme heebie-jeebies I felt before going on that river trip. It wasn't guaranteed to be a bad trip. In fact, hundreds of people go down that river a day, without mishap.

But my sense of doom did not lessen. In fact, when I saw the boat we were assigned to, I felt the lock click into place.

I should have flung myself into another boat, and in doing so, the doom probably would have evaporated in an instant because I would have been fine.

Listen to your precognition. Don't talk yourself out of it. Just don't assume that your sensation is a foregone conclusion.

Ghost Light 8: When you receive a precognition, you might be sensing a soul-level transition.

Some of us, myself included, pick up on major life transitions that affect us on soul-level, such as when someone is going to pass away, when someone is about to become pregnant, about to break up from a significant relationship, or be fired from a job.

Think of someone in hospice, where the person's passing is a given. You can witness changes in the person's being as the soul transitions further and further away from the body. In the last day or so before that person dies, something changes. You can feel their death is imminent.

This sensation can also be trained. For example, ICU nurses are experts at sensing when someone is ready to pass away. Other nurses who have worked with babies can look at a woman and sense "She's pregnant" before the mom even has cause to know.

Usually, our conscious minds block the precognitive hit. So how else is such a sensation supposed to rise into our awareness? A dream.

Dreams About or with Departed Loved Ones

Why is my loved one NOT visiting me in my dreams? Have they left me behind?

Ghost Light 9: We might be meeting with our loved ones in spirit on a regular basis in the dream world.

This question is the most frequent one I receive about dreaming. I am certain, based on what I've been told through channeling, meditation, and readings, that we commune with the souls of our loved ones through dreams when we need to and when it's beneficial.

We might not remember it the next morning, however.

When we feel the closeness of a person while dreaming, then awaken to the hard reality that we're here on Earth without them physically with us, ouch. That pain is visceral. I don't think our loved ones pull back from us when we're feeling the pain of loss. Instead, I think our brain, to protect us from unnecessary grief, forgets we were just with them.

Ghost Light 10: If it feels like you met with a deceased person on a dream level, you probably did, but the interaction may seem mangled upon awakening.

I had a funny dream with my grandfather after he passed away. I was on a train that stopped at a station. The doors opened and Pops stood on the platform. He pointed at me and grouched, "You're not supposed to be here. Turn around and go back."

I felt very strongly that I had seen him, even briefly, and disappointed I was sent home too soon. I also suspected that there was more going on in the dream than I could grasp, like whispers you can hear with words you can't make out. Or, I only remembered that one wispy layer of the dream.

The point is, trust your sense when it deeply feels like you were with the person in your dream, even if other aspects of the dream feel off.

Ghost Light 11: Don't cling to your conclusions when you've dreamed of another person.

It's normal to dream of a person, living or deceased, then jump to a conclusion upon awakening **based on how the dream made us feel** or the interactions in the dream.

A frequent misconception is that the person we dreamed of, living or deceased, is mad at us, has abandoned us, or is otherwise not okay.

Witch Tip:
Be open to alternate theories existing at once,
because a lot of layering happens
within our dreams
that fall outside our logical, conscious way of thinking.

Dose of Magic: Be the rogue detective when it comes to analyzing your dreams.

Don't let someone else tell you definitively what a symbol or a dream means to you. Rather than go online searching for a dream topic right out of the gate, sit with or journal about a symbol or recurring dream activity first, applying the Ghost Lights above.

Tease apart the dreams that stick with you, and observe what comes up with curiosity. Don't discount any idea that pops into your mind!

When you're flummoxed, or you'd like additional suggestions to chew on, then go searching for possible archetypal meanings.

The practice of not knowing what our dreams mean, with certainty, strengthens our practice of Surrender, which tends to lessen fear. Over time, we can gain clarity with our personal symbols and dreamscapes. The more we learn the language of our unconscious minds, the more wisdom and wants can seep through into our daily choices.

Dreams are your soul's way of processing, healing, and guiding. Trust the wisdom that comes through — it's part of your spiritual toolkit for navigating life with more clarity and confidence.

For Further Inspiration:

 *The Master of Lucid Dreaming* Dr. Olga Kharitidi. This book is her second, and while it can be read independently of *Entering the Circle* suggested in the last chapter, I recommend reading them in order.

* If you're up for losing hours exploring science, research, and very cool anecdotal studies about all aspects of dreaming, both mainstream and theoretical, check out the International Association for the Study of Dreams (IASD), a non-profit organization with essays, a databank of FAQs, the scholarly journal *Dreaming*, and online courses and conferences. **www.asdreams.org**

✴ See also **www.Dreambank.net**: A repository of dream narratives for research and analysis using standardized scoring systems.

Credits:

Here's the citation for Rabbit's quote in Chapter 9 of the Story: "In 1989, less than a third of Americans admitted to consulting a mental health professional. The primary barrier to seeking help? Stigma." (American Psychiatric Association, "Mental Health in America Survey," 1990).

And here's the citation for Rabbit's information in these program notes: Radin, D. *The Conscious Universe: The Scientific Truth of Psychic Phenomena*, (HarperOne 2009).

CHAPTER TEN
PROGRAM NOTES

Gaslighting the Grief: What Not to Say
+ The Taboo Topic of Suicide
+ The Fairy Tale of Soul Contracts

❧

W
HEN YOU'RE IN pain and someone throws spiritually bypassing comments at you, at best, they are unconsciously dismissing you, your emotions, and your reality. At worst, they are intentionally GASLIGHTING you.

What Not to Say to Someone Grieving

It pains me deeply when I see "spiritual" people preach fluffy, positive thinking hooey when confronted with someone else's suffering. This practice only causes further pain to an already bereaved person.

People flit into spiritual bypassing when they can't stand to be confronted with another person's emotional situation. You see this on social media when, say, Lola shares that she's lost a job, or she's going through a rough time.

Suddenly, the dam bursts open with chipper phrases.

"Prayers!"

"Look at the bright side!"

"You're so beautiful! It will all work out!!!"

"Hang in there, Pookie Pie! Hugs!!!"

They want to "fix" the problem because they can't stand their own pain and suffering and, therefore, can't hold space for another person's true state.

When Lola loses a person or pet close to her, the Wrong Things to Say amplify.

"He's in a better place. Be thankful!"

Or, *"She's with God now!"*

My friend, who worked as a funeral director, nearly fell out when someone sent a floral arrangement in the shape of a telephone, with the note, "Jesus called! She answered!"

Ghost Light 1. When someone is in pain, try not to dismiss their emotions, even if others aren't comfortable with high emotion, or the situation, and they say all the wrong things.

It is true that there may be comfort to think of the deceased's soul as being in a "better" or "less suffering" state, surrounded by the Divine and other loved ones.

Comments that address only the deceased, however, dismiss the fact that the grieving person may suddenly have a hundred-pound weight threatening to cave in her chest, she can't gulp in enough oxygen, and she might be worried about how to pay her bills going forward.

In other words, such comments are not entirely helpful.

How about: *"Awww, they'll always be with you in spirit!"* or *"I can feel that they're always around you now."*

These are plain CREEPY and suggest that the Spirit World is watching us in the shower, which they're not.

Additionally, people in deep grief may not sense mystical signs after their loved one has passed, which we'll talk about more in the next chapter's Program Notes. So these comments about the deceased "always being around" can heighten a sense of abandonment and confusion.

This next one is particularly heart-wrenching: *"Friend, it's been a year already. You need to Move. On."*

A grieving person has barely relearned how to breathe after a year, sometimes five years. Yet, I hear from every single client who's lost a child that someone actually said this to them.

Y'all, let's do better.

How To Support Yourself and Others

Ghost Light 2: Grief isn't entirely about the person who's passed. It's about those of us left behind here.

Most of the phrases that do more harm than good focus on the deceased and ignore the living.

Tragic loss feels different from the loss of a person who lived a long life and deteriorated gradually. But loss is loss, and endings always bring grief. Just because someone reached the age of 90 Million Years doesn't mean they won't be sorely missed and create a painful hole in someone's life when they die.

Ghost Light 3: Trauma fatigue is real. Know yourself and how much you can emotionally handle when it comes to supporting another person.

If you cannot hold space for another person in a tragic situation or through loss, don't. You may do more harm than good to you both.

Take care of yourself first. Just don't say any of the above phrases out of your own overwhelm, and for crying out loud, resist the urge to send a bouquet in the shape of a telephone.

Dose of Magic:
Address the Living—if you're up for it.

1. **If you don't know what to say, stay silent.** If you're physically present, standing next to a grieving person may be enough.

2. **Do not try to "cheer up" a person in grief.** Instead, listen and meet them where they are, especially when they're crumpled in a heap, sobbing on the sidewalk. Traffic can wait.

3. **What To Say Instead:**
   a. "I'm sorry."
   b. "I keep thinking of you."
   c. "I can't imagine how you're feeling."
   d. "I know she lived a good, long life, but I'm sure you're going to miss the hell out of her."
   e. "Take all the time you need."
   f. "This massively fucking sucks" works wonders as well.

4. **Follow all the rules of dark humor, meaning, use it only where appropriate.**

When in doubt, keep those lips zipped.

A friend's dad died while standing in line at customs after returning from a trip out of the country. At the funeral, another friend noted, "No one wants to go through customs."

It landed well, primarily because this use of humor wasn't to falsely cheer up the grieving, and it did not dismiss anyone's emotions.

5.   **Check in on the person in the months and years after the funeral.**

Particularly when someone loses a loved one tragically, or after a lifelong marriage, there's a lot of attention paid to the family in the immediate aftermath, then crickets as time wears on, as if their loss has been forgotten. Clients have told me, "It's like the whole world moved on, and I haven't." All you need to do is send a note or say, "You've been on my mind. How are you coping?"

⁂

When we're the ones grieving, there are two natural, long-term reactions that we should pull into our conscious awareness every now and again, like a wellness check. As you see from the pages of this book, I am guilty of both.

Ghost Light 4: We place the Deceased on a pedestal.

This one is inevitable, and in some cases, healthy. But other times, the pedestal placement can be a way of bypassing harsh realities of life with that person, and over a period of years, it can become a way to avoid intimacy in our other relationships.

Ghost Light 5: Because of the Pedestal Placement, we focus more on the deceased than on the living.

Again, totally normal, as grief can be all-consuming. Over the years, however, check to make sure you're devoting enough energy and attention to the folks still on Earth.

Occasionally, I've seen this with parents who have lost a child and truly don't have the energy or emotional resources to focus on their remaining children. In fact, that happened in my own family and had generational consequences, which is discussed in Chapter 17.

Reach out for all the help and support you need, in any form you can grab.

Give yourself time, and give yourself grace.

For Further Support:

* I have included the essay I wrote about grief and suicide in the appendix to this book, and on my website, I have an easier-to-digest free essay hitting additional points about grief: "Five Dirty Facts About Loss." **www.andreasaintamand.com/free-resources**

* For an excellent deep dive on loss, hope, and healing by tending to all parts of our soul, see *The Wild Edge of Sorrow* by Francis Weller.

Understanding Suicide Beyond the Stigma

When grief involves suicide, the complexity—and potential for harmful responses— multiplies.

Ghost Light 6. There are varying reasons that people die by suicide. Sometimes people die by suicide in the slowest, most agonizing manner possible: by living eight decades in a state of quiet despair.

Most people assume suicide is always an act of desperation or mental illness. While those are common drivers, the choice to die can stem from:

- ✳ **Mental health struggles:** Depression, addiction, manic episodes, or medication effects

- ✳ **Safety fears:** Abuse, trafficking, criminal threats, or feeling safer dead than alive

- ✳ **Health-related:** Terminal illness, dementia, or untreated physical/emotional conditions

- ✳ **Perceived burden:** Believing family and caretakers would be better off

- ✳ **Quiet despair:** Living decades in emotional numbness or hopelessness

Ghost Light 7: Reactions to suicide vary widely.

Beyond grief, people experience nothing, anger, confusion, endless unanswered questions, judgment (toward the deceased and survivors), and sometimes relief. All can exist simultaneously.

Ghost Light 8: Don't let the end swallow the whole.

We tend to let the final moments erase years of memories, laughter, and love that came before. Notice if this is happening in your thought patterns and work to balance the last moments with everything that preceded them.

Are we obligated by "Soul Contracts" even beyond the grave?

Ghost Light 9: "Soul Contracts" are a fairy tale. That doesn't mean fairy tales don't come true.

There's an idea that our souls made agreements with ourselves and with other souls to do X, Y, or Z upon incarnating here on Earth. It's a romantic notion that can alleviate the responsibility that comes along with making choices.

But here's a secret.

All souls have free will.

Therefore, **any soul can break a contract at any moment in time. Without penalty.**

Soul contracts come up A LOT after someone has passed tragically. Such as, "We had a contract that he wouldn't live long, and part of my lesson is to learn how to survive the pain."

This might be 100% accurate. We don't know. It is possible that some bodies aren't built to last as long as others, regardless of genetics, environment, diet, exercise, and health.

This notion can help with our grief-healing journey tremendously, by making sense out of the unknowable and reaffirming there is nothing further we could have done to prevent the inevitable. If this resonates with you down in your bones, run with it all the way across the finish line.

Where this idea causes harm is when we hold ourselves back from what we truly desire in life based on a belief of inevitability and unwanted obligation. So many people don't get divorced, don't heal certain traumas, or don't remarry because they believe they made a soul contract with someone else and now must honor it, bearing a cross for the remainder of their lives.

Witch Tip:

A soul contract will never disagree with your heart.

If you feel obligated by the notion of a soul-level contract or promise, and you desire something different, break the contract! There will be no court of law judging you, and no penalties, except the pain you're causing yourself by not breaking free.

"But what about soul mates?"

The Soul Mate Ghost Light shines in the next chapter!

In fact, what if your "lesson" or situation your soul wants to experience is the sensation of breaking free from obligations that no longer serve you?

Dose of Magic:
Reflections and Journal Prompts

1. Have you felt a sense of inevitability regarding a situation or relationship, particularly after someone has passed? Did it bring you comfort or cause more distress?

2. Have you stayed in a situation or relationship you wanted free from because you felt overly obligated on soul-level, beyond any Earthly promise you may have made?

    a. Were you able to break free?

    b. If not, does it help to think of a soul contact as a fairy tale that you no longer need to believe in?

3. Have you felt comforted knowing that a painful, yet seemingly inevitable situation may have led you to strengths you wouldn't otherwise have?

For Further Inspiration:

* *Destiny of Souls* Dr. Michael Newton. This author has placed tens of thousands of people under hypnosis to learn about our souls, concepts of destiny, agreements, experiences, and so forth.

Credits from the Story:

Rabbit's statistics on the Satanic Panic comes from Richardson, J., Best, J., & Bromley, D., "The Satanism Scare," *Aldine Transaction*, 1991.

CHAPTER ELEVEN
PROGRAM NOTES
Shock & Signs,
Soul Mates & Spirit Guides

⟐

I F YOU'VE LEARNED anything from this book so far, it's that conflicting truths exist in our minds and hearts simultaneously and intensely, particularly during a tumultuous time. So let's parse apart a few of the more confusing ones.

Why am I not receiving any signs from my Person who Died?

This is the question I hear most often. You're already in tremendous sorrow, and it feels like a cruel trick that when you want to hear from your person more than ever, all you get back from the Universe is white static.

"Psychiatric shock" or "psychiatric injury due to a traumatic event" is the term for my brain wiping itself clean of all memories of Jason. I read about it in a novel six years after Jason died, and it was the first time I'd ever heard it was a thing.

If you've experienced it on any level, it makes perfect sense, even though it's discombobulating at the time.

Ghost Light 1: All forms of grief will have some element of psychiatric injury, which is why we have a harder time perceiving signs from someone in the weeks and months after they've passed, if ever.

Placing grief to the side for one moment, imagine that in the best-case scenario, communicating between dimensions is like a glacier pulling itself up off the Earth to interact with a wisp of steam floating in the sky.

We're the glacier, incarnated into bodies with dense energy, and the spirit world is steam.

Now think of how much heavier we feel in grief, and how our brains feel like the neural pathways are clogged with molasses. Even when we're anxious, can't sleep, and our minds are bouncing all over the place, we can't focus clearly. In that state, it becomes even harder to pull our glacier selves up into the sky to hear the steamy whispers.

That said, sometimes, in the immediate aftermath of grief, we can be hyperfocused on the spirit world, receive very clear signs and sensations, but as the days turn into weeks and years, the signs dissipate as we slog through our grief.

When we don't receive signs or sensations that resonate with us, it can feel like the person has left us all over again.

Ghost Light 2: It's us, not them.

It's common to blame the spirit world during times when we can't sense its existence. In my experience, however, the signs and sensations of their presence are always there. We have to keep training our awareness to perceive them.

When we're in grief, we don't always have the energy to do so. Be easy on yourself. Our awareness can sharpen, and the signs will come.

And remember from earlier chapters, we have to be open to the many forms signs can come in, rather than insisting on a specific message or sensation.

Ghost Light 3: There is no such thing as time in the spirit world.

"Is it too soon to communicate with my loved one?"

Conversely, "That person has been gone for so long! It's probably too late to hear from them now."

Nope and nope. I've had souls communicate immediately upon passing and within the days that follow — and decades later. The timing depends on us, not them. When we're ready for the communication, and we've hoisted our glacier selves out of the Grief Well enough, we'll become aware of the mystical occurrences around us.

Revoking Permission

In previous program notes, we touched on telling the Universe, "Never mind! Not today!"

In this chapter in the story, I was clear to the Powers That Be (which may be my own brain's receptivity) that I wanted no more precognitive dreams about someone dying. Even though my Auntie Maude's passing was peaceful and the dream was lovely, I couldn't take any more additional awareness at the time.

But I still wanted signs from Jason and other mystical winks.

Ghost Light 4: You can tailor your revocation of permission to your needs in the moment.

You can tell the Universe, your loved ones, and your Higher Self, "Hey, I do want signs, but I don't want any bad dreams."

Or, "I'm overwhelmed. Shut down the entire operation. You're driving me batty."

Witch Tip:
Being aware of our emotional state
is already a WIN!
Being aware of whether we want
to consciously grant or revoke permission
to the Divine is a BIG WIN!

Dose of Magic:
The HALT Method

My colleague and brilliant scholar, Rev. Dr. Katy Valentine, created a rule of thumb when to NOT try to serve others or to tap into your intuitive abilities for yourself or others: when you're HUNGRY, ANGRY, LONELY, or TIRED.

In my experience and that of other professional practitioners, our intuition becomes murky when our cortisol levels are raised.

When we're in deep grief or overcoming a trauma, we're pretty much angry, lonely, and tired all of the time, and our cortisol levels may be higher than normal. We also tend to be overwhelmed.

Trying to tap into our intuition during these times may result in frustration with ourselves and a deeper sense of disconnection — and may cause more harm than good to everyone concerned.

When it doubt, HALT.

The signs are there and will appear when you're ready and have enough energy to perceive them.

I lost my soul mate to death or divorce.
Am I destined to be alone forever?

I was fortunate to have a few soul-level connections in the short period of time immediately following Jason's death. We can't force these connections, but we can't deny them either.

Ghost Light 5: We might have many soul mates over the course of lifetimes.

A soul mate isn't a one-and-done phenomenon. No one can replace another person, but if you've lost Your Person, you can still connect with someone else, should you so desire.

The more we understand ourselves, the more we can connect with many people, on varying healthy levels, at the right time.

Sometimes, we might feel the soul-level love, but Lord help us, we cannot live with that person! A friend of mine found her Person in high school, but through college, they blew up and broke up. Decades later, they reconnected and have been happily, peacefully married ever since. They recognized their connection at first sight, but had to mature with other life experiences before they could live under the same roof.

On the other hand, I've witnessed people stay in volatile, unhealthy relationships because their partner was their soul mate or "Twin Flame" and they didn't feel like they had permission to leave.

Witch Tip:
**Remember: even if someone is connected to you on soul-level,
you are never obligated to tolerate harmful behavior.
Break the bond if it no longer serves you.**

Revisit the bit on Soul Contracts in the previous chapter's program notes if you need to.

A Primer on Spirit Guides, our Trusted Advisors

Who knew the oompa-loompa fellow that made me giggle during my French exam was also my childhood friend, Man-Toy, my Joy Guide! I didn't figure this out until decades later when I began to warm up to the notion of spirit guides.

Ghost Light 6: Imagine that we have a team of trusted advisors we can consult regarding everything going on down here on Earth, no matter how big or small.

The idea that we're not puttering around alone resonates with me. Guides also have a wider perspective than what we're allotted in our limited human form.

It makes sense to me that our Guides may be communicating advice through our subconscious minds, only a fraction of which drips into our conscious awareness.

Think of when the traffic light turns green, yet your foot doesn't leave the brake—then a car runs a red light into the intersection right in front of you! There was a reason you didn't barge ahead. It may have been your Guardian Guide talking through your instinct, suggesting that you pause.

Ghost Light 7: Guides may feel quieter than the sensations of our deceased loved ones and the signs we receive from the Universe.

Guides tend to feel subtle compared to our deceased loved ones, who come with trunks full of shared emotions and memories, including the memory we have of their physical presence. With Guides, we won't remember why they are on our team or "who they are" in terms of personalities or names.

In fact, if names matter to you, you don't need to ask a medium what your Guide's name is! You can name them yourself.

Ghost Light 8: Guides will never tell us what to do.

We can ask for help and guidance, surrender as to how that guidance appears, then we can choose to heed the advice or toss it into the wind like bratty teenagers. Ultimately, a decision is ours to make.

Ghost Light 9: Think of Guides as fulfilling archetypal roles.

We may have numerous Guides, some closer to us at times than others. Roughly, let's say these are the main roles:

✳ **The Guardian:** the Guide who tries to keep you safe. If you choose a life of physical risk, your guardian can only help so much!

✳ **The Gatekeeper:** the Guide consistently closest to you. Think of this Guide as your personal consigliere.

✳ **The Healer:** the Guide who not only helps you heal, but also expands your healing energy to others.

✳ **The Teacher:** the Guide who nudges you when it's time to learn something new, then assists you in absorbing the information. (Teacher and Healer might have placed this book in your hands.)

✳ **Joy:** My favorite! The mischief-maker who alerts you to look in a certain direction to see flowers or puppies, or, as in my case, encourages you to laugh out loud in all the wrong places.

I believe that our Guide team can also include our deceased loved ones in areas where they excelled. For instance, Uncle Bobby, who was a financial guru, might drop in a message, and you suddenly think, "Time to sell."

Do you already have a sense for your Guides?

Dose of Magic: Meeting Your Guides Through Active Meditation

Grab your journal and a pen, then drop into your favorite comfy chair. Hit play on a monotone, shamanic drumbeat track. Turn the volume down. Set your timer for 7–13 minutes only.

Close your eyes, then make your intention to meet one of your Guides.

To give your monkey mind something to do, tell yourself that you'll either swoop into the sky, or down into the Earth. Along the way, you'll meet a Guide. Your Guide may be talking trees, animals, humans, any form imaginable!

Follow your imagination wherever it takes you. This is a funsy — no need for judgment on anything that comes up.

When the timer goes off, write down everything. You will forget later, and you might be surprised what you saw and who you met along the way.

You may need to repeat a few times. Just keep following your imagination.

⧈⧈⧈

When I first did this exercise, guess who I saw? My jaunty little orange-skinned, green-haired friend. I hadn't thought of him or Man-Toy since high school, and I instantly knew we were old pals.

I also saw a barefoot woman with ragged dark hair and muddy feet in a splendid dress layered with deep blue and green tulle and silk. I heard her name. Witch.

I knew she was my teacher of ancient wisdom, knowledge inherent in us all, and I sensed that she pushed me to explore the areas beyond my comfort zone. I also sensed I was safe with these friends.

The following morning, after seeing Witch, the first thing that appeared on my Facebook feed was a photograph of a magnificent Alexander McQueen costume. It was the dress Witch wore in my vision.

Dose of Magic: Spirit Animal Oracle Cards

If you feel like playing with cards, find an oracle deck with artwork that makes your heart soar. Working with animals to relay messages from Spirit Guides is my jam.

With any deck, set your intention — whatever it is — then shuffle the cards. One will either fall out of the deck, or you'll be drawn to pull one.

See what it says! Pay attention to the animal, the colors, or anything that pops out of you from the image in addition to the written message.

⁘⁙⁘

Alternatively, pay attention to what animals in nature continually make themselves known to you, either over the course of one day or repeatedly over time. Feel into what that animal might mean to you. Or draw the card of that animal and see what the message is.

Hold off on looking up the animal on the internet because you'll find a million conflicting messages. Instead, defer to your intuition or what the card pull might tell you.

⌘

The signs, the Guides, the winks from the Divine are all invitations back to wonder, to the knowing that Love transcends every boundary we can imagine.

Love didn't end with anyone's last breath. Trust that you have a team of Guides cheering you on, and most importantly, trust that your wounded heart is also your superpower.

Witch Tip:
Grief is not a problem to be solved
but a love story to be honored.
Magic is real.
You never walk this path alone.

For Further Inspiration and Support:

❋ This chapter in the story described a funeral laden with poisonous religion. If you've been raised with toxicity in religion and are conflicted about how to move through it to a magical spirituality, please see the work of New Testament scholar and metaphysical expert Rev. Dr. Katy Valentine.
www.katyvalentine.com

Not all words deserve an ear.

✴ My favorite animal spirit oracle decks are: *The Spirit Animal Oracle* by Colette Baron-Reid and *The Wild Unknown Animal Spirit Oracle Deck* by Kim Krans.

✴ If you're just starting out with reading cards, I recommend oracle decks rather than tarot. Tarot has its own meanings, which may be more difficult to learn as a beginner.

Credits:

RABBIT's sign in the story: "Complicated bereavement can freeze memories and emotions for years after trauma, affecting roughly 7% of those experiencing loss," came from Shear, M.K., "Complicated Grief," *New England Journal of Medicine*, 372(2), 2015.

CHAPTER TWELVE
PROGRAM NOTES
Dracula & Drivel: Drivers Toward Success
+ The Roadblock of Over-Responsibility

❧

HAVE YOU STAYED in a relationship or job because a voice in your head nags that if you leave, you'll be deemed a failure? Or, you reach for a goal to prove you're not a failure? I've never regretted my years dancing professionally. That said, it wasn't until those boxes were checked that I realized I had nothing further to prove to anyone or myself. Only then could I authentically check in with my desire: Did I want to keep dancing at all?

Ghost Light 1: Unconscious drivel may be driving your achievement.

If it's healthy, great! Such as, "I am NOT stopping until I hit that milestone. When I'm tucked snug in my grave, I'd be mad at myself if I gave up now."

But if it's unsustainable and trapping you in a situation too long, bring it into your awareness, and let's kick it to the curb. Such as:

✴ **Naggie Nelly:** I've already invested so much time and energy and money into this decision/career/relationship, I can't walk away now.

    ☾   Counter: Maybe I should stop throwing good money and energy after bad. I can cut my losses and free myself.

✴ **Naggie Nelly:** Push on, girl. What are you, a quitter?

    ☾   Counter: I've already achieved everything I want from this endeavor. It's wearing me down instead of inspiring me.

✴ **Naggie Nelly:** You're REALLY good at This Thing. Besides, what else can you do this well?

    ☾   Counter: Thank you for acknowledging how kick-ass I am at This Thing. If I achieved This, I can achieve the Next Thing.

✴ **Naggie Nelly:** Boss Man still looks down on you. Don't you want to prove yourself to him?

    ☾   Counter: Does his approval matter to me anymore? Nope.

✴ **Naggie Nelly:** BUT YOU'LL GO BROKE! YOU'LL BE HOMELESS BECAUSE YOU DON'T KNOW WHAT'S NEXT!

    ☾   Counter: I hear you. I'll figure it out.

Ghost Light 2: "I'm done" feels different from "I give up."

"I'm done" feels like there's no blood left to squeeze out of the experience, given your personal desires and life goals.

Giving up feels like turning your back on a large holiday buffet when you're starving. Giving up will have twinges of regret. We give up on a goal for a variety of reasons, when Naggie Nelly's yammering gets too loud, when others don't believe in us or share our vision, or when we're faced with repeated rejection, time, or financial constraints.

Witch Tip:
The critical question to ask yourself is:
Even if I succeed wildly within this venture,
is it an experience I still want to pursue?

～⁓⚬⊰⊱⚬⁓～

Alternate Guides Can Nudge Us Toward Achievement, Particularly When We Don't Know What's Next

Dracula emerges from the shadows and makes his presence known to me too often to be chalked up to coincidence. So I've adopted him as my alternate, imaginary Guide.

I have a client who noticed that Secretariat, the Triple Crown winning thoroughbred, showed up over and over in her life, and she wasn't even a horse person. So she researched him, allowed herself to feel connected to him, and now allows the spirit of this great horse to guide her toward strength and freedom.

Maybe the guidance comes from our subconscious or our imaginations. The source doesn't matter if the nudge works to inspire us to fuller, more authentic lives.

Ghost Light 3: Fictional characters, historical people, and animals can serve as Guides.

Sometimes, feeling playful with our Guides is more effective than over-rationalizing it or trying to box an energy into an archetype.

We may see a character as possessing traits and achievements that we'd like to bring into our lives. Or something mystical about the character may deeply inspire us.

If my Guides, my Departed Loved Ones, and my Subconscious all know that the way to move me in the right direction is to send in Dracula, aren't they going to use him?

Dose of Magic: Is there a recurring character in your life, fictional or historical?

Make note of all the times a character has repeatedly appeared in your life. You may have pooh-poohed it as coincidence. See if the character emerges again. It will be a synchronicity, I guarantee, and over time, a pattern will emerge.

What is it in that character's essence that is alluring to you? Your answer may change over time, and it will reveal what you're being nudged toward.

Over-Responsibility for Others Can Be a Roadblock to Hearing Our Truth

Ghost Light 4: Trauma can lead to an exaggerated sense of responsibility for others.

Traumatic experiences tend to make us feel out of control, or even at fault. We can then take on excessive responsibility for the emotional well-being of others to the detriment of ourselves.

I've seen this A LOT in people who were abused as children. On the surface, it appears as people-pleasing, but when the person ignores their own life goals in favor of someone else's dreams, it's self-destructive. It's a tough pattern to break, but not impossible once you're aware of it.

Ghost Light 5: You are allowed to take what's yours and leave what's theirs.

In this part of the story, Mom sure did nail it when she delineated for me what was my responsibility and what wasn't when Dad called in a crisis.

It's really hard to walk away from perceived responsibilities when a loved one is hurting, but sometimes, drawing a healthy boundary is the best thing to do for all concerned.

Sometimes, you aren't the right person to call.

Dose of Magic: Trust Your Knowing When Others Disagree

Distinguishing your voice from the noise is a process, but trust what you know.

Here's a checklist:

* What boxes do you have to check in life? Do you still want them there?

* Have you reached authentic completion on certain experiences?

* What are you continuing out of habit compared to desire?

* Are you engaged in endless proving?

* Are you giving up because you don't want to tackle all the road-blocks between today and your future goals? **If you gave up, would it feel disappointing, or like a relief?**

* What new boxes would you like to create?

Dose of Magic: Your Future Self as Your Guide Exercise

Naggie Nelly might argue vociferously with our Draculas and Secretariats, but she can't argue with our future self.

This one is my personal go-to when determining whether to go for the gold or walk away. I've left relationships and even sold houses and moved out of state when I felt that Future Me would feel stifled if I were still in the same place thirty years from now.

There are also times when I've known that Future Me would be disappointed if I didn't try for something, even if I splooted face-first.

Here's how we can use our future selves as our Guide.

Can you imagine your future, much older self? What kind of life has she led?

If you can't conjure it, think of an elderly person you admire greatly. Someone who has no regrets, feels proud of their accomplishments, is comfortable with their so-called failures, and left no stone unturned.

If you're that person, looking backward through time at the You Today, what is the Future You's advice?

Will she be proud that you reached for the stars and still managed to land on the moon? Will she tell you it's time to rest and give yourself a pat on the back? Or will she tell you to take one more leap before you head back to Earth?

Witch Tip:

**When your boxes are checked,
the signs align and your Future Self nods approval.
That's your green light,
regardless of who thinks you're making a mistake.**

CHAPTER THIRTEEN
PROGRAM NOTES
Witchcraft & Curses

W ITCHCRAFT TENDS TO have too many rules for me. I can't even follow a cookie recipe.

I argue with the ingredients and amounts, and I do the same every time I've tried to follow a complex ritual and cast a spell.

That said, rituals can provide comfort in times of uncertainty and helplessness. Particularly if it seems that someone else has more knowledge of the craft and a better handle on the unknown forces in the world than we do.

Like Warlock to Daisy.

Simultaneously, the idea of witches, spells, and curses conjure the dark side of the unknown. They seem to promise a greater power, yet come with a risk of danger.

Let's pull back the curtain on spell-casting and the energetics of curses to reveal the truth: the real magic isn't in following complex rituals — it's in understanding the energy behind them.

Spell-Casting 101

You're already familiar with how to cast a spell. In the Program Notes for Chapter 8, we learned to set an intention, erect boundaries, then surrender to the outcome.

Why does witchery seem different?

Ghost Light 1: Witchcraft requires more physical actions, rather than a mere mental exercise.

Spell-casting typically entails:

⚹ A desired outcome;

⚹ Ingredients, including the elements of fire, water, and earth;

⚹ Doing something with those ingredients, such as boiling, lighting a flame, placing objects in a jar, a pouch, or a specific locale outdoors;

⚹ At a specific time of the day, month, or season;

⚹ The use of symbology; and

⚹ Speaking your intention out loud, through chanting, songs, or prayer to a deity.

The idea is that if you take physical actions, in addition to a mere mental exercise, then you're speaking and activating your desire into 3-D reality.

Therefore, your intent has much more power.

Ghost Light 2: Surrender takes a back seat.

Usually, witchcraft rituals are geared more toward tangible manifestation. The energy might feel more like an active direction of our will. When you're feeling uncertain and helpless, surrender feels frustratingly passive.

Ghost Light 3: "Praying to" or asking assistance from strange deities can make us uncomfortable.

It's common to feel resistant to the idea of asking a specific deity for help, particularly if it's a being with whom we have no resonance and may have never heard of.

If you feel this way, don't do it!

On the other hand, there are beings, historical and mythological, that may embody qualities we want to draw into our own lives. Clients have whispered to me, "I've never told anyone, but I feel drawn to Hecate. Should I research her further?"

YES.

Dose of Magic: Reflection

If you are pulled to a Being, like the Guides we discussed in Chapter 11 Program Notes, then explore what aspects about that persona intrigues you.

It may be that you're wanting to draw those qualities out of yourself. It's easier to do so when we have a role model who already embodies those traits.

Ghost Light 4: Witchcraft has been viewed as requiring a deal with the Devil.

The Devil myth stems from religious teachings that we mere humans aren't powerful souls in our own right, that we need supernatural help, and because we supposedly can't access the Divine directly, we must be turning to the Devil.

This is nonsense.

Unless you specifically want to work with dark forces, witchcraft doesn't require it. When you cast a spell, or ask for help from a Being with whom you resonate, you're not accidentally making a deal with the Devil. You're simply exercising your divine birthright to create change in your life.

Ghost Light 5: We've also been taught that getting what we want requires giving up pieces of ourselves.

What a brilliant way to keep people disempowered!

Yes, we make conscious trades daily, such as exchanging time and freedom for a high-paying career. But that's different from believing you must sacrifice something precious and unknown to receive your desires.

Don't assume manifesting what you want requires a dangerous payoff. However, be realistic: Does what you want require new responsibility or changes to your current life?

That's not a curse. That's growth.

Ghost Light 6: Historically, witchcraft has been viewed as manipulative.

There's a difference between voicing a desire and inflicting that desire on a specific target. For example, love potions and their accompanying rituals tend to be directed at an individual, ignoring that other person's free will to fall for you or not.

A better practice would be to perform the love potion focusing on the qualities you want in a partner, rather than fixating on attracting one person.

Dose of Magic: Be your own Witch

It took me a long time to realize I was fine with making up my own rituals and leaving out the parts that feel superfluous, inauthentic, or creepy to me. In fact, our intentions are likely to be clearer to the Universe when we follow our own nudges about how to express them.

The basics of intention setting, erecting boundaries, then surrender remain the same, and in my experience, the most effective.

Here's my go-to ritual that you can practice on a daily basis. Feel free to make it your own:

1. Set your intention. Write down or speak out loud, "I want _____." It's important to bring this intention out of your head and into physical reality. It's also important to focus on the qualities or big-picture outcome rather than on a particular individual.

2. As you speak, or just after you've finished writing, light something on fire. Strike a match, a lighter, a candle, incense, pick your favorite.

3. Wave it in front of a window or around your room, and ask for help. You can direct your request to your Guides, the Universe, Bigfoot, any Being with whom you feel comfortable to play.

4. Surrender. The Universe knows better than you how to bring your intention to your doorstep.

5. Close it out: "In the highest and best good of all beings everywhere, so it is. Thank you, thank you, thank you."

6. Blow out the flame.

Curses

Ghost Light 7: Curses epitomize the height of manipulation.

Curses target an individual, with the goal of rendering that person helpless to the will of another, with intended harmful results.

A curse will feel like a specific person energetically — and purposely — vomited on you in a WHOOSH! It's a tidal wave of energy directed from one person to another, beneath the words.

We can see this sometimes from commenters on social media. We'll see a spew of angry hatred that seems way too personalized — given the content — and carries a frightening amount of energetic severity that doesn't match the words.

If this ever happens to you, delete, delete, delete. Do not engage, and don't overthink it. If the person continues spewing on your feed, block them. Even if that person is your relative.

Bye bye, Felicia.

Ghost Light 8: You cannot be cursed without your permission.

You are a divine being with free will. A curse will only work if it targets a perception of yourself THAT YOU ALREADY BELIEVE TO BE TRUE. Usually, these self-beliefs come attached with stigmas and shame.

For example, if you deeply, even subconsciously, believe that you are undeserving of love, you will either welcome relationships into your life that prove the belief, or you will unconsciously take steps to ensure that you remain single.

Then, a fortune-teller says, "You're cursed in love." Or an ex hisses at you, "You will never find love again."

If it's the energy of a curse, you'll feel the WHOOSH. If it lands, you'll feel a burning shame of being exposed for your deepest desire and your most vulnerable weakness.

You'll feel a tangible block in yourself that exists between you and what you want. And that block feels inevitable.

Ghost Light 9: You are not helpless. You can remove a curse. But only you can do so.

How? Change your behavior and your self-belief system. Disentangle yourself from actions and people that sabotage your goals and desires, from stigmas and shame.

In the story, Daisy felt cursed, but she also had options as she grew into adulthood to confront the many instances of abuse in her life. That healing would have empowered her.

In her defense, I believe that's what she was trying to do with Warlock, by looking for redemption in "forbidden" practices. Understandably, she fell prey to coercion at that point in her life.

For another example, if your identity is that of the martyr and a penniless victim, you might feel cursed. But only you can take steps to change your self-view, change your relationship with money, and stop allowing people to take advantage of you.

Over time, you'll become more empowered. Your former mates won't like it, but that's their problem.

Witch Tip:
**Any feelings of a curse —
even if someone else tries to place one on you —
will slide off when you no longer believe
a false narrative about yourself.**

Dose of Magic: Reflection

Think of a nasty breakup. Were there times you could sense your ex sending extreme angry vibes your way? Such as, they wanted you to fail, or never find love again?

Did you outgrow it at some point and realize you moved on? You no longer engaged in thoughts of him or her and discovered that whatever ill they wished you, you no longer cared?

Ghost Light 10: If someone tells you that you're cursed, don't engage. Move on.

A lot of fraudulent "fortune tellers" make money by telling clients that they're cursed, then offering to "remove" the curse for money. Another face of this scam is that they tell you they see something "special" in you that they can unlock, promising love, riches, or fame.

This is all malarkey.

Scammers generally are brilliant at sensing a victim's weak spot, or greed, and playing into it. They are not psychics, nor are they seeing hidden starbursts in you.

Like all other fraudsters — from Charles Ponzi, to Bernie Madoff, to possibly the corner fortune teller — they are trying to manipulate you. They are experts at talking — usually overly quickly or over-sharing — and experts at eye contact and reading body language and reactions.

They will mimic your words, movements, and even pretend they share your same experiences in order to create a bond.

Don't engage. Make no eye contact. Keep walking. You can even raise your hand and dismiss them with a wave. Poof!

Practical act of witchcraft there.

Dose of Magic: Letting Go
Visualization to Dissipate Anyone
Else's Lousy Energy or Ill Will

This is another one of my go-to's. A quick meditation to get anyone else's ill intentions, or their own junky energy, out of my auric field. Once you learn this one, you can visualize it in an instant or take as many breaths as you need.

Place your feet firmly on the ground. Barefoot, outside is best, but not necessary. Close your eyes and take deep breaths.

Imagine everything that no longer serves you dripping from your head, down your arms and body, down your legs, and into the Earth like dirty water. You might see chunks of stale energy falling off of you.

The Earth is vacuuming away everyone else's "stuff."

All of that energy falls to the very center of the Earth. There, energy gets transmuted into hot, white, pure energy.

The energy then shoots back up into you. You can imagine pillars of light, or tubes covered in diamonds or crystals, sparkling with perfect, healing, Earth energy.

The energy comes into your feet and into your hands. It shoots up your legs and into your root chakra.

If you are familiar with chakras, see each chakra as a full ball of color, feel each one as a clear ball of color. You might feel tingling, particularly up your back and sides.

Allow the energy of light to erupt from the top of your head and flow around you like a glowing waterfall.

Now imagine pulling more energy from the top of your head back into your heart. Imagine pulling more energy from the Earth up into your heart. All that perfect energy is now filling your heart where it will expand into a full bubble that grows outside your body. You are now in a perfect bubble of light and pure energy.

Open your eyes, touch your face and hair. Return to the present.

Dose of Magic: Affirmation —
I rise, I rise, I rise

J.E. McTeer served as the sheriff and as a witch doctor in Beaufort County, South Carolina for fifty-three years. He helped people find jobs and love, helped with financial issues, and with removing curses through the practice of witchcraft.

He had one rule: he worked witchcraft only to enhance someone's belief in their own empowerment. The aggrieved person had to conduct the spell himself, on himself.

When asked how a sheriff could believe in such silliness, he answered, "It doesn't matter what I believe. It matters what you believe."

The opposite is also true and is wonderful when someone tries to pull you down or sends you less-than-high-vibe wishes.

In conjunction with the above Letting Go Dose of Magic, this simple affirmation works wonders:

> *It doesn't matter what you believe.*
> *It matters only what I believe.*
> *I choose to rise.*
> *I rise.*
> *I rise.*

Another option:[8]

> *I arise today*
> *through the strength of the heavens,*
> *light of the sun,*
> *splendor of fire,*
> *clarity of ice,*
> *speed of the wind,*
> *depth of the snow,*
> *stability of the Earth,*
> *firmness of the rock.*
> *I rise.*

Remember: You already have everything you need. The question isn't whether you can access your own power. It's whether you'll choose to trust it.

---

8   Susan Pesznecker, *Yule: Rituals, Recipes & Lore for the Winter Solstice*, (Llewellyn Publications, 2015), 81.

Dose of Magic:
Readers' Guide Reflection

✳ Why did Daisy go back to Warlock? Do you think it was because he allowed her a space to explore something "wicked"? To explore her beliefs? Even though she was repulsed by him as a person?

✳ Or to cement her beliefs that witchcraft, or free spirituality outside religion, was repulsive?

✳ Have you ever met a Daisy?

✳ Has there ever been a season when you were a Daisy?

For Further Inspiration:

❊ If you can find it, *Fifty Years as a Low Country Witch Doctor*, or *High Sheriff of the Low Country*, both by J.E. McTeer.

❊ *Witch: Unleashed. Untamed. Unapologetic* by Lisa Lister.

Credits:

In the story, Rabbit's comment that "Readers are drawn to vampires because these monsters touch something primal within us, reflecting our own repressed desires and fears" came from: Nina Auerbach, *Our Vampires, Ourselves*, (University of Chicago Press, 1995), 6.

CHAPTER FOURTEEN
PROGRAM NOTES

Who's Driving this Train Anyway? Our
Subconscious, Mental, & Emotional Bodies

༄

EVER WONDER WHY you sabotage what you *say* you want? Why you pick the "logical" option but feel hollow inside? At some point, we all shove our hearts into a trunk, locking them away for safety or survival. That's why so much of this book is about freeing them.

In this chapter in the story, I made the conscious choice to pack up my heart. But even then, Big Doors swung open in ways I never saw coming.

So something else — a deeper, unseen force — seemed to take over, as happens to us all. Sometimes, that force moves us forward. Sometimes, it derails us. Often, both.

Let's meet the internal forces quietly running our lives from backstage. And the best part? Let's learn how to stop fighting them and start partnering with them.

Ghost Light 1: There are three distinct, internal drivers of our life experiences: our subconscious desires, our mental machinations, and our untamable emotions.

They live together in a sloppy menage-a-trois.

Unbeknownst to Mental and Emotional, Subconscious is the conductor, laughing at the other two, who quarrel like codependent lovers.

Mental assumes rationality rules and comes across to Emotional as a condescending know-it-all. Emotional, however, is the Diva and won't hesitate to throw a hand grenade into Mental's perfectly organized sock drawer.

You and I are left to go about our business in the world with a straight face, pretending that everything going on inside of us is hunky-dory. But in truth, we're a reactive mess, struggling to bring what we want into our lives.

Shadow Work:
Bringing the Subconscious Conscious

We discussed the fear of our desires in the Program Notes to Chapter 4 and we'll go a little deeper here into the concept of Shadow Work.

Ghost Light 2: Shadow work is based on the premise that we've repressed memories and desires into our subconscious for varying reasons. Until we give them conscious attention and reconcile these pieces of ourselves, these subconscious drivers will rule our lives.

When the subconscious drives the train, we may find ourselves in inexplicable, repeating patterns that sabotage what we think we want.

Take, for example, the Law of Attraction, a misunderstood manifestation practice. Most people think, *I want to attract a lot more income and I'm willing to do whatever it takes. If I keep that desire in my conscious mind, it will eventually come.*

But what if Subconscious doesn't want the responsibility that comes with extra income? What if Subconscious loves life the way it is, on a tight budget, and the more that desire is suppressed, the more Subconscious will cling to it?

What if the Law of Attraction brings in what Subconscious wants, until those desires are given attention and pulled out of the shame closet?

Here's where shadow work becomes essential. Shadow work means bringing your unconscious desires into the light — not to judge them, but to understand what they're really asking for.

In the story at the end of Chapter 13, we learned that the characters in *Dracula* experienced taboo aspects of themselves through relating to the "monster."

Then they killed him, shoving the so-called wicked parts of themselves back underground. Which meant they spent the rest of their lives secretly yearning for him — and probably subconsciously manifesting self-sabotaging events so they could experience the thrill of the monster again.

Because when we shame our shadows instead of integrating them, they control us from their hiding spot.

Our Mental & Emotional Bodies

In their purest form, our mental body is our thoughts, and our emotional body is, of course, our feelings.

A silly example: Emotional says, "I WANT TO GO SWIMMING RIGHT NOW!" Mental responds, "I hear you, friend. A hurricane just made landfall down the road, and we might get struck by flying alligators. How about tomorrow instead?" Emotional pouts but agrees.

Usually, though, each is highly influenced by the other, particularly when we fall into unhealthy thinking and emotional patterns.

When we develop a pattern of talking ourselves out of our wants because we deem our desires to be irrational, eventually, Emotional will flip out. Other times, we allow Emotional to behave like an undisciplined toddler without stepping back to allow Mental to offer logical observations.

If they're so tangled up in unhealthy patterns that we can't separate the two, then we spiral into paralysis, depression, and anxiety, which is what cognitive-behavioral therapy targets.

At all of these points, Subconscious has full rein. But we're so distracted and confused by Mental and Emotional mud-wrestling, we can't understand what's happening in our lives.

Ghost Light 3: JEALOUSY is a no-fail shortcut to discern exactly what Emotional wants without Mental's input.

Jealousy is my favorite reactive emotion ever. When we're jealous of another person, their accomplishments, their boyfriend, their handbag, their hair, ZING! That's what we want.

It's not that we necessarily want to steal their boyfriend, and we might not even want the handbag. We do want something that the relationship, the item, or the accomplishment represents to us.

For example, if you're jealous of someone's book deal, you might think it's about money or recognition. But dig deeper. Maybe you want the courage to share your voice, or the feeling of being taken seriously as a writer.

Unfortunately, we're told jealousy is bad, so we shut it down without further ado.

These are typically the times when we behave badly based on jealousy. In these instances, we're actually acting out of insecurity, which can lead us to be controlling.

If we take a breath and stand back, however, the underlying jealousy is still trying to send us a truth bomb. Maybe we're not getting enough attention from a relationship. Maybe there's a part of ourselves that we're not paying enough attention to.

Maybe we need to work on our self esteem, or maybe we need to acknowledge that a relationship is shredding our self-confidence and we need to leave.

Tease apart the jealousy from the insecurity, and you'll find a whopper of a wise nugget.

≈≈≈≈≈≈

When we allow ourselves to luxuriate in jealousy and desire, we may learn that we simply want to experience the feeling of desire without the responsibility of taking action. Or, a path forward suddenly becomes clear to us on how to go after a new goal, or how to leave a situation.

Witch Tip:
Jealousy is Taboo,
the desire it raises in us is Taboo,
and, therefore, it might be Subconscious winking at us.
Wink back.

Dose of Magic: Reflection

When was the last time you felt jealous?

What caused it?

No overthinking and no self shaming!

Ghost Light 4: Mental wants you to allow conflicting thoughts.

Our thoughts become really clear when we allow them space to be conflicted. The problem arises when we jump to shutting down trains of thought and insist that only one line of thinking must be accurate.

This is where writing out the good ol' pros and cons list is helpful. Not that you should make your decision on which choice has the greatest pros, but at least you're giving yourself permission to see everything in black and white.

Witch Tip:
If you can't make a decision,
you either don't have enough information,
or you're not yet ready and need more time.

Ghost Light 5: The absurd hiccup is that we tend to "feel" facts and "think" feelings.

One of the hardest exercises I was given in therapy later in life was to get grainy on discerning thoughts from feelings when both were wrestling in the Upside Down. With observational practice, clarity eventually came to distinguish the two—but it was not easy.

When we're in a quandary, or our mind is muddled in confusion, we'd love to pretend that we do this:

"I think XYZ about this situation. I feel ABC."

Instead, we find ourselves saying, "I feel the light is red. I think I'm angry about it."

Funny, but common.

Most of the time, it looks like, "I feel like I should take this promotion. But I think it's not a good fit."

The more honest version is, "I think this promotion offers opportunities to obtain a new skill set and make more money. I feel like it's not a good fit because I don't want to devote my time to that skill set, and I'll be miserable every day."

If I had perfectly performed this exercise at the time discussed in the story in Chapter 14, I would have said, "I really want to stay in Charleston and in South Carolina. I feel rejected by my home state, but I'm worried it's not a good fit to stay here for law school. I feel so disappointed that I have to leave.

"I also want expansive experiences, not restrictive ones. I think it's better for me to head to Chicago. I don't like it, but that's what I'm doing."

My heart and thoughts were given full voice, and apparently along with my subconscious, the manage-a-trois were all at the table because the Big Doors of a fancy law school opened that ended up broadening my view of the world and changing how I saw myself.

Dance with the Manage-a-trois

Being aware of our multiple internal influences can help us understand our current circumstances, especially the ones we think we might not want, then make more authentic, proactive decisions going forward.

Ghost Light 6: Allowing equal space for thoughts and feelings will help you also allow the suppressed nudges from Subconscious to become more obvious. You can then make proactive choices rather than staying stuck in reactive, suppressive patterns.

Take, for example, Sarah. She wanted to start a coaching business but kept "forgetting" to post on social media.

Consciously, she wanted clients. Subconsciously, she feared judgment from her corporate colleagues and desired their respect. She told herself their opinions of her didn't matter, but, in truth, it did matter.

Her emotional body felt excited about using her skills to connect with people in a new way, while her mental body spun round and round, not understanding why she wasn't getting clients through word-of-mouth, all while beating herself up for forgetting to make posts.

Once Sarah recognized the manage-a-trois at play, she could address each part. She finally acknowledged, "Ahhhh, I hate it, but Subconscious desires respect from Ernie and Ed at work."

Sarah could then further acknowledge, "There are lots of people in the world with the traits of Ernie and Ed who WILL respect my coaching skills, even if Ernie and Ed don't understand. And YES, I want respect from people with those traits. By the way, I'm jealous of coaches who already have the respect of those folks."

She could feel excited, deliciously jealous, and allow her mental body to create a strategic plan that felt productive.

Result? She stopped "forgetting" to make marketing posts. Her business launched successfully because all three parts of herself were aligned instead of fighting each other.

Ernie and Ed were probably secretly jealous.

Or, take the patterns of millionaires, for example, who repeatedly fall into bankruptcy and start over, gaining success each time before losing it all again. Subconsciously, the millionaire isn't afraid to fail and secretly loves the creative process of building under pressure.

But once she earns the next million, the pressure goes away, so the creative process changes. She then subconsciously brings failure into her life.

When she recognizes her true Subconscious desire, she can manufacture other ways to keep the creative process fiery. In one such case, the entrepreneur handed the finances over to her husband, so her creative process — and her view of success — wasn't tied to money in the bank. Instead, she could pressure her creativity with notions of *How do I create more boldly, more originally, in more useful ways to humanity?*

Subconscious was thrilled with the tough pressure, and she made millions even faster, joyously and mentally stimulated, without the financial roller coaster.

Dose of Magic: Reflection/Journal Prompt

- If you take this concept of a Secret Subconscious driving your life, do aspects or times of your life make more sense now?

- Have you been through periods where you did everything by the book and nothing worked?

- Were there relationships that "made sense" but fell apart anyway?

✳ Have you been rejected by your desired hometown, and it pushed
    you toward an opportunity that offered a greater fit?

✳ Have there been times when you were overwhelmed and your
    body (or Subconscious working through your body) decided
    your next steps for you, like when I had a debilitating migraine
    at the thought of staying with Mr. Dynamic? Or like when Mom
    passed out when she nearly married the wrong guy?

⚶⚶⚶⚶

Now let's invite Dracula to dinner.

Dose of Magic: How would Dracula tempt you?

Dracula has a lot going for him, mentally and emotionally, and all
his vexing subconscious desires are conscious. He knows how to use
each element of his internal self with ease.

How are we mere mortals supposed to resist?

We're not. And because we have access to all of these same super-
powers, let's play.

**If Dracula knocked on your door in the most irresistible form
imaginable, how would she or he lure you outside?**

It's just you and Dracula. You don't get to involve another person.
You can't use Dracula to force someone else to do something, such as
*I'll walk with the ol' vamp under the moonlight if he makes my husband
be more emotive and romantic.*

Instead, tease yourself with:

What desire am I not allowing myself? Maybe it's creative freedom, recognition, or simply permission to rest.

What is the most taboo thing you can think of that wants to be expressed within yourself?

What makes you jealous? What are your conflicting thoughts over it?

Do you feel unsafe exploring the world with Dracula?

You can journal these answers, but ... I think it's best to do the Big Heart meditation mentioned in Chapter 3 program notes. Play music, drop into your comfy chair, close your eyes, and allow desire for something to well up inside of you.

When I can't quite grasp what I want with clarity, I imagine green or purple mist flowing through me, swirling around, then I surrender to a mystical feeling for a few moments.

Sometimes, what we want is to simply feel magical — or safe in the mystic sea. Allow your Dracula to help with that.

Your Dracula will push *something* into your awareness, because with him or her, all of your internal drivers are welcome to the party — Mental, Emotional, and Subconscious.

Witch Tip:
**You don't need to be afraid,
because in this scenario,
your Dracula is You.**

CHAPTER FIFTEEN
PROGRAM NOTES
Shangri-La and Snake Oil Salesmen:
Reading Space + the Suspicion of Flakes

☙❧

I TOILED AWAY with my summer associate projects in K&E's D.C. office, hunched over my desk under fluorescent lights, missing Charleston's gas lanterns.

We've all felt the pull toward Somewhere or Some Thing. A place or set of circumstances that feel like home before we've even arrived. We tend to dismiss these longings as daydreaming, but longings are our soul's GPS trying to guide us home to ourselves.

During the law years, I didn't have time or emotional energy for anything other than Very Serious school, then Very Serious work. Any longings outside those bounds seemed superfluous. Sound familiar? In my experience, this is when we start dreaming of Shangri-La.

What is Shangri-La?

It's a fictional, harmonious, magical place that exists far away.

We ALL have access to our personal Shangri-La, and learning how to be aware of the energy of space is one of the easiest ways to tap into our intuition and to the messages from our Souls and from the Divine.

Reading the space around us also alerts us to unnecessary or overly cumbersome compromises we've made that need to change.

The Energy of Space

When we start dreaming of a vacation or traveling to exotic locales, these imaginings are SAFE. Therefore, we indulge in them easily. Maybe we want to escape from our current lifestyles. Maybe we merely need a break. Sometimes, we plan the trip. Sometimes, fantasizing is enough.

Ghost Light 1: When we are so busy in our daily lives that we can't find where we buried our dreams, we always have Shangri-La.

When Dad took pictures of me in the offices at Kirkland & Ellis with the White House in the background, my shoulders were slumped! I was so exhausted, I couldn't sit up straight for the length of a camera click.

I never stopped dreaming about returning to Charleston. I tried to sell myself the Life in D.C. Package, but I couldn't buy it.

Pretty sure my droopy posture was the weight of all my dreams that I tried to ignore bearing down on my neck.

My classmates and colleagues couldn't understand why I felt drawn to a sleepy southern town that most folks back then confused with Charlotte. Charleston was my Shangri-La for reasons I couldn't explain.

Ghost Light 2: A magical space

✴ feels like Champagne for the Soul

✴ or consistently re-energizes us, regardless of our circumstances,

✴ because it reflects something in our soul back to us in physical reality.

Our Shangri-La doesn't have to be perfect, yet it will seem like the air sparkles, or that we feel home. It's as if we can fully breathe, even momentarily.

It doesn't have to be an entire city. It may be one corner, one cathedral, one park or market, maybe even your backyard. It may be a place that existed twenty years ago that is now overrun with crowds. It may be a place you have never visited.

Ghost Light 3: By contrast, the wrong place drains us or feels flat.

Someone's Shangri-La might be your Shangri-Blah. One of my clients was so excited about her new, at-home consulting business, but she found that every time she entered her home office, she felt heavy.

We realized the space held the energy of her previous corporate career — the very thing she was trying to escape. Redecorating wasn't enough. She had to change her mindset, and the structure of her business offerings, so her business resonated to freedom and creativity rather than obligation. It was the space that clued her in to the notion that something was off.

Witch Tip:
The energy of space is not objective.
It's subjective.

And you don't need to justify how you feel about particular spaces to anyone else, or even explain it to yourself.

For example, many people love the southern coast, but over time, they may start to feel the weight of the historic plantation system and the good ol' boy network. It's as if the energy of those formerly enslaved are reaching up from the ground and encircling your ankles like kudzu contrasted with the oppression of those in power.

I felt that energy intensely, yet I loved its complexity and richness. Other people can't escape fast enough.

In contrast, the West Coast is dramatic, the air feels clean and light, yet ultimately, to me, falls flat.

Dose of Magic Reflection:

What is your magical place? Where have you felt most like yourself — even if you couldn't explain why to others?

Have you ever outgrown it? Were you able to return?

Where is a place you lived that required you to compromise, such as moving for a job or a spouse, that didn't feel like home to you?

Ghost Light 4: We can stumble into our Shangri-La by accident or we can intentionally create it.

Both require awareness that you are in your Place. Therefore, pay attention to every single spot that brings you joy, inspiration, guidance, sanctuary, completeness.

The spots may be mere moments, with certain people, that are not recreated.

The place may be a moment crossing a bridge, when the moon or the sun hangs in one corner of the sky.

Or, it's a building, or an entire city that never lets you down.

It's possible that the energy of your Place is wholly affected by the people around, or that no one can shake your sense of sanctuary in a given space.

How to Read Space for Yourself

Ghost Light 5: The energy of place is your mirror.

This sounds deceptively simple, but paying attention to how you feel in any surrounding is a shortcut to your intuition and messages from your soul.

How you feel in any given space will mirror back to you what's happening deeply in your heart or the recesses of your mind. As a rule of thumb, know that you are projecting onto the air, the ground, or the building what's inside of you.

When you are in a space that makes you feel bored or uncomfortable, it's because the vibrations of the area are not in alignment with you. By extension, it may mean that the energy of the other people in the place, both current and historic, are also not in alignment with you.

⁊⸝⸱⸱⸱⸱⸱⸱⸱⸱⸱

When you feel inspired, as if your heart, body, and soul are at one and the space feels like a sanctuary, you are in complete alignment, at least in that moment, with the space.

This is true even when we feel agitated and upset and seek the sanctuary of our magic space. When we're drawn to the beach — or the bathtub — and we feel anxious, we know the sand or water will calm us.

That calming is actually coming from within our own souls, amplified by the space around us.

For me, Charleston consistently provided inspiration and sanctuary, even as I outgrew careers and relationships.

Ghost Light 6: Ask — Does the space need to change? Or do I need to change?

When the shadows stopped twinkling in my consistent Shangri-La of Charleston, I knew that was a red alert that something in my life needed addressing and maybe the problem was me. Because I couldn't sense the magic around me, I knew I needed to check whether I may be falling into a mild depression or a less-creative state of being.

During this time, I also noticed a glaring difference between how I felt even looking at a courtroom or walking past a theater. I didn't care how rickety the theater was. I felt inspired and exhaled deeply.

In a courtroom, even in the United States Supreme Court, I felt my throat constrict, my breathing become shallow. But walking past even the rattiest community theater? My chest opened, and I could suddenly breathe again. My body was giving me information my mind wasn't ready to hear.

I tried mental gymnastics to see a courtroom as a theater and never succeeded in deluding myself. The point: my entire being reacted to a courtroom, alerting me that practicing law could not be my final endeavor. I needed to get right with myself.

When I addressed the root cause of the magic around me dimming, such as my heart's pull toward change that I was repressing, the twinkles came back to life.

It's worth noting that a lot of folks make compromises on where they live for jobs and families, then tell themselves they're perfectly fine. To do otherwise might require a hard conversation with a spouse or with themselves about much-needed life changes.

It's common, then, that we suppress our dissatisfaction with our surroundings — that is probably indicating a greater dissatisfaction with big areas in our lives.

Witch Tip:
Try not to let the fear of change prevent you from listening to what the space around you is trying to tell you.

Dose of Magic: Reading and Creating Your Magical Space

Once you recognize the difference between magical and flat spaces, you can start intentionally creating your Shangri-La.

Keep a running list of every single place that inspires you. I recommend writing it down.

For the next seven days, carry a small notebook. Each time you feel energized or drained by a space, jot down: Where am I? What's my energy level (1–10)? What does my body feel like?

You'll forget some, and revisiting those places as you reread your list will bring you joy. You will also notice a pattern.

Repeat with places in which you automatically relax and breathe. These spaces may feel simpler than the inspirational spaces. Or they may be one and the same.

In contrast, your Shangri-Blah spaces will stand out.

One of the easiest ways to bring a spark into your day is to stop going to the grocery store that feels blah and go to the market that puts a spring in your step.

Remember, there's no need to justify your feelings about any place to anyone else.

You'll also notice that you take yourself with you wherever you go. Note: Are there days or periods in your life where no space is magical or relaxing? If so, it's not the space. It's you.

The point is to consciously observe your atmosphere, whether it's your region, your town, or even your local grocery store, and how you, uniquely, move through each space — without numbing out or making subliminal, unnecessary compromises.

Dose of Magic: Clearing You and Your Space

Entire books have been written on this topic alone. But here's the quickest way to clear your head and your space.

Snap and clap.

That's it.

If you want to disrupt thought patterns that are unhelpful and dragging you down, snap quickly around your head. You're literally telling yourself, "Snap out of it!"

Want to recharge your home or office from energetic dust bunnies or when company leaves? Walk around clapping, with your intent set to "Let's gooooooo!!! Out!"

If you really need to reactivate your home or personal space, then try this exercise, in conjunction with the Letting Go Visualization in the Program Notes to Chapter 13, and the energetic boundary setting in the Program Notes to Chapter 8, and you'll be all set.

I clear my head space at the end of every day that I see clients. I do the Letting Go visualization at least once a week, and I check in to strengthen the energetic boundaries of my residence and work space about twice a year.

You can always light a candle, or burn sage or palo santo while you're doing these exercises, but it's not necessary. Your intent alone is powerful enough.

Quick ethical note: You can only clear space you energetically own, meaning space you own, rent, or is dedicated to you, such as your work space.

Without permission, you can't clear your boss's stressy, junky office, or your daughter's house because you don't like her boyfriend — even though they might sorely need it. We have to respect the boundaries of others.

Of course, if they ask for your help, have fun and go gangbusters.

Why We Resist Our "Unsafe" Desires

The most common, unsafe Desire Demon has nothing to do with the want itself. Instead, it's the idea that if we pursue what we want, THE SKY WILL FALL DOWN!

We fear that everything we painstakingly built will collapse like a house of cards. So we either hide our hearts under a packed tight schedule of Too Busy or Too Distracted.

At this point in the memoir, I still felt like I carried more emotional baggage than most people my age. Therefore, I made the common mistake of repressing all parts of me that I found cringe-worthy, including my creative and spiritual desires.

In creating a tight safe space for myself, everything I repressed felt dangerous to me. You might have experienced this in earlier exercises where we played with inviting our desires back into the room. It feels life threatening to open the lid to Dracula's coffin.

But that's precisely when all the magic whooshed right out of Charleston. No sparkles. No twinkles. I created a Shangri-Blah bubble around myself in which I trekked through life.

Dose of Magic Reflections:

Have you ever feared that if you started something new, whether it's a career or following a personal interest, that your whole house of cards would collapse?

Have you gone through times where you didn't trust your own voice? Times where speaking up might threaten those around you?

What would you attempt if you knew everyone was secretly rooting for you?

Ghost Light 7: More people are rooting for your success than your failure.

If you don't perceive this to be true about the actual people in your life, then it's still true about humanity. You just haven't yet met ALL the people who need you to be the most authentic version of yourself, the you that lives full time in Shangri-La.

One year, I was asked to be the medium at an invitation-only, private event on Halloween where I would hold an old-fashioned seance from the stage in front of a large and very discerning group of people.

As soon as I said yes, my colleagues warned me that because of the nature of this particular event, I would be laughed off the stage, and that no matter how good I was, it wouldn't be enough. It would be a career-ender.

I freaked out, even though I trusted my Yes to the event.

My husband calmly said, "No one is paying over $100 a ticket to see you fail. Every single person in that audience wants you to succeed wildly."

Mind blown. From that point forward, that disruptive truth changed how I approach public speaking and large group readings events. I could see the audience as a support system, rooting me on, rather than judging me.

That Halloween event turned out to be more than overcoming fear. The space itself was charged with expectation and hope, which taught me to accept the energy of a room full of people who wanted magic to happen — even under the tremendous pressure that I was the one who had to deliver it.

Obviously, opportunities don't arrive at my doorstep without me doing years of training and developing a solid reputation in my field. It's a given that whatever endeavor you're going to undertake will require you to cobble together tools for your success.

That said, don't let those tools or the looming mountain of change overwhelm you. Just. Get. Started.

The longings of Shangri-La don't lie.

Dose of Magic: The What If Game — Feel the fear and do it anyway (at least in your head).

I know this next bit might feel like toxic positivity or spiritual bypassing. It's not.

We're not ignoring real obstacles. We're temporarily removing the limiting belief filter to see what our souls are actually telling us.

What are the new interests or new set of circumstances that you're afraid of exploring? Or, what are the things you're afraid to say out loud?

No need to psychoanalyze the fears. Let's just flip the script.

What if... instead of humiliating failure or misunderstanding, you are 100% certain to be well-received? By EVERYONE.

What if... everyone is rooting for your success and no matter how terribly you face-plant, **you are still safe and a guaranteed success?**

What if the words you speak fall on grateful ears?

What if when you speak and give into your dangerous desires, that instead of your life crumbling like a sandcastle in the surf, a fortified castle arises?

How do those WHAT IFs feel compared to the fear?

Let your imagination run wild on this one. If you are as anxiety-riddled and be-prepared-for-the-worst-case-scenario as most lawyers are, feel free to do this exercise every single day for the rest of your life.

Navigating Spiritual Suspicion
(Snake Oil Salesmen)

Asking for any type of help as we move toward change typically awakens suspicion of frauds and flakes. That's precisely what happened to me at the end of this chapter in the story. Feeling suspicious of spiritual beliefs and mystics who don't resonate with you is common.

Hopefully, that suspicion leads to discernment so we recognize the snake oil salesmen. Unfortunately, too many people have one bad or shallow experience, then they conclude everything mystical is baloney.

In turn, they then don't embark on the journey to find their soul or intuition at all, and are too distrusting to ask for help along the way.

I get it!

Ghost Light 8: You have a personal flaky factor, and it changes as you grow.

To me, flakiness is shallow positivity that ignores pain and fear, grief and raw emotion, and pretty much everything that life on Earth presents that's inconvenient.

Such as, folks who spew puppies-and-rainbows messages and spiritually bypass everything. Especially the exchange of money.

There are a lot of leaders out there who aren't afraid of the messiness of our existence, who may accept payment for services in different ways, and who may rediscover the miracles of puppies and rainbows, but they aren't bypassing any fragment of our reality.

I've learned, however, that people I dismissed as flakes early on may have something valuable to share with me and vice versa. Sometimes, I've outgrown the people I used to look up to.

Ghost Light 9: The snake oil salesman might be a fraud.

The snake oil salesman makes claims of miracles, preys on our needs and curiosities, then betrays our trust by taking our money or energy in exchange for hot air. I see this a lot with "fortune tellers" who say to unsuspecting passersby that they're cursed, then offer to lift the curse for loads of money.

Just because someone claims to have knowledge in a mystical

area that you don't have, doesn't mean they're an expert, or that they are the right person for you to interact with.

Like any industry, some practitioners are fabulous, yet you may not resonate with them. Some might not be so great, but you absolutely love them. As with the energy of space, pay attention to whether a guide or a mentor is supporting you to trust your own intuition or is trying to shove dogma down your throat that doesn't taste right.

Dose of Magic: Identify your personal flaky and fraud factors.

What are qualities that turn you off about the mystical world? Is it the person? Their voice? Their outfit? Yes, you are allowed to be totally turned off by someone's shoes.

Or is it an inexplicable feeling?

On the other hand, are there mystical people out there who you adore and you don't even notice the details of their body or clothes?

What is your Shangri-La? Who inhabits it?

If a gentle dragon flew to you in Shangri-La, would you instantly be suspicious? Or would you welcome it?

The more you open yourself up to your version of the mystical world, the more you'll trust your heart and soul to lead you on this journey.

That slumped-shouldered woman in the D.C. office? She needed someone to tell her that her longing for Charleston wasn't escapism — it was her soul's GPS pointing home.

Witch Tip:
Your Shangri-La isn't frivolous.
It's sacred information about who you're becoming.

CHAPTER SIXTEEN
PROGRAM NOTES
Resonance & Integration
of the Unwanted

◦◦◦

W HAT IF I told you that your body already knows how to detect lies, spot authentic people, and guide you toward decisions that truly align with your soul? In this chapter, we'll turn you into a human lie detector and show you how to integrate the parts of yourself you've been hiding under the bed.

You Can Be a Human Lie Detector

Here's the science that backs up what your intuition already knows. According to research by Dr. Paul Ekman, the pioneering psychologist who trained FBI agents to detect deception, **the human body can give off up to 50 different "microexpressions" that last only 1/25 of a second but can reveal when someone is lying.**[9]

Holy cow.

---

9   Edman, P., *Telling Lies: Clues to Deceit in the Marketplace, Politics and Marriage*, (W.W. Norton & Company, 2009).

One twenty-fifth of a second is only perceived by the subconscious mind. We're not talking about big body language here.

Note that Dr. Ekman **had to train** the agents. I'm assuming the agents needed to learn how to tune into their subconscious spidey senses and de-tune the loud chatter of the brain that scoffed at what the body, heart, and intuition knew to be true.

These exercises aren't about becoming paranoid, and, in fact, many people speak inauthentically without consciously "lying." Rather, these practices are designed to help us learn to trust the wisdom our bodies already possess by discerning authenticity.

Ghost Light 1: Words have a vibration.

We can sense whether the vibration of the spoken word feels in alignment with the person speaking them and whether the vibration is in alignment with us.

Ghost Light 2: Use your body, not your brain. Your brain won't be accurate.

Learning to detect inauthenticity is a somatic exercise, meaning, your body will alert you to dissonance.

Usually, when your body signals something is off, your brain argues, "She has no reason to lie. She's telling the truth."

Or, if you distrust someone, you'll have a bias against them and won't be able to believe them when they are telling the truth.

For instance, listen to any politician talk!

No matter how apolitical you are, you'll have a bias toward or against their policies or even their voice, making it impossible to detect when they're lying or being honest.

The best way to practice how your body discerns resonance from dissonance are in situations when you don't have a dog in the fight. Keep in mind that this exercise is not about being right. It's about learning your body, over time, and how your body reacts to authenticity or falsity. It's subtle.

Ghost Light 3: The danger of becoming adept at sensing resonance is that you won't be able to lie to yourself anymore.

Your status quo, if it no longer suits you, will become obvious.

Your statements of, "I want . . ." will readily seem authentic — or false, if you're trying to please others or talk yourself into a situation that you don't truly desire.

When we live in a state of dissonance for too long, that out-of-alignment sensation starts to feel like anxiety, which begets more discomfort and more anxiety.

When we still continue ignoring the signs our bodies give us, our bodies grow louder. This is usually when we fall ill to sicknesses that don't make sense at first, such as a healthy person having stress-related heart issues, inexplicable generalized pain, lingering allergies that don't clear up, and so forth.

To be clear, I do not buy into the belief that every single illness is somehow our own fault. I do believe, however, that some physical symptoms are caused by unresolved emotional issues and lifestyles that don't fit our soul's longings.

So let's move out of dissonance and into resonance.

Dose of Magic: Resonance with Words

Practice on yourself first! Speak a lie out loud. No one has to hear you.

Try stating a fact that is verifiably false and isn't even true in your fantasy world.

For me, such a fact might be, "I went to medical school at Tulane University, and I'm now a brain surgeon at Carnegie Mellon."

What does that feel like?

Does saying something untrue hit a part of your body?

Does some place in you tense up?

Do the words sound funny to your ears or taste weird in your mouth?

Do you feel like giggling?

To me, dissonance hits my ears or my throat tickles, and I start to feel a little foggy.

I get the same sensation during a reading when I misspeak. I can feel when I've said the wrong word or an incorrect fact.

Now try stating facts that are verifiably true.

Do those words flow from your mouth with more ease?

Does your body relax?

⸗⸙⸘⸙⸗

You can also practice with a friend. To eliminate your brain guessing — and getting it wrong — start with your friend telling you, "I'm going to lie for the next ten to twenty statements." Have her speak slowly as she lies to you. Feel where and how your body reacts.

Repeat with statements of the truth.

This is a fun exercise to go back and forth with because you'll detect dissonance versus resonance in your own bodies whether you're the speaker or the listener.

I will warn you that a side effect of this exercise is becoming aware of dissonance in your daily activities as well...

Acknowledge Your Left-Behind Parts
as You Move Toward Integration

Now that you've felt the difference between truth and lies in your own body, let's explore what happens when you turn this awareness inward. Here's where this body wisdom becomes both a gift and a challenge.

The more we follow our journey into creating a life that resonates with our hearts and souls, the more our intuition may jump up and down with pesky past issues. Like, "Hey! Don't ignore this big chunk of You that got discarded on the side of the road twenty years ago!"

To me, those are UGH moments of awareness. My reptilian brain that wants everything to remain the same forever balks, "Seriously? Can't I just run forward?!"

Those tossed away chunks of your past self could be dusty desires or painful traumas that, yep, still need to be resolved before you can evolve into your wiser iteration. They might also be a trauma that you swore you resolved, but there it is again, popping up with a different angle.

Ghost Light 4: If you suspect that some piece of you is left behind, ignored, or holding you back, well, then, it is.

I frequently hear clients say, "Ohhh, that was so long ago. I should get over it." Or, "That was just the silly dream of a little girl." (Cue eye roll.)

As you know from this chapter in the story, these are not successful routes toward healing or living fulfilled. Instead, these "ugly" and unwanted parts of ourselves end up as the monsters hiding in the underbed. Let's drag them into the light where they can transform into lovable fluff muffins.

Ghost Light 5: The simplest way to identify parts of you that might need more attention is to see yourself as someone else in the same circumstances.

We tend to place our current knowledge, insights, biases, and beliefs onto our younger selves, forgetting what it was really like to live back when we made decisions with the limited information and experience we had at the time.

When undergoing PTSD therapy, I had to imagine a different young person, objectively, in the same circumstances. Only then could I fully acknowledge a child's innocent wants and unfair traumas.

I also discovered how much pain I still carried over my old dreams!

Witch Tip:
**Feeling grief or the sense of failure
over lost dreams
is as common as the pain from past traumas.**

Dose of Magic/Journal Prompt:
The Someone Else Cognitive Trick

Is there a part of you left behind? Go through each chapter, era, or decade of your life and view your younger self as a different person, someone you love dearly — maybe a beloved niece or a nephew — or even a public figure for whom you have tremendous admiration and compassion.

From the outside looking in — or from the Catwalk peering down onto the stage — how do you feel about that person's circumstances?

Do you want to encourage him to run wildly toward his hopes and dreams?

Do you want to fight for her? For her pain or her desires?

Do you want to protect that person?

Do you feel desperately sorry for what that person has experienced?

Do you want to hold her hand and help her seek healing?

What other sensations and thoughts do these ponderings elicit?

Ghost Light 5: Integration of all your cringe-worthy and shameful parts is the secret to a life of authenticity.

Interestingly, this topic of integration is finally being given a loud voice with regard to plant medicine experiences! Ayahuasca and other plant medicine uses are becoming more popular. Frequently, people unearth buried traumas during these ceremonies and glimpse a path toward understanding them.

However, they then hop on a plane back to their daily routine and wonder why their lives haven't changed after the cathartic experience. **The same wounds and triggers reappear in inconvenient** places because they haven't integrated their experience into their current reality.

They've shoved them back under the bed instead of continuing to work with them.

Acknowledging pains does not get us all the way toward integration. Working with these ugly and unwanted parts of our experiences does. Because integration isn't a solo sport, with the help of trusted experts, we can learn how to accept and love those parts of ourselves.

Gathering a Band of Warriors

Ghost Light 6: Don't go it alone.

From all of the exercises leading up to this moment, you'll have a good sense of who resonates with you as an expert when you start looking.

And you'll have a good sense of who not to share with, such as my decision to not bring Dad into my band of warriors at that time in my life.

The one thing that stood out in my PTSD healing curriculum was the emphasis on education and somatic — physical — exercises, rather than talk therapy alone.

The program addressed my physical, emotional, mental, and spiritual needs with the purpose of fully integrating every aspect of myself into my current reality. We went to work on tools and exercises for each of those aspects, and we did a deep dive on the biochemistry of PTSD and anxiety.

Momentary drop down here into two tips I learned during this period that helped me work through anxiety.

1.   Apparently, anxiety looooooves itself. Meaning, we get anxious, then we get anxious because we're anxious.

    If you know how anxiety feels in your body, you won't be anxious over the feelings alerting you to anxiety. You'll be able to recognize anxiety for what it is.

    I remind myself that a full-blown panic attack can only last 8–10 minutes. That's it! If we recognize it, we can observe it, knowing it will pass.

2.   We might feel anxious because we're not getting enough oxygen distributed to our brain or throughout our body. Then, when we get anxious, what do we do? We hold our breath.

    Like I said, anxiety loves to create more of itself. So when you feel anxious, breathe. Super simple, yet the first thing we forget to do.
    Then we're ready to address the underlying issues causing the anxiety.

❦

I was a full two months into the program and fully armed with knowledge and breathing techniques before I ever delved into the abuse and tragedies themselves.
That's integration.

Even outside of extraordinary trauma therapy, I subscribe to the "it takes a village" approach to life. Your village might include a therapist who gets your spiritual side, a coach who challenges your limiting beliefs, a friend who holds space for your ugly cries, and a mentor who sees your potential when you can't.

I use and recommend having a regular stable of teachers, coaches, mentors, healers, confidants, and inspirers.

And they have changed over time.

Witch Tip:
**The key is choosing people
who can handle all of you,
not just the polished, acceptable parts.**

Most significantly, when we coax out the pieces of ourselves that we viewed as ugly monsters lurking in the past or the underbed and integrate them into our daily lives, they become tame. They turn into gentle balls of fluff needing love.

The monsters under your bed aren't your enemies. They're the parts of you that got scared and hid. When you bring them into the light with the right support, they transform into the very qualities that make you unstoppable.

Your resonance practice starts now.

For Further Inspiration and Support:

✻ Stephanie Burg, a trauma and plant medicine integration coach, started writing about the potential pitfalls of plant medicine retreats without integration coaching and counseling afterwards at the same time I was writing this chapter! She's also a breathwork expert. Please see her work for further education and support: **www.stephanieburgcoaching.com**

CHAPTER SEVENTEEN
PROGRAM NOTES
Fallout + Acceptance
+ Surrender = Miracles

ॐ

H ERE'S WHAT NOBODY tells you about personal growth: the people closest to you might not like the new version of you. Friends, spouses, even family may resist your integrated, confident, less-easy-to-be-manipulated self.

Hang in there. The gains that come from acceptance and surrendering to the unknown and the unknowable overshadow the growing pains.

Parting Ways with the People We Love Most

Ghost Light 1: We can outgrow tools and people.

Most of our real-world guides offer a specific set of tools that we eventually outgrow. I was disappointed when the PTSD therapy was over. I felt like I still needed guidance, but the doctors shooed me out the door, telling me it was time to trust myself.

The same has happened with teachers and mentors. I wanted to work under them forever, but they, too, told me to spread my wings.

But what about our best friends? Or our spouse? Our parents? Shouldn't we all be movin' and shakin' together through life?

Ghost Light 2: We don't make change in a vacuum.

There is usually fallout when we make life changes. It doesn't mean your entire life will collapse, but the fear of that is very real.

We worry about making people uncomfortable. We can't see how a bigger version of ourselves fits into our current life, whether life is tidy or in full chaos. We're desperately afraid of rejection.

On the other hand, we can't stop growth once the momentum is rolling! Expanded consciousness is like toothpaste — you can't put it back in the tube. (Harken back to Chapter 1 Program Notes where we discussed the notion that **we don't go backward in consciousness.**)

We're excited about our changes, our new perspectives and levels of awareness, and need to share them with our besties. It's devastating when their enthusiasm doesn't match ours.

In fact, it feels like betrayal when our loved ones don't grow with us.

But here's where it gets really challenging...

Hard Acceptance

Ghost Light 3: We can't force anyone to accompany us on our path, on our timeline.

When I was drowning in confusion during the last years of my marriage to Mr. Perfect, wondering how it was possible that we were growing in different directions, someone asked me, "When you're little, who's your best friend? The kid that twirls, giggles, and rolls down the hill with you? Or the kid that stands back, looks at the hill with disdain, and discourages you from going down?"

Obviously, there are great friends and partners who might not want to roll down the hill themselves, but will loudly cheer you on while you do so. Those are the keepers.

One of the most bitter pills I ever had to swallow was acknowledging that Mr. Perfect had no intention of skipping down a new path with me or cheering me on — at least not on my timeline.

That's a lonely place to be for everyone concerned.

Ghost Light 4: We can't force anyone to embark on their next journey either.

I see this truth the most often when people are involved with addicts or abusers, and they are desperate to make the other person heal. But it also rears its head in more subtle situations when we think we know best what another person needs, even if our intention is innocent.

Such as, when we're excited about a new venture, and we think our new discoveries can help others — but our pals aren't interested.

Like, "I just took this class on intuition — you should take it too!!!" Or, "I had an amazing session with this medium — you have to go!"

If our friends try it before they're ready, they wonder what your hullabaloo was all about. We then may attempt to appease our loved ones, and second-guess our raw and real first reaction, downplaying our authentic exuberance.

We tell ourselves, "Yeah, I guess it wasn't that big of a deal, after all."

Putting a lid on your excitement with something that resonates with you is the same as trying to shove toothpaste back in the tube. Know that your experience was not flat, even if your friend's was.

Witch Tip:
**We can't push the river
on other people's personal development
any more than we can slow the flow of our own.**

And remember, when you try to stay in dissonant circumstances, the anxiety tumbleweed rolls into town. Revisit last chapter's Program Notes if necessary.

Dose of Magic Reflection / Journal Prompt: Have you stayed in a situation past its expiration date?

* Have you found yourself in growth spurts at different times than your loved ones?

* Did you stay in the relationship anyway, hoping they would change and grow? Or you dismissed your own inevitable growth?

* Did staying eventually make you depressed, anxious, or physically ill as it did me?

If you answered yes to these questions, pull out that casserole of grace and serve yourself a heaping plateful. It's happened to all of us.

Surrendering to the Unknowable, Part 2

So if we can't control others' timelines, what CAN we control?

A lot of people think surrender means giving up altogether, and that by doing so, your knight-in-shining armor will finally appear. Not exactly.

During my breakup with Mr. Perfect, a therapist called me to the carpet in the first session. "No one's coming to rescue you," he said.

Phhbbbttt. "I didn't expect so," I retorted.

"Sounds like that's what you're waiting around on."

That was a humiliating blow to my self-image — and dead-on accurate. I had tools to heal the past, and I was still miserable with my current life. And even though I had my band of warriors gathered 'round, and my heart was screaming at me to change, I was still acting like Sleeping Beauty in a hundred-year slumber, waiting to be rescued.

We discussed the concept of Surrender in the Program Notes to Chapter 8 in the context of spirit communication. Let's revisit how to use Surrender when making real-world changes, and during the excavation process of truly resolving the past.

Ghost Light 5: "Surrender" means taking every step in your control toward your desired life, then releasing your grip on a particular outcome.

Surrender requires three things: showing up completely, particularly in the face of an unknown future, listening to your nudges, then taking action — even when it doesn't make rational sense.

Surrender requires you to *do something*.

Surrender allowed me time and space to recognize that I still needed to have a face-to-face with myself regarding all the muck I carried around the topic of suicide. But once I surrendered to that truth, I had to do something about it, with the tools I had from my PTSD therapy.

No one else was going to extract my irreverent, impolite, and angry observations for me. And if I didn't do it, they were going to stay as monsters in the basement.

Surrender got my slumbering butt out to my friend Stefaney's retreat. But if I hadn't paid attention to the pull of the Ibo Point story, particularly when it made no rational sense, I never would have had my first experience with channeled writing of a historic event.

You have your band of warriors, both in this world and in spirit, but you're the CEO of your life. Without taking the action that Surrender requires, you'll stay sleeping for another hundred years.

Witch Tip:
**When you're really lost,
the action you are pulled to take
might not seem rational
and might seem unrelated to your goal.**

For example, I had a client with business interests in many different directions, but he wanted to make a certain revenue goal by year's end. He was frustrated because his businesses weren't producing on the trajectory he expected. Still, he was bound and determined to stay the course and stick with what he knew.

During a reading, his soul told him to sell off the extraneous interests and use the extra time to go surfing. Alone on the water each morning, he could recharge and hear his own Inspired Knowing about how to attend to his primary business, which was his first love.

He reached his financial goal by that September, four months earlier than previously planned.

The lesson? When he stopped forcing outcomes, took new action, then created a surrendered space for clarity, money flowed naturally because all of his actions were then energetically aligned with him.

Dose of Magic: RADICAL BRAIN DUMP!

When we're stuck, can't see an answer, or when our thoughts loop around a topic in a way that we can't see past, the best way out is a radical brain dump on the topic. By this point in our exercises, your imagination should be bopping around the block without a leash, like a happy dog on the loose.

Grab a sheet of paper or a whiteboard with lots of colored pens.

Set a timer for 15 minutes. Write without stopping. Include ridiculous options — sometimes the "impossible" ideas contain kernels of truth.

What are all the steps you can take to change your circumstances?

No need to confine yourself to this reality.

I see a lot of clients who want to change a job or career but haven't even started Googling alternatives or talking to people to get the word out. You may feel so burned out or beaten down by your job that you can't see readily available actions.

If you are at your wits' end, hire a coach, or a friend to brainstorm with you.

Otherwise, go crazy on your whiteboard with all the colors in the pen box. At least one action item will resonate. Take steps toward it.

Dose of Magic: The Something-Unexpected-This-Way-Comes Experiment

If you're as stuck as I was during this part of my life, do the ritual in the story.

Write on a piece of paper "Something unexpected this way comes…" As you're writing, invoke feelings of hope and curiosity, trust and resolve. Feel as empowered as you possibly can.

You're not inviting misfortune, so if you find yourself sliding into disempowerment or doubt, set the paper on fire and try again when you feel better.

You can place this affirmation on the fridge, the bathroom mirror, or next to your car keys if you want it as a reminder. Or place it in the bottom of a bowl filled with coarse salt and decorate it however you desire.

Importantly, keep your eyes and heart open for the pull. Know that your intention will come with the responsibility that you take action when it appears. Such as going surfing.

If you need help, ask for it!

Spiritually Bypassing, Part 2

When my cousin Shaun died, I discovered something crucial about grief and spiritual tools. I had enough tools — and because in the previous year, I had also brain-dumped into the essay in this Appendix everything I needed to say about suicide — that I didn't spiral into habitual, obsessive thought patterns that weren't helpful.

I knew how to sit with my jagged regret and grieve.

Ghost Light 6: Just because you have tools to deal with life and loss doesn't mean you get to bypass the grief.

It always shocks me that when I'm in grief, some people respond, "This must not be that hard for you. Being a medium, and all."

What?! As if I'm now a robot, not crumpled in a ball of tears when someone passes away? Or a breakup happens?

Y'all, no. When you're fully in your spiritual cups, you'll feel ALL the feels, and way deeper than most because you're not afraid of your emotions, your thoughts, and every last one of the creepy crawlies in the grief basement.

You know you have the tools to resurrect yourself when — and only when — you're ready.

For Further Inspiration:

✳ Henry Rollins has a great quote that helps me get through those times when I know change is coming, but I don't know where I'm going: "**You have to take it upon yourself to be an infinitely fantastic person every single day. There will be times when it will be a bitch to be so awesome, but you'll handle it.**"[10]

✳ "A Good Rain," the essay I wrote on suicide, appears in the Appendix to this book if you want to rip off the bandaid and dive into the swamp of grief and everything that bothered me at the time regarding society's reaction to the topic. I wrote it as if no one would see it, so it remains unedited.

✳ *The Surrender Experiment* by Michael Singer.

---

10 Henry Rollins. "White America Couldn't Handle What Black America Deals With Every Day," *LA Weekly*, July 16, 2016.

CHAPTER EIGHTEEN
PROGRAM NOTES
Empathy, Hypersensitivity,
& Neurological Reactions

❧

I DEDICATED YEARS toward getting my crap together, planning to leave the law firm, and STILL had skyrocketing anxiety and those atypical migraines.

Turns out, something further was happening — that I was too skeptical to accept — that explained why the volume on my anxiety ratcheted to full blast.

Even to this day, the neuroscience behind facets of our sensitivity is overlooked. Let's dive into the misunderstood, murky waters of being an empath AND being hypersensitive.

Empathy

How many times have you heard someone claim to be an "empath," but it comes off as attention-seeking or an excuse to remain disempowered by the world?

When this happens, I have to reign in a big eye roll and resist the urge to blurt out, "Get a grip, sister."

Many high-performing people, including myself, don't want to be perceived as victimized by our own sensitivity. Unfortunately, then, many empaths will hide under a rock, embarrassed, and futilely trying to stifle their overwhelm instead of gaining knowledge that can turn this brain function into a superpower.

Been there, done that. I'm going to break it down for you.

Ghost Light 1: Empathy is not compassion. Empathy is not sympathy. Empathy is a brain function.

The word "empathy" is frequently misused as a synonym for sympathy and compassion, even in scientific journals reporting on behavioral symptoms rather than brain functions.

Sympathy and compassion can — and should — be developed in every human. These states of awareness allow us to **intellectually and emotionally comprehend** others' circumstances.

In contrast, as Dr. Judith Orloff has well-documented in *The Empath's Survival Guide*, "**Empaths have an extremely reactive neurological system.**"[11] The brain of an empath lives in a constant state of overstimulation.

Additionally, the empath brain can't tell the difference between The Thing happening to someone else and The Thing happening to the empath herself. In other words, an empath will physically feel the emotions, sensations, pains, and joys of other beings on the planet — as if the stimulus is happening to the empath in that moment.

---

11   Judith Orloff, M.D. *The Empath's Survival Guide: Life Strategies for Sensitive People,* (Colorado: Sounds True, 2017).

**Ghost Light 2: Empathy only affects approximately TWENTY per-
cent of the population, and the degree of sensitivity can vary.[12]**

Statistically, many folks who think they're empaths are probably
not. They may be highly sensitive, and, more likely, that sensitivity
comes from unresolved trauma that triggers them in a variety of
situations.

Additionally, research has shown that only a THIRD of the population is neurologically affected by "stress contagion." Meaning, if
one person in a group grows anxious, causing a cortisol spike in his
brain, only a third of the rest of the group will also experience a cortisol spike.

Understanding these statistics becomes even more fascinating
when we consider the evolutionary perspective. Scientists theorize
that empathic sensitivity and stress contagion served crucial survival
functions for our ancestors.

> *Note the use of the
> word "reactive" in Dr.
> Orloff's statement above.
> As you'll remember,
> reactive = instinctive
> = survival mode.
> See Program Notes to
> Chapter 2.*

---

12 Orloff, *The Empath's Survival Guide.*

For example, some people in a tribe may have been empathically reactive to changes in the atmosphere that indicated oncoming bad weather. Others may have been empathically sensitive to an impending stampede or attack.

Their brains would react, thereby causing a cortisol spike in one third of the rest of the tribe — enough that the entire tribe would be alerted to prepare.

Likewise, some members could react to others' health or emotional issues before the rest of the tribe even noticed a problem. The same reactive sensitivity can be extended to understanding the energies of plants and animals.

In modern times, these statistics help explain why most of the developed world can easily watch action movies or round-the-clock news, where only up to 20% of us fall into a panic attack while viewing a made-up fight scene or one photograph of destruction.

Because this book ended up in your hands, my guess is that you're more likely than not to be either empathic, hypersensitive (discussed below), or both.

Ghost Light 3: Empathy can cause tremendous anxiety.

If you're an empath, you're overrun with the world's noisy energy — both good and bad. When we're surrounded by too much energy, all those heightened sensations can feel a lot like a jumbled mess of anxiety.

If you don't understand what's happening to you, in your brain and in your body, as an empath, you might believe that you have an anxiety disorder, particularly if you've already done all the integrative work on past harms and traumas.

Instead, you may need to create a lifestyle with a lot less external stimulation.

Ghost Light 4: Many of us have a hard time accepting that we may be empaths.

When "being an empath" became trendy amongst the melodramatic, disempowered crowd, I scoffed that empathy was even a thing. Many of us do the same thing because we don't want to be perceived as weak or "overly sensitive," as if we can't get a grip on ourselves.

In my experience with clients, sensitive folks — particularly men — learned as children to internalize their experiences and build a fortress around themselves. As children and even adults, an unaware, untrained empath genuinely cannot stand the intense emotions — and proven neurological responses — that erupt in his or her body when facing another person's suffering **that the rest of the world doesn't feel as deeply**!

When we don't understand what's happening to us in these situations, we can shut down in overwhelm.

Witch Tip:
**All this said, empathy and brain functions
are not excuses to avoid getting your act together,
or to avoid living your fullest life.**

However, if we don't know whether we're empathic, we won't know where to start.

⊙≈⊙⊂⊚⊃⊙≈⊙

I think empaths may be more likely to develop PTSD, as PTSD has a large, neurological component geared toward survival.

While writing this book, I found a lot of research devoted to understanding compassion and its effects on healing the behavioral aspects of PTSD. However, this research only looked at behavioral and social functions that could be changed proactively — not the body's neurological reactions to stimuli. The research also conflated "empathy" with sympathy and compassion.

That's frustrating.

If, like me, you've done a ton of work to understand your cognitive and behavioral issues, you still fall prey to neurological reactions that seem hardwired, then those reactions can be downplayed by therapists or the scientific community.

The good news is that the more we're aware of our brains and bodies as a neurological contributor to our thoughts and reactions, the more we can choose to either unleash or harness our empathic instincts.

The bad news is, we don't get to use our hardwiring as an excuse for poor behavior or hiding under a rock forever. Sorry.

What's the solution? Let's see who here is an empath, then let's make this brilliant neurological system work for us.

Dose of Magic: Are You an Empath?

Color me shocked when a friend shoved Dr. Orloff's book in my hand and said, "This entire book is about you, dummy."

Because empathy as a neurological reaction is backed by science that I understood from my PTSD experiences, I could finally embrace that all the things going on with me weren't mental health failures and emotional weaknesses that I couldn't seem to conquer.

In fact, **empathy can be a superpower,** which Dr. Orloff teaches.

She also includes numerous quizzes in her book to help you determine whether you're empathic, and, if so, which direction your sensitivity leans in, such as emotional, physical, plants, animals, etc.

I have posted onto YouTube several short, free videos walking you through a few of Dr. Orloff's quizzes where you can tally your responses and determine where you fall on the empath spectrum.

Note: some of you may score low on the empath scale, but this does not mean you're not highly sensitive and intuitive! In fact, I think some of the best psychics, mediums, and healers in practice today are not empaths, yet they are tremendously compassionate and gifted.

Find my videos here: **youtube.com/@andreasaintamand**

Or see: *The Empath's Survival Guide, Life Strategies for Sensitive People* by Judith Orloff, M.D.

Hypersensitivity

Ghost Light 5: Hypersensitivity is a state of awareness, of consciousness.

Hypersensitivity operates differently from empathy. Hypersensitivity requires an expanded awareness rather than feeling others' experiences as your own.

Where empathy is an emotional and physical download system, hypersensitivity is more like having enhanced psychic and mediumistic reception.

Hypersensitivity can mean you're intuitive to the spirit world, to precognition, telepathy, psychic, and mediumship phenomenon, or a whole host of intuitive outlets outside empathy.

Think of all the non-verbal children researched in *The Telepathy Tapes* referenced in the Program Notes to Chapter 8. They may or may not be empathic, but they are certainly operating through a different state of consciousness, which may have been learned precisely because they are not verbal.

To further illustrate the difference between hypersensitivity and empathy, let's look at Edgar Cayce and Anthony William, both renowned medical intuitives.

Through a reading for a client, both men would turn their awareness to a heightened state of consciousness. They would then simply "know" the root cause of a client's medical issue and suggest a dietary cure.

Both men showed heightened intuitive abilities at a young age, which could have easily been squashed. Instead, they devoted years of their lives to developing a higher state of conscious awareness so they could channel accurate information.

As far as I know, neither of these men relied on empathy, meaning that they did not feel a client's medical problem in their own bodies. Instead, they accessed knowledge through their heightened awareness.

On the other hand, a physical empath might start feeling that her left knee hurts. If she's trained and aware, she'll know that someone around her has a problem with their left knee. If she's not aware that she's empathic, she'll schedule a doctor's visit and the doctor will find nothing wrong.

Ghost Light 6: Hypersensitivity can also feel like anxiety or nausea.

I learned this nugget from the Long Island Medium! Theresa Caputo once said that she thought she had an anxiety problem, until she learned that she was becoming more sensitive to the energy around her, particularly to the discarnate energies of the spirit world.

As we grow more intuitive, whether it's to the spirit world or the people around us, the vibration rate in our body rises. When that happens, it can make us feel fluttery, our palms sweat, our chest tightens, our mouth goes dry. It can be a generalized, prolonged sensation, or a sudden burst.

If we're not accustomed to an unexpected whoosh of energy, or to our newly heightened awareness, we can mistake these sensations for anxiety or even feel sick.

Take the Old City Jail in Charleston, South Carolina, for example. The building housed thousands of inmates and workers over a century. Then, in recent times, hundreds of people toured the building every day, 360 days of the year, with their imaginations on fire, hunting for ghosts.

From those aspects alone, the energy of the locale was high and intense. So much so that some untrained, yet hypersensitive people who weren't used to an abrupt force of high energy would spontaneously vomit or feel nauseous upon stepping foot in there.

Witch Tip:
Heightened awareness of energy can also cause headaches, toothaches, visual migraines, and ear ringing.

Dose of Magic: Countering Energy Overwhelm

For 911, in-the-moment triage:

✳ BREATHE. Breathing creates space between you and the stimulus. You don't need to explain yourself on this one.

✳ If you have to talk, use the phrase, "Give me a minute."

✳ Place your bare feet on the ground, or your hands on a tree and — yep — breathe. The electromagnetic energy of trees has a calming effect on our own raggedy energy when we're overwhelmed.

For overall care:

✳ Bathtub soaks with epsom salts;

✳ More downtime without external stimulation;

✳ Walks in nature without headsets;

✳ Soft, comfortable fabric on your skin at all times! From your clothes to your pillowcases and towels. Indulge here.

✳ Breathe — did I say that already?

Again, the Letting Go visualization in the Program Notes to Chapter 13 is my consistent go-to for a variety of issues. As this quick meditation takes you through, the best practice is to release all of the old energy first, then reconnect with the Earth and your own Divine Soul power.

Witch Tip:
**Stand in your power
and radiate that power
back out into the Universe.
The Divine will respond.**

Dose of Magic Reflection:

During those final years of practicing law, empathy, plus a growing awareness of the spirit world, felt like unconquerable anxiety to me. Have you experienced anything similar? Even when you've done all the therapy and self work?

If so, it's time to investigate empathy, turn it into your superpower, and develop your own intuitive sensitivities on a deeper level — with a teacher or mentor to guide you.

I remind people that Lady Gaga might have been born with a talent for singing, but she still had teachers and a voice coach. So yes, you need a teacher or a guide on intuitive development, particularly when you're starting.

But really, the development never stops!

Additional Ghost Lights on the Divine

Ghost Light 7: Sometimes we can pick up on a loved one's transition into the afterlife. Sometimes we won't.

Even if you're sensitive to transitions, you may not always sense when a loved one is about to pass. This has been confusing to so many of my clients who have awareness of an impending passing, but not consistently.

As one of my mentors always says, none of us have access to the ultimate truth. And none of us have access to the full truth. We'll get hits of Knowing, sometimes more than others, depending on a whole host of circumstances going on in our lives and the lives of others at the time.

Ghost Light 8: Do the Sacred Self Work. Sit in Silence with your Divine Being.

There's no bypassing learning about yourself and your vessel — without judgment. I am not aware of a high caliber psychic or medium who skipped the self knowledge part. Many spent a year or more in meditation, as I did, before the miraculous-level spiritual awareness blossomed that could be harnessed or turned off on command.

In fact, the pursuit into Self applies to many successful human beings, athletes, leaders, artists, lawyers, parents, and spouses, regardless of their occupation.

Witch Tip:
**If you skip this part,
your intuition,
sending messages to yourself,
will project itself
onto other people and spaces.**

The number one mistake that psychics and mediums make, either when they're just starting out or because they've never undergone rigorous training, is that they read themselves, not the client, the spirit world, or the space.

Because they don't know themselves well enough, they can't discern the subjective messages from a factual message from an objective communicator.

Ghost Light 9: All timing is Divine, Including Your Readiness for This Knowledge.

The fact that you're reading these words now is no accident.

Your nervous system and your intuitive abilities are all part of your unique design. The work isn't to fix or suppress these traits, but to understand and harness them as the powerful tools they are.

You are not too sensitive. You are not broken. You are exactly who you're meant to be, reading exactly what you need to read, at exactly the right time.

Dose of Magic: Ongoing Personal, Intuitive Development

There is no one-size-fits-all. Go where you're pulled. Straight up psychic and mediumship development has been the only route that works for me.

For example, I thought I would love astrology. I tried so hard to learn about it, but I can't retain one aspect, other than the fact I'm an Aquarius. So I leave it to my friends who are brilliant with it.

What's for you? Astrology? Mediumship? Dream interpretation? Tarot cards? Tea leaves? Writing? Art? Animals? Plants? Music?

It's all legit, as long as you're legit with yourself.

Because you've reached the end of this book, you are well on your authentic Divine Path, with a significant effect rippling out in the waves of our planet and our existence.

I thank you, and the worlds, both physical and spiritual, thank you for being here.

For Further Inspiration:

✷ For a short video on stress contagion, see:
www.facebook.com/ScienceNaturePage/videos/1348684565263798/

✷ *The Empath's Survival Guide* by Dr. Judith Orloff

✷ To learn more about Edgar Cayce, who was a remarkable human being, please see a fabulous biography, *There is a River: The Story of Edgar Cayce* by Thomas Sugrue.

✷ Intuitive development for beginners:
   ☾ I have a basic, self-led video course on my website, if you prefer to learn at your own pace, that includes many of the topics we've covered in this book. See **www.andreasaintamand.com**
   ☾ I highly recommend interacting live with a teacher and other learners, however, and my first beloved teacher was Carol Cottrell. She offers in-person and online courses, workshops, and mentorships. **www.carolcottrell.com**

- ✻ After a thorough, beginner-level course, if you are drawn toward developing intermediate and advanced evidence-based psychic and mediumship skills:
  - ☾ For two years, I mentored under Anthony Mrocka. **www.anthonymrocka.com**

  - ☾ For another two years, I then mentored under Andy Byng. **www.andybyng.com** Two very different mediums with different teaching styles, but both are exacting, rigorous and heart-driven.

- ✻ Workshops and classes with Lisa Williams are always enjoyable. **www.lisawilliams.com**

- ✻ Sporadically, I offer workshops and courses on personal development, and my favorite, a Paranormal Party, is designed to teach you how to read space and radically release your imaginations. Join my mailing list to stay tuned on all these opportunities and more: **www.andreasaintamand.com**

APPENDIX

⦿

THIS ESSAY IS included here at the suggestion of several people who thought it might be healing for others.

It is graphic and gloomy.
It was never meant for outside eyes.
But it did serve to exorcise demons.
Please view with caution.

A Good Rain
(*Originally Written September 2008*)

We need a good rain.
You look puzzled.
This will make sense if I can show you the way I see things.
A good rain would wash it all away. That way, someone wouldn't
have to go out there with a hose. The neighbor or God help us, Mr.
Dewey himself.

They don't clean it up, you know. They just move the body and any major parts lying around. Who do they think will clean up the rest of the mess? No one comes to clean it all up. At least, they didn't used to.

Of course, that's years ago when obituaries read like news reports and stated the cause of death: "Dead on arrival from a self-inflicted gunshot wound."

The "arrival" part of these obits always struck me funny. Like, before the "arrival" to the who-knows-where, everyone's standing around scratching their heads, uncertain about the dead part or the cause part.

Wonder if they quit doing the obits that way because of what you forget. It's crazy that you never forget the dead part or the what-caused-it part, but the life can get completely wiped out.

Even though the death is one instant and the life is years and years. The basics even go away, like his full name. It's so embarrassing. This is the stuff no one talks about.

But now, the obituaries help out a little. You can read the obit and maybe find a nice picture, some information that might remind you of who he was.

It doesn't matter that you spent every waking minute with him for the last three months or the last eighteen years. It's gone. It's all gone. Except for that last triggered instant. There's no mention of the cause of death in the obit now, but you remember that forever anyway, so it's ok.

Still, there needs to be someone to clean it up. So they wouldn't have to wash it away themselves.

And this one, the pieces could sneak up on you because this kid fell in the grass. You can't walk out there by the water now, even a good twenty yards away because you might look down and find a piece of rotting flesh lying between the blades of grass. Perhaps animals will come in the night.

This is why we need a good rain. That way no one would have to do it. No one connected with him anyway.

You know, I would though. If something like this happened to one of our neighbor's kids, like Macon's kids, I'd be out there first thing cleaning so the family wouldn't have to see it or watch someone washing it all away.

Yes, I would.

It's not just a body to people who knew *him*. It *is* him. That's *his* blood and *his* flesh and *his* head blown to smithereens. And it's all we have left.

No one who ever laid eyes on that child should have to go out there and see these remnants, then wash away what's left of him like he is now nothing. Something dirtying up the yard that's not supposed to be there. It's like erasing him.

Even though he's not supposed to be there. Not in pieces anyway.

Maybe they do clean it up. Maybe all those years ago, Jason's mom told them to leave the room as it was. Maybe she didn't let them stay long enough. His blood splattered on the ceiling, dripping down the wall and pooling where his headless body fell and stayed for hours, surging, well, it was all we had left of him.

Maybe she didn't want it cleaned up right away. It was *him*. Not something dirty and shameful to be hosed off, erased like he never happened.

It would be different with a rain. Rain would make it all right.

There's a goddam drought now. Dryest month on record. Even nature gets frustrated when some fool goes and lops himself off too soon.

See, nothing's right. Just like in the funeral procession and you got your lights on and some jackass on a cell phone cuts the line and nearly causes a wreck.

How dare that person even go on living in the hum drum routine? Shouldn't the world stop until you at least get to the fucking cemetery? I mean, that's not too much to ask, is it? Lives have been ripped up here. For chrissake, isn't there enough decency to halt everything for just a few seconds?

Let us catch our breath. Figure out how to get our legs back underneath us and proceed from here.

Like, how do we go about waking up in the morning and sitting up in bed and swinging our feet over to touch the floor? Can everything just slow down for one minute so we can figure this out?

No. The driver on the cell phone disregards the glaring endless line of car after car after car in the procession and cuts through anyway. Everything is upside down but people go on acting like nothing happened. Worse, like they don't care. Nothing is right. Mother Nature herself is frustrated. She can't even make it rain.

Guess he had a right to die as sure as he had a right to live. But he sure didn't have the right to shatter that beautiful face. That was for us, for the rest of the world to see and touch and read and love. And that wasn't just any head. It housed the great mind of a great love. He destroyed something we had a stake in. Without our permission to boot. That's not right.

Then for someone to have to go outside and hose it all away so quickly, it's embarrassing.

Suicide's funny like that. Everyone gets hollowed out and confused. Everyone left alive, together as a group, gets pulled into the same swamp. It doesn't help that you're all in that suffocating horror together because everyone's trying to figure out where to point fingers and wondering, *why?*

If you know why, they wonder why you didn't do anything to stop it. And if you don't know why, they wonder how the hell you could miss it when the poor soul was right there walking in and out of your day, every day, in and out.

Forget that it's his fault. Or no one's fault. We never forget that it's our fault. And there's no way around it because there's no answer to the *why*. That's the funny shame part of suicide.

And then there's the surprising force of the destruction.

Not his.

Ours. Lying in wait for only one small something to come softly unhinged. There it is, so close.

Suddenly, everyone thinks their own hidden destructive force is wide open for everyone else to see. Everyone can see right inside to the evil in me that caused *him* to do this.

Doesn't make sense when you see it in black and white, does it? Crazy. But we each feel responsible — alone.

You just can't reach out from all this. Because if you do and no one's there, no one responds and you've reached out, well.

See, for me, I don't call because I want to protect you from your own terror and gruesome visions. Maybe I don't want you to really know mine.

Shit, I don't want to know mine. And I will have to know mine to reach out to you, tell you about it and ask you to help me. I feel sick.

Knowing all this, even after all these years, I still do exactly what everyone else does. I have to know every detail of this boy's death. All the facts. When? Where? No, exactly, precisely, where? How was the yard laid out? Where was the water?

How? With a gun. Where was the gun? Under his chin? In his mouth? On the side of his head? Jason used to say there was only one sure way to end it so you wouldn't end up a vegetable the rest of your life. Under the chin so the bullet would go through your brain and out the top of your head, guaranteeing death.

He educated himself on this matter. Apparently, there are conflicting schools of thought on the subject.

What time of day? Was it in desperation? Was it planned? What triggered him in that precise moment? Anything? Anything at all?

The statistics are that, by far, the successful suicides are impulsive, not thought out. How crazy is that? And how do they know? I mean, the only people left sitting around to respond to this survey are the folks who don't die after they've tried. Think they're actually going to admit, nah, man, I've been trying, thinkin' up ways to knock it off for a while, and I'm such a freakin' failure, I can't even kill myself.

Don't you think after an unsuccessful go at it, they might ruminate, think out the next attempt? If it's successful next time, the statistics can call it impulsive. How will they know you sat around for a while and figured it all out?

Who found him? When was he found? How did they take so long to find him?

Had he known when he woke up that morning that he would never lay down in his bed again? Had he known when he was hanging around throughout the evening, talking with friends, when he was in the car heading downtown, did he know he only had a couple hours left? Was he doing a countdown?

Was there a thought of, hey, maybe I'll stick around one more day to hear if Billy really does bag that babe tonight and what he says about it in the morning.

Did he find himself worried about his math test next Thursday? And then check himself with a chuckle and say, oh yeah, no worries, I won't be around Thursday. Did he feel relief or trepidation in that instant? Did he wonder, "am I really going to do this?"

Did he wonder who would find him? He must have because he went outside. In the dark and down by the water's edge.

Perhaps he really didn't want to wake his family. Perhaps he just wanted to disappear quietly into the dark. Maybe his body would have fallen into the water, fallen under the surface and he'd be clean by the time they found him.

He wouldn't have known that detail though. They never show you on TV or in the movies what a bloody mess a shot to the head really is.

All these details. It's obsessive.

Everyone's scampering around looking for another detail, just one more, 'cause each detail is another brick to fill in that canyon, the one where your rib cage blew apart and left that hollowed out space between your tongue and belly button and your chest and spine. Where your guts and lungs and heart used to be.

So if you brick in that hollow space with facts, it will all go back to normal. Maybe you can even eat and breathe and live again.

But first, demand the most important brick of all: *Why?*

Get that brick. Then that rotting putrid feeling will go away. The one that will infect every thing from here on. Every thing.

Then the parents. They will carry shame and guilt for the rest of their lives. His brothers too. Even his friends. Hope he didn't have a girlfriend.

Here's the worst part of the shame that goes with suicide. There's this other guy a few weeks later, same age, same tons of friends and loved ones. That guy goes and wraps his car around a tree at 3 AM. *He* ends up on the front page of the paper. Swear to God, he does.

Everyone publicly grieving about the tragedy, what a loss, lines of people and cars outside his home supporting his family, signs and shit posted, "We love you, Ricky."

As if he died from some accident, like, oh I don't know, drinking himself blind, then falling into the driver's seat of a car. No one asks his mama . . . *why?*

But our suicide? Buried in the back of the obits. Nothing but whispers. Same friends and loved ones. Same loss. No one lined up around his home. Yet everyone looking at his mama . . . *why?*

Come on, now, is there really one more destructive or less intentional?

It's hard to know where to put all these awful words. It's hard to put them all on *him* since he's no longer here.

But you can't reach out from all this horror, so they end up just staying put. Heavy, heavy on the rest of us. Everyone gets left with the lonely sickness of fear and guilt and shame that rots through us all.

I'd rather wade in to the swamp waist deep and circle your body. Hold your hand. I don't even know who I'm talking to. Anyone else in the swamp with me. Please, anyone?

Everyone's paralyzed in the confusion and no one rescues anyone else.

But wouldn't it still be better if I reached across my own rotting gruesome visions into yours and you'd know I'm here and you're there and we're not alone?

Right now, it's hard to breathe, really, for more than a moment at a time. Suppose that's how you get through a swampy forever. One moment at a time.

Since we can't rescue anyone right now, it sure would help if we just had a good rain. At least take care of the clean up for us.

Sooner, and again and again and again later, we'll dive in, head first. Yeah, right in the swamp. Float, fixate on the details of the trees and their roots. Each detail to brick in that hollowed out spot. Brush a toe across the murky bottom and recoil in disgust.

Sometimes there's quicksand and you can sink slowly, luxuriously. Deeper and deeper under the thick water into the rot.

Someday, after the rain, it will be all we have left.

ACKNOWLEDGMENTS

Shew! So many.

First off, *Ghost Light* owes its 3-D existence to my book coach and editor, Meg Calvin, and her team.

Meg's intuitive, patient guidance coaxed more out of me than any other editor or writing mentor I've worked with. I particularly appreciated our forays into snark and sarcasm that she then encouraged me to nuance into raw truth. Our sessions included gales of laughter, chills of resonance, and a reluctance for our time to end. The only bad part of finishing a book is that I'll miss my creative time with Meg. Thank you, friend.

Next up, if Meg was awesome, her whole team then proceeded to blow me away. Emily Werner illustrated the book cover, and wow, baby, does that cover speak for itself. I never imagined something so lush and gorgeous, and I cried when Emily first showed it to me as a "rough draft."

Jodi McPhee line edited, book designed, and added the words, fonts, and final magic to the look and feel of the pages and the cover.

While she was highly communicative, I swear that most of how she intuited what I wanted, she plucked telepathically straight from my brain. She performed this exacting work with such excitement, her energy got me over the finish line.

Along the way, Cassidy Lee swooped in, brought her own ideas of Rabbit to the table and created a mystical creature that leapt off the page and into my heart. When Cassidy sent the image that became our prototype of Rabbit, I opened it a million times that first day, until I crashed my computer and soaked my supply of Kleenex with happy tears.

Standing ovation, ladies. I am honored you joined my carnival.

⁂

There are so many people from my life who need acknowledging and thanking. My mom, dad, Grandma, and Pops, all of my extended family members — including the stepmoms, dads, and siblings — and all of those relatives long dead by the time I arrived on Earth. In return for your support, I hope I've provided bits of enduring, albeit, at times, unexpected entertainment for you. Y'all certainly have for me. No one's ever called any branch of the family boring.

All of my colleagues in my various professions — the theater, the law, storytelling, and the spiritual — particularly those of you who became treasured mentors and lifelong friends.

A shout out to my deep, rich community of personal friends that I am so fortunate to have. Most of you didn't make the pages of the book because you haven't brought enough conflict and upheaval into my life. Thank you for that. (But also thank you to everyone who did contribute to times when my life turned upside down, because clearly, there wouldn't be a story to tell without you.)

I carry a ginormous, trunk full of gratitude to everyone who has trusted me in psychic and mediumship work, sacred endeavors of the soul. My heart is with all of you — those of you still incarnate, and those already in the Spirit World.

Finally, Fire Horse. The book begins and ends with you.

www.ingramcontent.com/pod-product-compliance
Lightning Source LLC
Chambersburg PA
CBHW051255120626
46547CB00015B/1960

* 9 7 9 8 2 1 8 7 8 8 8 9 6 *